P9-BYC-421

Integrating Climate, Energy, and Air Pollution Policies

Integrating Climate, Energy, and Air Pollution Policies

Gary Bryner with Robert J. Duffy

The MIT Press
Cambridge, Massachusetts
London, England

© 2012 Massachusetts Institute of Technology

All rights reserved. No part of this book may be reproduced in any form by any electronic or mechanical means (including photocopying, recording, or information storage and retrieval) without permission in writing from the publisher.

MIT Press books may be purchased at special quantity discounts for business or sales promotional use. For information, please email special_sales@mitpress.mit.edu or write to Special Sales Department, The MIT Press, 55 Hayward Street, Cambridge, MA 02142.

This book was set in Sabon by Toppan Best-set Premedia Limited, Hong Kong. Printed on recycled paper and bound in the United States of America.

Library of Congress Cataloging-in-Publication Data

Bryner, Gary C., 1951–2010
Integrating climate, energy, and air pollution policies / Gary Bryner ; with Robert J. Duffy.
  p.   cm.
Includes bibliographical references and index.
ISBN 978-0-262-01812-8 (hardcover : alk. paper) — ISBN 978-0-262-51787-4 (pbk. : alk. paper)
1. Air—Pollution—Government policy—United States. 2. Greenhouse gas mitigation—Government policy—United States. 3. Energy policy—United States. I. Duffy, Robert J. II. Title.
TD885.B79   2012
363.739′25610973—dc23
2012007799

10 9 8 7 6 5 4 3 2 1

Contents

Preface   vii

1   Introduction   1

2   Fragmentation, Policy Integration, and Policy Change   17

3   US Climate Policy   41

4   Reducing Greenhouse Gas Emissions from Generating Electricity   71

5   Increasing Energy Efficiency and the Use of Alternative Energy   101

6   Transforming Transportation   129

7   Integrating Agriculture, Energy, and Climate Change Policies   155

8   Climate Change, Policy Integration, and Ecological
    Sustainability   177

Notes   201
References   205
Index   223

Preface

This book was conceived by Gary Bryner, who produced two drafts of the manuscript and worked on it until his untimely death in March 2010. When it became clear to Gary that he would be unable to complete the project, he asked Clay Morgan of the MIT Press to consider finding someone to take it over because he did not want it to "simply disappear," and suggested me as someone who knew his work and might share some of his ideas. I was flattered because I did not know Gary well and I would not presume to say that we were friends. We had chatted at conferences, exchanged occasional e-mails about our common research interests, and I was fortunate to have shared an enjoyable lunch with him in Fort Collins during one of his visits to Colorado. In all of these circumstances, Gary was friendly, expressed a genuine interest in what I was doing, and was very generous in offering helpful ideas and suggestions. Although these connections were limited, I greatly admired Gary's work and, like many others, was impressed by the breadth and depth of his research agenda and by his intellectual curiosity, so vividly displayed in his many books, articles, and chapters. I still do not understand how he managed to master the details of so many disparate issues—in addition to his environmental work, Gary wrote expertly on welfare reform, regulation, bureaucracy, and the US Constitution, and somehow found the time to earn a law degree and open an environmental law practice in Provo, Utah.

So when I was approached to complete the manuscript, I agreed, although I also have to admit to a certain level of apprehension because the topic—integrating climate, energy, and air pollution policies—was, to say the least, typically ambitious and involved policy issues (clean air) that no political scientist knew more about than Gary. Fortunately for me, Gary left fairly detailed notes on how to respond to the reviewer's comments and suggestions, which were enormously helpful as I went through the manuscript, as were the reviewer's comments themselves, which were thoughtfully provided to me by Clay Morgan at the MIT Press. In the course of completing the book, I learned a great deal from Gary and from those whose work informed his thinking.

The basic outlines of the book—the themes, the major arguments, the order of the chapters—remain as Gary envisioned. My contribution consisted primarily of updating the manuscript, streamlining some of the arguments, highlighting others, reorganizing some chapters, incorporating the reviewer's suggestions, and so on. Throughout, I tried to remain faithful to Gary's vision while recognizing that events since early 2010 required adjusting some of the ideas presented here. For example, some sections of the manuscript were initially written during the early days of the Obama administration, when many, including Gary, thought US action on climate policy was imminent. That did not come to pass, and, if anything, climate change is an even more polarizing issue than Gary thought; the prospects for congressional action now seem even more remote.

In addition to the anonymous reviewers, I would like to thank Susan Geraghty for doing a superb job copyediting the manuscript, and the many individuals at the MIT Press who worked so diligently to shepherd the book to completion. In particular, I would like to thank Susan Clark for her help in promoting and marketing the book, Miranda Martin for going out of her way to assist with permissions and figures, and Deborah Cantor-Adams for walking me through the various editorial and production stages. I also owe a debt to Chuck Davis, Sandra Davis, Michele Betsill, and Denise Scheberle for providing comments and feedback on various aspects of the manuscript. I would also like to thank Colorado State University for supporting this project with a sabbatical leave. Most important, I want to thank Debbie, Julia, Marissa, and Sarina for providing the inspiration for this and other projects and for allowing me the time to complete it.

Robert J. Duffy
Fort Collins, CO
Spring 2012

1

Introduction

The idea of the interconnectedness of nature and that "everything is connected to everything else" is at the heart of environmental science. Indeed, the very notion of an ecosystem suggests elements are linked together and act in harmony. At the same time, there may also not be any word more descriptive of US policy making and governance than that of *fragmentation*. The constitutional structure of separated powers and checks and balances combine with divergent ideological views, geographic representation, and political competition to fracture and diffuse governmental power.

Environmental protection imperatives clash with political institutions and values in other ways as well. Environmental problems are often long-term concerns, with causes that are rooted in well-established patterns and practices and solutions that typically require long-term thinking and action, which are major challenges for a political system famously dominated by short-term thinking and parochial concerns. Yet another challenge is that the benefits of environmental policies may not be realized until well into the future and the burdens of preventive costs and behavioral changes fall on current voters.

Environmentalism is also rooted in the idea of restraint, in ensuring that human activity remains within bounds set by ecological conditions and that resource consumption and waste production do not overwhelm ecosystems. By contrast, there may be no political value more universally embraced that that of economic growth, and no presumption more pervasive than the belief that government's primary imperative, after national security, is an ever expanding economic pie.

Nowhere does this mismatch between the nature of the problem and the capabilities of government pose a greater challenge than in the threat of disruptive climate change, which has implications for energy use, air quality, and a host of other environmental problems. Although there is an almost infinite array of climate policy choices, it is essential to pursue them in an integrated fashion. Many of the sources of greenhouse gases (GHGs), for example, also produce conventional air pollutants that threaten public health, and coordinating regulatory efforts can produce more efficient and effective ways to reduce the threat of climate change while also improving air quality and reducing adverse health effects from polluted air. Similarly, energy policies aimed at increasing domestic production and energy security may also release more GHGs, making them much less attractive than they initially appear. This interconnectedness means that we cannot afford to pursue policies that appear to remedy one problem while creating or exacerbating others. It is also important to understand that it is the co-benefits of reducing GHG emissions that help strengthen the political case for taking action, especially for those who are not yet convinced of the seriousness of the threat of climate change. The more political constituencies that can be allied together to support a wider array of benefits, the greater the probability that effective policies can be enacted and implemented.

This book seeks to contribute to the debate over climate and energy policies by focusing attention on the importance of policy integration. We suggest that policy making at all levels of government requires careful attention to assessing policy options in terms of their consequences for climate change, energy, air pollution, agriculture, forestry, transportation, land-use planning, and other issues. The task of environmental policy making has for decades been twofold: what kinds of policies are most likely to produce the kinds of environmental benefits sought and how can sufficient political support for these policies be generated? We want to know what kinds of policies we should pursue to secure a more ecologically sustainable society and what kinds of political changes will produce and implement those policies. More specifically, how can our policy-making capacity be expanded so it is better equipped to set long-term goals and put in place short-term policies that will accomplish those goals? The focus here is on one slice of the broader debate: how can policies aimed at addressing air pollution, climate change, and energy use be effectively integrated, and how can the modest political support for action in each of these three areas be integrated in some synergistic fashion to advance policy making? Although the discussion centers on three policy issues, which are nested within an even larger effort to secure an ecologically sustainable future, how efforts to integrate these three overlapping policies can, in turn, help inform broader environmental policy making is the ultimate question this books seeks to address.

Ethanol and the Need for Policy Integration

Ethanol provides an illustrative example of the importance of fashioning a more integrated policy effort to address climate change and the challenges to doing so. In order to promote domestic energy supplies and energy independence, Congress passed a law in 2005 requiring that domestically produced biofuels displace 5 percent of total gasoline used in the country by 2008. To meet the 5 percent goal, US farmers produced large quantities of ethanol from corn grain that was then blended with gasoline and sold in fueling stations around the nation. Unlike many public policy goals, that goal was met easily and well in advance of the deadline, driven by a combination of tax incentives and the productivity of US farmers. Corn prices doubled between 2006 and 2008 and farmers responded by planting more corn; the 2007 crop was the largest planted in more than sixty years and surpassed the previous year's crop by 20 percent. Against this backdrop, US production of ethanol increased by nearly 400 percent between 2000 and 2007. By 2008, there were nearly 150 ethanol refineries operating in the United States, producing a total of 8.5 billion gallons, and another fifty were under construction that promised to increase production by an additional 5.1 billion gallons. By the end of the decade, the United States was the world's largest ethanol producer, exceeding Brazil's sugar-cane ethanol production.

Buoyed by this success, the 2007 Energy Act set a much more ambitious target of producing 36 billion gallons of biofuels by 2022. Production of biofuels was encouraged by a 51 cents per gallon tax credit (lowered to 45 cents in the 2008 Farm Bill); imported ethanol has a 54 cents per gallon tariff that also serves to encourage domestic production. The 2008 Farm Bill provided $1 billion in funding for bioenergy programs, including $320 million in loan guarantees for biorefineries, $300 million to expand production of biofuels from crops and residue, and $120 million for biomass research and development (Siikamaki 2008).

The ethanol boom was interrupted by the 2008–2009 recession, which led to a dramatic drop in energy demand, lower prices, and a decline in ethanol production. But the bad economy was not the only challenge facing ethanol producers. Some studies of corn grain ethanol concluded that it takes more energy to produce ethanol than the resulting product actually contains. One study, for instance, concluded that three units of fossil fuel energy are typically required to produce four units of ethanol energy. Biodiesel, by contrast, is more efficient, requiring only about one unit of fossil fuel for three units of biodiesel energy (Paustian et al. 2006).

There is great hope that newer biofuels such as jatorpha and miscanthus can be used to produce ethanol because they can be grown on marginal lands, use much less water, and thus do not compete with food production as corn-based ethanol does (Barta 2008a).

Another problem with corn-based ethanol is that it does not significantly reduce GHG emissions. According to one estimate, every gallon of corn ethanol used reduces GHG emissions by about 20 percent, but that depends greatly on the kind of fuel used in the conversion process (Center for Climate and Energy Solutions 2012). Most existing ethanol plants use natural gas, and ethanol produced from those plants results in GHG reductions of 28 to 39 percent. As natural gas prices rose, however, ethanol refineries increasingly turned to coal-fired power, which has much higher GHG emissions. If corn-based ethanol usage increased to twelve to fourteen billion gallons a year, equivalent to about 10 percent of US gasoline consumption, it would cut overall US GHG emissions only by less than 1 percent. If, however, cellulosic ethanol can be commercially produced, emissions could be reduced by 80 or 90 percent compared with emissions from gasoline (Siikamaki, 2008).[1]

Another key trade-off is the way in which expanding crops for biofuels puts pressure on farmers to grow crops on environmentally sensitive lands. Nearly one-quarter of the nation's corn crop is now used for producing ethanol. It is clear that technological breakthroughs are required for biofuels to play a significantly larger role than they do now in displacing gasoline. Turning cellulose into biofuels is a top priority for entrepreneurs and researchers because it would use crops for biofuels that are not used for food. There is, however, no commercial-scale cellulosic ethanol facility operating anywhere in the world (Tollefson 2008).[2] Globally, farmers are converting forests and grasslands to grow more corn but that decreases the role of those lands in absorbing carbon from the atmosphere.

The US Agriculture Department Conservation Reserve Program's goal of keeping environmentally sensitive lands out of production clashes with the demand to grow more corn. Higher prices have encouraged more intensive production techniques that reduce soil conservation, carbon storage, and other environmental benefits. And if cellulosic ethanol becomes viable, it could place additional pressure on environmentally sensitive lands, forcing trade-offs between expanding biocrops and protecting or expanding croplands, grasslands, and forests. It is not clear which will have the greatest climate benefits—more lands cultivated for cellulosic ethanol or more lands protected as forests for sequestration (Siikamaki 2008).

Ethanol's impact on agriculture so far has been mixed. Higher food prices reduce the federal subsidies that must be paid to farmers under the price support program but increase the cost of the revenue-guarantee program established in the 2008 Farm Bill to help stabilize farm revenue. At the same time, increased demand for corn increases the cost of feed for livestock producers and helps drive up the price of other crops and the value of farmland (Barta 2008b). Doubling the price of corn from the average price during the past twenty years increases the price of poultry by about 5 percent, pork by about 10 percent, and beef by about 17 percent. The impact on other domestic food prices is much smaller because so much of the cost of food is independent of crop prices. For example, the corn used to produce a box of corn flakes costs only a few cents; most of the final cost comes from packaging, processing, advertising, shipping, and so on. Doubling the price of corn only increases the price of corn flakes by about 1 percent. The rise in corn prices help inflate the price of wheat and other crops but the cost of these crops as well only make up a small part of total food costs. Internationally, however, crop price increases are much more likely to translate into higher food prices because the cost of crops is a greater share of food production, grains are a larger part of the diet, and food takes up a larger part of a family's budget. As a result, growing demand for ethanol has only a small impact on prices in the United States and other wealthy countries but a much larger impact in poorer countries (Siikamaki 2008).

A 2004 study by the UN's Food and Agricultural Organization found that about 860 million people in the world were food insecure—defined as not having enough food to be able to live productive, working lives. Studies demonstrate that although the world is producing more food than ever before, the problem is largely the lack of income poor people have to buy the food they need. As many parts of the world grow wealthier and move higher up the food chain by eating more meat, the pressure on poorer people only increases, leading to additional degradation of natural resources (Pinstrup-Anderson and Herforth 2008).

Global food prices rose 83 percent between 2005 and 2008, resulting in rioting to protest the cost of food in Egypt, Cameroon, Ivory Coast, Senegal, and Ethiopia. Troops were called up in Pakistan and Thailand to protect fields and warehouses from theft. At a meeting of world finance ministers in April 2008, many laid the blame of high food prices on efforts by the United States and others to expand the production of biofuels such as ethanol, which diverts cropland to energy production. Rising food prices are actually a result of a number of factors, including biofuel production, higher oil prices that make farm equipment fuel and fertilizer more expensive, and rapidly growing demand for food in the developing world. World Bank president Robert Zoellick warned that thirty-three countries were at risk of social violence as a result of high food prices; for many of the world's poor, three-fourths of their income goes for food and there is "no margin for survival" (Davis and Belkin 2008).

The case of ethanol illustrates how energy, climate, and air pollution policies overlap and how policies in one area can affect the others, often in ways policy makers do not intend. It also illustrates why an integrated approach in these areas is necessary and desirable. If we are to achieve policy goals in any of these areas, it makes abundant sense to understand how they interact. Finally, the ethanol example demonstrates the many challenges to integration; sorting through the maze of laws, regulations, agencies, and levels of government will not be easy.

Science, Politics, and the Prospects for Policy Change

The challenges facing scientists in assessing climate change, understanding its causes and consequences, and projecting future impacts are daunting. Just as difficult are the obstacles to designing and implementing effective policies and finding political support for them. Nowhere is this clearer than for climate change. A scientific consensus has emerged about the seriousness of the threat and the need to develop an immediate and sustained effort to reduce greenhouse gas emissions but the political response has been slow and tepid (DiMento and Doughman 2007). The precautionary principle has become largely irrelevant; scientists warned nearly two decades ago that global warming was underway and that reducing GHG emissions was essential as a precautionary measure. There were many uncertainties, to be sure, but there was enough agreement to prompt prudent, preventive action in the face of evolving science.

The evidence that has accumulated since then is strong and compelling. Rather than taking action in the face of considerable uncertainty as insurance against the risk of serious harm, however, we have done very little to reduce emissions. Now that there are clear signs that climate change is occurring, it is too late for precautionary action. The question is whether we will act now to ensure that the risks do not become so significant and far reaching that they become unmanageable. Many climate scientists argue that greenhouse gas emissions should be reduced by 50 to 80 percent from 1990 levels by midcentury in order to significantly reduce the likelihood of catastrophic climate change. In a December 2005 lecture, NASA climate scientists James Hansen (2005), a leading figure in climate debates, summarized the situation this way: "the Earth's climate is nearing, but has not passed, a tipping point, beyond which it will be impossible to avoid climate change with far ranging undesirable consequences" (p. 1).

Climate policy needs to be rooted in a clear understanding of climate science. Much of the paralysis in policy making is a result of confusion over the science of climate change. There are tremendous uncertainties that permeate climate science, such as whether climate changes that have already occurred can be attributed to GHG emissions or to natural climate cycles, how fast global temperatures will rise and what the increases will be in specific regions, whether feedback mechanisms will accelerate warming trends or reduce its magnitude, and, perhaps most important, what the impact of climate change will be overall. There are also questions about whether climate change will be a slow, gradual process that will allow for a relatively painless adjustment or abrupt and catastrophic.

It is worth noting several aspects of climate change that make policy making particularly challenging. To begin, climate change policy is inevitably a moving target because occurring events alter the policy-making environment. The severe economic downturn in 2008, for example, significantly altered patterns of energy use and GHG emissions. In recent years, hurricanes and accidents in the oil production and refining networks in the Gulf of Mexico have sent energy prices skyrocketing. Similarly, it is conceivable that unambiguous or catastrophic evidence of global warming could result in a dramatic breakthrough in climate policy. Despite these jolts, however, the basic trends and forces that shape the use of energy and production of pollution have been quite predictable. They are relatively easy to project into the future and, concurrently, very difficult to alter. The focus here is thus on these long-term trends and projections in energy use and emissions of GHGs and other pollutants that will shape the major policy choices confronting the United States in the decades ahead. The US focus of this book is admittedly too narrow for the global reach of climate change but there are sufficient policy challenges in the United States to justify this and many other books.

Although the debate over the causes and consequences of climate change continues, just as important is the debate over what kinds of actions we should take to reduce the threat of disruptive climate change and to adapt to its effects. Policy options for significantly mitigating and adapting to climate change are among the most challenging that Americans have ever undertaken. The broad and far-reaching activities that contribute to climate change occur throughout society and are intertwined with fundamentally important processes of producing and distributing goods and services. Climate changes are largely driven by emissions from the production and use of energy that fuels virtually every aspect of US economic life. Policy making in this area requires an unprecedented level of coordination and a greater collective commitment to political change than has ever occurred.

The prospects for a transformation in climate policy and in our politics are not encouraging. Although we know far more about environmental problems than we did in the 1960s, our policy making has languished. Rather than addressing the issue, Congress has instead enacted legislation in recent years that seeks to stimulate increased fossil fuel production and gives only modest support to alternative forms of energy and improved conservation and efficiency. US Department of Energy spending for energy research and development peaked in the late 1970s but then dropped by more than 85 percent in real terms between 1978 and 2005 (US Government Accountability Office 2008). In the waning days of 2007, Congress passed an energy bill that raised the national fuel efficiency standard to a fleetwide average of thirty-five miles per gallon (mpg) by 2020, the first time it had raised the standard since 1975. Throughout its two terms, as the scientific consensus over the threat of climate change solidified, the Bush administration emphasized voluntary programs for US firms and voluntary agreements with other nations to develop alternative energy technologies. Although the policy vacuum at the federal level has been partially filled with state and local policy making, primarily in cities and states in the Northeast and West, the current level of national policy commitment falls far, far short of the level of concern among climate scientists.

Once marked by consensus, the environment is now a political wedge issue, shaped by Republican politicians and their consultants who warn that increased environmental policy efforts require bigger, more intrusive government that limits personal choices and profits. In Congress, climate policy has been held hostage by political tactics and ideology, with Republicans in the late 1990s and early 2000s enacting appropriations riders that prohibited the Environmental Protection Agency (EPA) from even *studying* climate change. Officials in the Bush administration instructed scientists not to discuss climate change with reporters and reports were edited to replace scientific judgments with political ones. This was not just a problem that showed in climate change discussions but happened throughout other parts of the administration. Former surgeon general Richard H. Carmona, for example, testified before Congress in July 2007 that political appointees in the Bush administration repeatedly sought to weaken or suppress the release of public health information and had prohibited him from speaking about issues such as stem cell research, emergency contraception, and global health problems (Bryner 2000; Harris 2007).

Several other factors contribute to the science-policy gap as well. For example, the political challenge of transforming energy policy in response to the threat of climate change in the United States is rooted in a political system that is notoriously oriented toward short-term political incentives, dominated by powerful interests, and divided by ideological cleavages. Climate policy deadlock has also been blamed on political responsiveness to well-heeled fossil fuel interests, the political difficulty of imposing immediate costs when benefits accrue in the future, and the failure of advocates of action to demonstrate, as they have on other issues, the practical threats climate change poses to people (Victor 2004).

Many observers have suggested that transformational policy change in energy or any other issue will not occur unless there is some kind of crisis that propels the issue to the top of the policy agenda and compels a response. In most measures of US public opinion, environmental quality is broadly embraced but is rarely seen as a top priority. Some polls have even shown widespread concern about climate change but little support for taking any costly action to reduce the threat. Public support for climate policies is much stronger in Europe, perhaps because of the way in which disruptive climate changes have already affected Europeans, but Hurricane Katrina's devastating impact on New Orleans did not prompt a US call for action on climate change.

The deeply held faith in economic growth is also a critical challenge to effective policy making in climate, energy, and air pollution. The primacy of the political imperative of economic growth typically eclipses other concerns; growth is seen as the great social stabilizer, diffusing conflicts over the unequal distribution of resources by holding out the hope that a rising economic tide will lift all boats. But the widely accepted view that continued economic growth as currently conceived is possible, inevitable, and desirable is itself not sustainable, given the scientific consensus surrounding climate change and other problems. Political leaders, economists, and others have been slow to understand that if the climate is seriously disrupted, conventional expectations of economic growth will be shattered.

Although wealthier nations have made considerable progress in reducing some forms of pollution such as air and water pollution, the solution to environmental problems is not simply more economic growth. It is true that regions of greater affluence have more resources to invest in cleaner technologies and improved energy efficiency. At the same time, though, securing clean air and water continue to be among the most pressing environmental problems for the world's poorest residents. Growth in greenhouse gas emissions and toxic wastes, the decline of habitat and biodiversity, the loss of topsoil, and the depletion of aquifers are examples of environmental threats that inexorably increase with global economic growth (American Association for the Advancement of Science 2000). Our consumption of natural resources is not sustainable, especially if people in the developing world increase their consumption and begin to approach the levels of resource use in the wealthy world. These problems not only threaten people now but also pose a tremendous challenge as we think about the effects on the life chances and opportunities of future generations. Those who believe that we can grow our way out of environmental problems must reject widely held conclusions drawn by environmental scientists that the planet cannot sustain current levels of consumption and waste, particularly if developing countries follow the model of economic growth pursued by the industrialized nations. The changes in lifestyle that environmentalism prescribes are, for some, simply too inconvenient or disruptive of practices they have come to embrace and seek to protect from change.

The globalization of markets is intertwined with growing global environmental threats, and poor people are most vulnerable to the consequences of environmental decline. Poverty in developing countries is often a reflection of inadequate natural resources such as good soil and water, and farmers depend on a healthy ecosystem for their survival. Short-term economic pressures lead poor farmers and others to engage in practices that produce immediate but unsustainable benefits. Such results are to be expected, given globalization's ideological emphasis on unfettered markets and blindness to the threats posed by prices that fail to reflect the true costs of production, and fail to provide the kinds of signals that are essential for making efficient decisions about the use of resources.

The most immediate environmental problems are typically found in the less developed nations, where poverty and environmental decline are inextricably linked. People who struggle to survive often engage in environmentally unsustainable practices, and they are particularly affected by air and water pollution, lack of sanitation, and loss of local biodiversity. Addressing these problems is a profoundly important moral imperative for all of us.

Science and technology scholars have produced numerous studies of the ways that engineers and other have shaped technological outcomes and how political processes and institutions reciprocally interact with technologies that help illuminate the obstacles and opportunities for policy learning (Jasanoff 1998). Democratic politics is a means to sensible and wise—as well as normatively desirable—governance of science and technology because that is the best hope we have to promoting prudent decisions and acceptable compromises by those who are likely to be affected by the resulting actions (Lindblom and Woodhouse 1993). One of the primary challenges we face is how democratic policy making can address the concerns and needs of nonexperts who must nevertheless address complex scientific and technological issues (Woodhouse and Nieusma 2001; Fischer 2003).

Finally, climate change poses a unique policy challenge because of the tremendously broad scope of activities that contribute to greenhouse gas emissions. The ways we transport ourselves, produce and use energy, consume products, produce food, and use and develop land are all central to the debate over climate policy. Because climate policy is to a large extent energy policy, climate issues are thus part of the broader debate over national security and how to ensure a stable supply of energy resources. The potential of climate change to disrupt life, engender conflict, and produce refugees around the world makes it a pressing priority for international relations and global policy making. Given the scope and magnitude of the challenge, integrating policy efforts is essential, and that is the primary focus of this book. Policy integration is required to ensure that efforts to reduce the emissions of greenhouse gases are economically sustainable and that the financial resources required to sustain life and fund the transition to an ecologically sustainable future are available. Because of the magnitude of policy changes required, those efforts must also be as cost effective as possible to allow their implementation.

The Plan of the Book

The importance of policy integration, we hope, will become even clearer in the chapters that follow. The key questions are how can policies aimed at addressing air pollution, climate change, energy use, and related areas such as agriculture and land use be integrated more effectively and how can the modest political support for action in each of these areas be mobilized in a synergistic fashion to move policy making forward? The case of ethanol cited previously is but one of many examples in which policy making requires careful integration to ensure that trade-offs are clarified, policies are designed to maximize co-benefits, and implementation takes into account the wide range of related issues. The chapters that follow suggest how the policy options and choices that are being debated can be framed and assessed in ways that encourage policy integration.

Chapter 2 examines the key concepts underlying policy integration and then explores ways of institutionalizing the concepts in national policy-making processes. Policy integration is a matter of degree; accordingly, we show that integration already takes place in some areas, albeit at a modest level. We argue that there are incremental measures than can be pursued now that can pave the way for more far-reaching efforts to integrate policy across the three issue areas. To date, much of the climate change policy debate has focused on which policies are consistent with a growing economy. The idea of economic growth remains paramount and as a result climate, energy, and other policies are ultimately measured by their contribution to growth and other conventional economic measures. The nature of the threat posed by climate change to current and future generations, however, compels a different starting point, one that begins with the goal of ensuring a stable climate and allows only the kinds of economic activity that are consistent with that ecological goal. This stronger commitment to a stable climate is built on the assumption that we need to put environmental quality and stability first because it is a precondition for all other human activity and well-being. Reducing GHG emissions is a massive, complex undertaking that will require careful coordination and integration with virtually all areas of economic activity and unprecedented institutional capacity to coordinate efforts, make trade-offs, and set priorities.

Chapter 3 examines the evolution of the debate in the United States over the goals of climate policy, what overall strategies are required to achieve those goals, and how policy integration can help clarify and assess policy options. Although there are a host of climate change policy options, the discussion here focuses on the two that have received the most attention from policy makers: a carbon tax and a cap-and-trade program.

The chapters that follow focus on four major climate change and energy policy issues—reducing carbon emissions resulting from generating electricity, increasing energy efficiency and reliance on alternative energy, reducing carbon emissions from transportation, and agriculture's role in generating and sequestering greenhouse gases. Chapter 4 centers on the debate over burning coal to generate electricity. Existing coal-fired plants generally produce electricity more cheaply than any other source, and new coal plants are regularly proposed because coal is the most plentiful domestic fossil fuel. But it is also the dirtiest fuel in terms of carbon emissions and in generating other pollutants that are public health and environmental hazards. One climate policy option is to quickly phase out using coal but alternative sources are not currently available in quantities required to avoid massive shortages and blackouts. More feasible is an integrated approach that employs climate, energy, conventional air pollution, and other policies to reduce emissions and shift toward cleaner fuels.

Chapter 5 explores the debate over how to increase energy efficiency and foster the development of renewable energy sources. There is widespread agreement that improving energy efficiency and reducing energy use through conservation is the most promising way to reduce the threat of disruptive climate change. Energy efficiency avoids the environmental and other costs associated with alternative energy sources and produces co-benefits such as reducing traditional pollutants that threaten public health. Alternative energy sources all have some environmental side effects that must be balanced against their climate benefits, though, and emphasizing policy integration can help identify costs and benefits.

By themselves, energy efficiency and renewables will not be sufficient to meet projected energy demand and thus coal will continue to play a key role in electricity generation for the foreseeable future. Because burning coal also produces pollutants that contribute to acid rain, urban air pollution, and public health problems, there are significant co-benefits that come from either climate or clean air policies that seek to curtail its use. But there are also perplexing trade-offs. For example, installing control equipment aimed at reducing particulates, which are responsible for the most serious threats to public health from air pollution, also reduces the efficiency of power plants, thus requiring that more fuel be used and more CO_2 emissions released. Barring a dramatic technological breakthrough in cleaner fuels, climate, energy, and air pollution policies will need to be carefully integrated in pursuit of cleaner coal burning and increased carbon capture and sequestration.

Chapter 6 focuses on how to reduce emissions from transportation. Reducing GHG emissions is one of the key climate policy priorities but has been a vexing challenge because there are currently no control technologies to remove CO_2 from tailpipe emissions, so gains must come from reducing fuel use and miles traveled. One of the major successes of the Clean Air Act (CAA) has been the reduction of conventional pollutants (but not CO_2) from motor vehicle emissions. Cars manufactured today are more than 95 percent cleaner than those produced before the act took effect; clear standards, developed by Congress and administered by the EPA, helped to dramatically reduce emissions. By contrast, the CAA has not been very successful in reducing vehicle miles traveled. As one would expect, it is much easier to devise technological fixes than it is to change people's behavior but both are needed for an effective climate policy.

Chapter 7 examines how agricultural policies interact with climate, energy, and air pollution policies. Agriculture is unique in that it is a source and a sink for greenhouse gases. Agricultural policies such as conservation programs and no-till farming and forestry policies governing timber harvesting have significant effects on carbon emissions and sequestration. Subsidies to encourage certain agricultural practices are well established and can be adapted to the pursuit of climate goals but they are also politically durable and difficult to change once in place. Planting trees and other methods of sequestering carbon are popular climate policies because they promise to offset emissions from power generation and transportation, thus avoiding the need for painful emission-reduction efforts in those sectors. But the effectiveness, permanence, and other characteristics of terrestrial sequestration are not well understood.

The final chapter discusses several crosscutting issues raised previously. For example, because of its central impact on the economy, energy policy will likely dominate the climate policy debate and whatever climate policies we pursue will largely take place within the context of energy policy making. It is thus critical that whatever energy policies we pursue over the next decades also contribute to achieving climate goals. US climate policy-making efforts must also be integrated with global actions. The United States occupies a key position in the future of international efforts to reduce the threats posed by climate change. Thus a credible effort by the United States to design and implement policies to reduce its own emissions will allow it to then work with other nations, developed and developing, to devise their own policies.

Policy integration has long been a part of environmental policy debates but we have made only limited progress in increasing the capacity of governments to take a more coordinated approach in environmental and other policies. The case for integrated policy making has been reinforced by the growing commitment to ecologically sustainable development. The final chapter broadens the climate policy discussion to explore how thoughtful policy integration can serve as a major step toward the goal of sustainability. Climate change issues are nested within even larger challenges of designing effective and efficient policies, securing sufficient political support, and developing the requisite institutional capacity to design and implement the kinds of policies required to secure more ecologically sustainable societies. Two goals are central to the policy debate: integrating climate with related policies to ensure that solutions are effective and efficient and securing a sufficiently healthy biosphere in which current and future generations can flourish. If climate policy is effectively integrated with these other kinds of policy concerns, we will be making significant progress toward a more sustainable world.

Climate policy is inevitably a moving target. By the time this book is published, the scientific and policy debate will have shifted, climate science will have evolved, and new policies will be in place. Barring some energy technology breakthrough, though, climate policy will be on the agenda for decades. This book seeks to provide a timely assessment of a contemporary policy debate without becoming dated as environmental problems and policies rapidly evolve. To strike that balance, this book seeks to provide a framework, rooted in the idea of policy integration, which can be used to assess the policy choices that arise during the next several years in the debate over the causes, consequences, and cures for climate change.

2

Fragmentation, Policy Integration, and Policy Change

As we have seen, air pollution, climate change, energy use, agriculture, and land use are all intimately connected. Air pollutants that pose major public health threats are not the same ones as those that pose global climate threats but they often come from the same sources, and reductions aimed at protecting public health can also reduce greenhouse gas emissions. More broadly, economic activity and environmental quality are inextricably linked through emissions of fossil fuels and other sources of greenhouse gases and traditional air pollutants. Indeed, as Holdren (2001, 10) argues, the steady increase in carbon dioxide emissions that is driving the threat of climate change is "deeply embedded in the character of civilization's current energy-supply system." Climate change and other global environmental threats are so complex and challenging that there is a need for creative policy experimentation to learn how best to create incentives for companies, governments, and other decision makers to make ecologically sustainable decisions.

The world's fossil fuel-based energy infrastructure will need to be fundamentally transformed by the middle of the twenty-first century in order to reduce significantly the threat of climate change. That infrastructure—power plants, transmission lines, and other facilities and equipment—typically lasts from twenty to fifty years, so investment decisions made today will have consequences for years to come. Transforming energy consumption to make it more efficient will similarly require massive shifts in technologies, building and equipment, and the ways in which energy is used throughout the economy. Climate policy imperatives will also have to permeate air pollution regulation, agricultural and forestry policies, and land-use planning. All this will require a fundamental transformation in the policy-making process as well and a dramatic increase in the capacity of governments to integrate and coordinate policy efforts. The dilemma is that the interconnectedness of these problems and challenges clashes with the fragmentation of the policy-making process. In the United States, these issues are largely addressed by separate statutes, federal agencies, and congressional committees. State-level policy making is typically just as fragmented. As a result, policies aimed at one problem may make others worse; that is why policy making in these areas must be integrated.

This chapter examines the key concepts underlying policy integration and then explores ways of institutionalizing the concepts in national policy-making processes. Integration is a matter of degree; accordingly, the focus here is on noting that integration already takes place in some areas, albeit at a modest level. Ultimately, we must do much more to integrate climate, energy, and air pollution policies but there are incremental measures that can be pursued now. This chapter highlights some of them and makes the case for more ambitious efforts to integrate environmental policy.

Fragmentation and Policy Integration

The fragmented structure of energy, climate, air pollution, and agricultural policy is a significant barrier to designing and implementing more integrated and effective policies. The problem has been widely described in the literature on environmental law and policy. For some, policy fragmentation represents a failure to integrate efforts across a range of substantive problems. Davies and Mazurek (1998, 16), for example, summarized the problem this way: "The most obvious and important characteristic of pollution control legislation is its fragmentation. . . . The [EPA's] statutory framework consists of dozens of unrelated laws passed at different times by different committees dealing with different subjects." As a result, they argue, environmental law divides up problems and solutions according to different environmental media (air, water, and land) and shifts pollution from one medium to another, emphasizes control technologies rather than pollution prevention, and has evolved into a complex, often inflexible system. The single media focus, for example, encourages polluters to dispose of waste in the least regulated medium and gives regulators incentives to require disposal of waste in any medium except the one for which they are responsible. The focus on pollution-control technology is also problematic because it does not really reduce pollution; it simply shifts it around, changes its form, or delays its release into the environment. In addition, the fragmented system makes it impossible to set rational priorities among different programs or even among different control measures. Davies and Mazurek (1998) recommend an integrated approach, focusing on pollution prevention, as far more effective in obtaining compliance and reducing pollution. Pollution prevention is inherently multimedia and, at least for stationary pollution sources, usually involves changes in plant processes rather than end-of-pipe solutions. Such process changes would be much more feasible under an integrated approach.

Other analyses have emphasized the need for a new generation of environmental policies that move beyond the conventional regulatory structure of existing environmental laws to encourage greater environmental improvements (Kraft 2004; Mazmanian and Kraft 2009). Elements of the new environmental regulation, such as market-based regulatory instruments, giving polluters more flexibility in exchange for more stringent goals, and integrating otherwise diffuse regulatory requirements, are already visible in some places. For more than two decades the EPA has undertaken a number of pilot projects aimed at encouraging a more integrated approach to pollution control, including Project XL (for eXcellence in Leadership, an initiative to encourage innovative approaches to producing better environmental results), the Common Sense Initiative (developing programs focusing on the needs of industrial sectors), and others but they have not moved from the pilot project phase, and environmental statutes largely retain the fragmented approach (Kettl 2002). These reforms challenged the assumptions underlying traditional environmental regulation: that companies will comply with environmental regulations only if they are backed by sanctions, that an adversarial relationship between government and business is essential, that top-down bureaucratic control produces environmental results, that standards can be applied across sources of pollution nationwide, and that regulators' primary focus is conformity with rules and regulations.

Daniel Fiorino (2006) argues that although existing laws have contributed to major environmental improvements, they have outlived their usefulness and should be replaced by a new approach to environmental regulation. One of the key concepts underlying the new regulation is that of reflexive law; the goal is to "create incentives and procedures that induce people to continually assess their actions (hence the 'reflexivity') and adjust them to society's goals." Another is "social-political governance," which blurs the lines between public and private as governments act alongside companies in more collaborative and communicative ways that emphasizes learning, shared responsibility, and trust (Fiorino 2006, 19–20). Despite major environmental and political changes, though, virtually all of the major environmental statutes have technically expired and Congress has been unable to reauthorize or update any of these laws for well over a decade or, in some cases, much longer. At the same time, there is not enough trust and good will between Democrats and Republicans to reopen political deals that were struck decades ago in order to see if new compromises could be struck. Thus, although Fiorino's new environmental regulation is a promising blueprint for policy reform, the kinds of political changes that will be required before those reforms can be pursued seem daunting and distant.

Mazmanian and Kraft (2009) go further, arguing that the modern environmental movement can be best understood as three successive epochs characterized by different regulatory instruments, from conventional command-and-control regulations, through market-based innovations and policy integration, to a commitment to sustainability. They offer this conceptual framework as a way to explain what is otherwise a complex, chaotic set of developments. The framework serves as a roadmap for understanding and assessing past efforts as well as exploring the likelihood of the transition to the third epoch of sustainability. Although notions of sustainability are well established, experience in implementing its tenets and achieving its goals is only beginning, and the final chapter explores how policy integration and sustainability are mutually reinforcing ideas.

Another form of fragmentation is the failure to integrate efforts within a specific set of environmental problems. Ronald D. Brunner and his colleagues (2005) argue that the solution to policy fragmentation is *adaptive governance* (AG), the term they use to refine and develop the core concepts underlying community-based initiatives, civic environmentalism, collaborative conservation, and other labels for consensus-based policy making. The focus on governance, rather than the term *adaptive management* favored by some, emphasizes the political nature of decision making in contrast to policy making as technocratic decision making by experts. Similar to other forms of collaboration, AG integrates scientific and other forms of knowledge through open decision-making structures that reflect the unique situation of each community. Adaptive governance also reflects several dimensions that distinguish it from other collaborative efforts. First, it focuses on the goal of achieving the common interest, defined as the shared interests of members of a particular community reached through compromise and consensus building. Second, although it relies primarily on collaborative processes, it also employs other methods such as adversarial proceedings in pursuing the common interest. Third, it expressly promotes the diffusion and adaptation of successful initiatives, incremental reforms to traditional federal management and regulatory structures and processes (Brunner et al. 2005). If efforts to integrate climate, energy, and air pollution policies are to succeed, they will likely begin through this process of diffusion, where programs and ideas in one policy arena are adopted in others.

Moving toward greater policy integration will require a change in policy-making processes as well as in policy design. The literature on strong democracy, anchored by Benjamin Barber's book *Strong Democracy* (1985), lays out a strong case for participation by local citizens in decisions affecting them. Science and democracy studies such as Richard Sclove's (1995) focus on how scientific and technological decisions can be more effectively shaped through participatory politics and how community-level, participatory policy making can serve as an alternative to technocratic, bureaucratic, expertise-driven policy making. Policy scholars such as Deborah Stone (2001) emphasize the intertwining of politics and policy analysis and argue that they cannot be separated. The very large literature rooted in books such as Lipsky's *Street Level Bureaucracy* (1983) through the community participation movement of the 1970s to the policy devolution literature in the 1980s and beyond (Conlan 1998) all share much with adaptive governance in focusing on the strengths of community-level policy making. With policy making stymied at the federal level, the more participatory collaborative efforts could provide a pathway to policy integration elsewhere.

Policy Integration, Policy Change, and Policy Learning

Although these efforts to frame the issue of policy fragmentation are helpful, an additional body of literature largely rooted in European politics is particularly useful in thinking about environmental policy integration (Lenschow 2002; Jordan and Lenschow 2008, 2010). Lafferty and Hovden (2003) trace the concept to a 1973 European Community Environmental Action Programme that argued for including an assessment of environmental impacts for "any measure that is adopted or contemplated at national or Community level and which is liable to affect these factors" (3). The 1993 Maastricht Treaty requires that environmental considerations be integrated into other policies, and the principle is assigned its own article (Article 6) in the 1997 consolidation of the EU treaty. A 1996 EU directive required all members to move toward an integrated approach to controlling pollution (Council Directive 96/61/

EC, September 24, 1996). In addition, the EU's fifth Environmental Action Programme specifically identified industry, energy, agriculture, transportation, and tourism as particularly important targets for policy integration (Lenschow 2002). Policy integration is now a familiar concept in Europe and some have even suggested it is "the critical challenge confronting European environmental policy-makers at the dawn of the new millennium" (Jordan and Lenschow 1999, 31).

So what exactly is policy integration? Lafferty and Hovden (2003, 9) argue that policy integration should be defined as "the incorporation of environmental objectives into all stages of policy making in non-environmental policy sectors . . . accompanied by an attempt to aggregate presumed environmental consequences into an overall evaluation of policy, and a commitment to minimise contradictions between environmental and sectoral policies by giving principled priority to the former over the latter."

At its most basic, then, environmental policy integration refers to a greater awareness of how policies in one area affect another and encourages policy makers to prioritize environmental concerns. The idea of environmental policy integration therefore overlaps with that of sustainable development and its emphasis on integrating environmental and economic policy making. Lenschow (2002, 5) contends that the principle of environmental policy integration "may be considered a core application of the concept of sustainable development" and that this link has given the concept greater legitimacy in the European Union. Similar to sustainable development, though, policy integration is also a slippery concept, subject to multiple interpretations. Which environmental goals, for example, are to be integrated and which of the goals should have priority? As one might expect, people might disagree on which problems should take precedence and how conflicts among goals should be resolved. There are also questions about whether elected officials or bureaucrats should make those decisions and when integration should occur: when policy is being formulated, when specific policy measures are being adopted, or when policies are implemented (Persson 2009).

There are vertical and horizontal dimensions to policy integration. Vertical integration focuses on the extent to which a cabinet department or ministry places environmental goals as central to everything it does. The emphasis on the vertical dimension refers to administrative action "up and down within the arena of ministerial sectoral responsibility" from policy making to implementation (Lafferty and Hovden 2003, 13).

It compels officials to identify their major environmental challenges, to employ environmental assessments, and to regularly report environmental conditions. Horizontal integration, however, refers to a cross-sectoral strategy of integrating environmental concerns in every ministry. This includes the goal of sustainable development, a centralized authority responsible for supervising and coordinating environmental priorities, clear targets, and timetables for environmental policy, and regular environmental impact and strategic environmental assessments to guide all major decisions (Lafferty and Knudsen 2007).

The accumulated evidence thus far indicates that policy integration is difficult, which should not be surprising to students of politics. Integration is difficult for a variety of reasons, most important because it is a policy change, and securing policy change is almost never easy (Nilsson, Eckerberg, and Finnveden 2009). Entrenched interests resist changes that threaten cherished benefits and programs, and lack of attention and organizational inertia more often than not frustrate the ambitions of those seeking change (Baumgartner and Leech 1999; Baumgartner et al. 2009). Furthermore, as Owens (2009, xviii) notes, "integration is difficult because it forces us to make choices," and making choices creates winners and losers.

Studies of environmental policy integration in Europe illustrate other obstacles to its adoption and effectiveness. Lenschow (2002), for example, argues that the policy preferences of key actors and their relative influence in making decisions are also critical. She suggests that because environmental interests are often marginal players, success in policy integration depends on the commitment of actors from other sectors, and their commitment levels inevitably vary. The structure of the policy-making system also matters, with policy change toward greater integration more likely in centralized systems than in those where decisions involve multiple actors at multiple levels. Indeed, most studies point to compartmentalization in government as a serious obstacle to policy integration (Persson 2009). The United States is, of course, a federal system famous for decentralized and fragmented policy making with many decision points that provide ample opportunities for those seeking to derail policy change.

Nevertheless, policy change does happen and the changes are sometimes dramatic (Baumgartner and Jones 1993). In most cases, significant policy change results from external factors, such as crises or focusing events, but it can also stem from policy learning by actors in and out of government (Hall 1993; Sabatier 1988). Increased knowledge about issues, for example, can lead actors to understand them in new ways and to rethink their positions and policy preferences. In this way, political coalitions can be reshuffled and the balance of forces supporting or opposing change can be altered (Schattschneider 1960; Baumgartner et al. 2009).

The potential for policy learning as a path to policy change illustrates that neither policy preferences nor political coalitions are set in stone. In fact, both can be quite unstable and subject to intense maneuvering by political actors seeking to influence policy making in a given area. Rather than assume that efforts to integrate environmental policy are destined to fail because of existing political coalitions, it is conceivable that efforts to integrate policy could also shape those coalitions. As Nilsson, Eckerberg, and Finnveden (2009) suggest, governments can create constituencies, as they have through research and development programs for nuclear power and clean energy. In the United States, Social Security and Medicare are also prime examples of this phenomenon. Once programs are created, there are actors who benefit from them and who have an interest in their success and growth. As a political strategy, then, it is important to have actors within policy sectors who can benefit from policy change (Nilsson, Eckerberg, and Finnveden 2009). As an example, investments in the development of clean energy or new low- and no-waste process technologies can help create and penetrate markets. By stressing their commercial opportunities, advocates of new technologies can create an incentive system that is consistent with market values while simultaneously creating a political force for their extension (Geiser 2004). In this way, providers of green energy technologies can become advocates for policy change.

The use of policy instruments that facilitate integration such as environmental audits or life-cycle assessments can also contribute to policy learning and diffusion in other policy arenas and help broaden the coalitions pushing for greater policy integration. Procedural reforms, such as greater collaboration, can also make the integration process more democratic by providing more knowledge and by increasing the chances for acceptance of policy outputs (Persson 2009). Once established, these tools and procedural requirements can take on a life of their own; international efforts can push the United States to act and federal efforts could have a similar effect on states. Although it is clear that federalism can hinder policy integration, it can also allow for policy learning and reforms that might not have occurred otherwise. States, for example, are said to be "the laboratories of democracy," and have in fact been far more active in initiating climate policy than the national government (Lenschow 2002, 221).

Although the principles of environmental policy integration seem to have been widely embraced in the European Union, in practice its implementation has been spotty (Lenschow 2002; Nilsson, Eckerberg, and Persson 2009). Nevertheless, scholars have identified several factors that are linked to successful integration efforts. Perhaps most important are political will and strong leadership and commitment from the top levels of government (Persson 2009). In the United Kingdom, for example, implementation was most successful when integration had the support of the core executive, the only actor with the authority to impose its will on the various sectoral departments. By contrast, integration efforts faltered when the executive was not supportive and the departments were free to resist. Similarly, for integration efforts to succeed in the long term, they have to become embedded in the daily processes of governmental decision making (Jordan 2002), which itself would seem to assume strong support from political leaders.

Other studies have recommended institutional reforms as a path toward policy integration. Among the proposed solutions are integrating departments and functions, establishing new organizations, and assigning new mandates and accountability measures to existing organizations. Other recommendations include better communication and coordination in the absence of reorganization (Persson 2009).

Why Policy Integration?

Because climate, energy, and air pollution are so closely linked, it is essential that we integrate policy making in these areas and others. For example, given the importance of energy in the US economy and the pervasive awareness of the price of gasoline, energy policy is often framed as an issue of rising prices. But rising global demand and diminishing supplies of cheap oil make price increases inevitable, even as politicians promise to reduce oil prices, crack down on greedy oil companies, and root out price gouging by gas station operators. The fear that the United States is dangerously dependent on imported oil from unstable regions has prompted efforts to develop unconventional sources of oil such as tar sands and oil shale. But developing those resources requires massive amounts of energy and the new coal-fired power plants needed to fuel the transformation of oil shale to oil would only increase greenhouse gas emissions. Other shifts in policy that would require increased burning of coal also run the risk of increasing emissions of conventional pollutants that threaten public health. If these linkages are not recognized, actions taken to address one problem may exacerbate others.

In the case of transportation policy, for example, the weakening of fuel efficiency standards to accommodate growth in SUV and light truck sales has increased oil imports and GHG emissions. In the area of power generation, improved efficiency in producing power and in using electricity results in reduced GHG emissions as well as pollutants that contribute to acid rain and ground-level ozone, but there are some trade-offs involved in using pollution control equipment. Installing scrubbers to reduce sulfur oxide emissions, for instance, actually increases carbon dioxide emissions because of the extra power required for their operation.

Agricultural and land-use policies and practices are also intertwined with energy. Producing and distributing food uses more fossil fuel than any other kind of economic activity except transportation and electricity production. Clearing land for crops and tilling soil for planting releases carbon into the atmosphere. Chemical fertilizers are manufactured using natural gas, pesticides are produced with petroleum, farm machinery uses diesel fuel and gasoline, and the processing, transporting, and packaging of food products is highly energy intensive. Factory farms produce massive amounts of methane emissions that contribute to global warming as well as water pollution. Michael Pollan argues that in 1940, 2.3 calories of food energy were produced for every 1 calorie of fossil fuel energy used in agriculture; it now takes 10 calories of fossil-fuel energy to produce 1 calorie of supermarket food. "Put another way," he writes, "when we eat from the industrial-food system, we are eating oil and spewing greenhouse gases" (Pollan 2008).

It is thus critical that energy policy reflects the linkages of air pollution, climate change, and oil security. Improved energy efficiency is the most effective way to deal with all three problems because it prevents pollution, reduces energy consumption, and improves economic competitiveness as energy costs fall (see chapter 5). Raising energy prices so that they reflect more of the costs of production, distribution, and use is also essential so that markets can produce efficient results. This can be done through taxes on fuel (based on their carbon content) and on vehicles (based on their fuel efficiency). Energy use can be reduced through fuel economy standards and efficiency standards for electrical equipment and appliances, and new emission limits for stationary and mobile sources can reduce pollution. Improved monitoring, inspection, and enforcement can ensure that controls are maintained (MacKenzie 1989). To move in this direction, though, energy policy must be framed within the context of the threat of disruptive climate change.

This is not simply a matter of being green because the benefits to be realized if policy making is more closely integrated are also important to regulated industries and to the collective interest in minimizing the cost of achieving climate stabilization goals. Electric utilities could make long-term investments in capital and equipment aimed at ensuring their compliance with all relevant regulations and policy goals rather than the current process of designing and implementing plans for one set of regulatory requirements and policy goals while hoping that another set will not be imposed a few years later. This was the dynamic in the early years of the Obama administration, when utilities resisted new rules under the CAA in part because of concerns that the climate legislation then working its way through Congress would impose a different set of requirements. Furthermore, new technologies that reduce emissions and improve energy efficiency can be designed and implemented at lower cost if they are part of the initial design rather than required retrofits as new policies take effect. Finally, ensuring that prices reflect more of the true costs of producing goods and services is essential in gaining the benefits from markets, and incorporating energy, climate, and air pollution costs and benefits into those prices can help improve considerably the way in which markets work. Improved energy efficiency can be dramatically altered when the costs of disruptive climate change or the health effects of particulate pollution are attributed to fossil fuel–fired energy production.

There are a number of reasons why a coordinated approach to regulating greenhouse gases and conventional air pollution makes sense. For starters, both are often the product of the same sources; generating electricity, for example, is the major source of GHG and sulfur dioxide emissions and one of the largest sources of nitrogen oxides and mercury. Second, many of the chemical and physical processes important for understanding air quality are also important in climate change. There are numerous process-level similarities in the physics and chemistry of climate change and air quality; as a result, changes in climate could affect air pollution meteorology, leading to changes in the frequency, duration, and intensity of poor air–quality events. Similarly, increases in the concentration of GHGs such as methane and water vapor have global implications for atmospheric chemistry, and consequently, air quality. Changes in climate could thus affect the susceptibility of people and ecosystems to adverse effects from exposure to air pollution. For these reasons, Pennell and colleagues suggest a "one atmosphere" approach to address air quality and climate-change problems that promises to be more effective in protecting human health and the environment than the current fragmented approach. From this perspective, actions taken to address one problem will affect those taken in the other area (Pennell et al. 2005).

There are, however, some key differences between the two sets of issues, as summarized in table 2.1. Conventional air pollutants can

Table 2.1
Differences between Air Pollutants and Greenhouse Gases

Conventional Air Pollution	Greenhouse Gases
Most emissions are caused by process inefficiencies at the source or by fuel contaminants. Emissions can be reduced or eliminated via process improvements or control devices that treat emissions before release.	CO_2 emissions are an inherent consequence of fossil fuel combustion. Capturing and sequestering CO_2 before it is released into the atmosphere is complicated and costly, and achieving the magnitude of emissions reductions needed to deal with climate change will have a transformational effect on the global energy system.
Emissions responsible for most air pollution problems typically have relatively short residence times in the atmosphere. As a result, emission-reduction programs should yield fairly rapid results (i.e., within years or decades).	Several GHGs have very long atmospheric residence times: in the case of CO_2, as long as several centuries. Long residence times result in a considerable delay between action (i.e., increased or decreased emissions) and response (i.e., more or less climate change).
For some pollutants, there are threshold levels below which there are no statistically significant impacts on human or ecosystem health; for others, such as fine particles, there do not appear to be any safe exposure levels.	All GHG emissions that exceed natural removal rates will result in increases in atmospheric concentrations. Stabilizing the atmospheric concentration of long-lived GHGs thus requires that the net emissions from fossil-fuel sources must ultimately be reduced to zero.*

Note: *This does not require that fossil fuels be eliminated; they could continue to be used if CO_2 were captured and sequestered.
Source: Adapted from Pennell et al. 2005, 9.

usually be reduced through end-of-pipe controls, whereas CO_2 is more difficult to remove from waste streams. Conventional pollutants have much shorter atmospheric life times than GHGs, so reducing their emissions has more immediate impacts on atmospheric concentrations. Furthermore, most conventional pollutants are believed to have thresholds below which concentrations pose little risk; that is not the case with GHG emissions.

Others have demonstrated how reducing traditional air pollutants can also lead to lower GHG emissions. A report of the State and Territorial Air Pollution Program Administrators and Association of Local Air Pollution Control Officials (STAPPA/ALAPCO), now known as the National Association of Clean Air Agencies, concluded that fuel switching in stationary sources such as power plants increased fuel efficiency while reducing conventional air pollutants and GHG emissions. The same was true of carpooling, mass transit, and more stringent fuel efficiency standards as well as a variety of programs involving municipal solid waste, such as landfill gas to energy projects (National Association of Clean Air Agencies [State and Territorial Air Pollution Program Administrators, and Association of Local Air Pollution Control Officials], 1999).

Paths to Policy Integration

Existing programs could be adapted to integrate air pollution, climate, and energy goals as well. In voluntary cap-and-trade programs, for example, energy efficiency projects could be used to generate marketable credits for emission reductions. Under the acid rain cap-and-trade program, Congress created the Conservation and Renewable Energy Reserve as a way for power plants to meet acid rain emission–reduction targets by investing in clean energy; sources can earn SO_2 bonus allowances by developing energy efficiency and renewable energy projects. They can then use those allowances as credits against the emission reduction targets or sell them as excess credits to other facilities. Alternatively, governments could auction allowances in national and regional cap-and-trade programs and use the resulting revenue to fund clean energy investments.

Another way energy and air pollution efforts can be linked is through requiring companies to invest in renewable energy projects as part of supplemental environmental project settlements. These settlements result from government actions against polluters. Rather than pay penalties to government agencies for violating clean air rules, companies might agree to purchase a fixed amount of energy from renewable sources, invest in renewable energy projects such as wind farms that would otherwise be too expensive to undertake, help pay for renewable energy projects in public buildings, help fund the cost of research on renewable energy technologies and sites, or invest in green energy marketing campaigns (Kotas n.d.).

Integration through Life-Cycle Analysis

The debate over energy efficiency, renewables, air pollution regulation, and climate policies requires analyses that clearly identify the energy and environmental consequences of major projects. *Life-cycle analysis (LCA)*, also sometimes referred to as *life-cycle assessment* or *life-cycle inventory*, is rooted in energy audits and other modeling exercises from the 1970s that sought to identify the natural resources and environmental impacts associated with human activities. LCA is a systematic effort to examine the environmental impacts of the entire life cycle of a product or service, from cradle to grave. One report nicely summarizes the idea:

A product's life cycle can be represented as a circular movement that ties together resource extraction, production, distribution, consumption and disposal. In other words, all the phases of organized matter and energy that are in some way related to the making and use of a product can also be linked to an impact on the environment. (US Department of Energy, National Renewable Energy Laboratory 2007)

Life-cycle analysis seeks to shift policy making away from conventional command-and-control regulation to shared responsibility for environmental quality among all actors—producers, consumers, governments, and others—and to move away from end of the tailpipe treatment toward pollution prevention. It addresses many of the shortcomings of conventional environmental regulation by assessing upstream and downstream consequences of producing, using, and disposing of products; identifying and then comparing the resources involved in different input streams; and integrating the outputs across different environmental media (water, air, and land). In theory, LCA empowers consumers and industry officials to reduce the environmental impacts of the goods and services they use and helps government officials design more effective regulatory strategies (Frank and Rubik 2000).

Since the 1990s LCA has been adopted by public and private sector entities. To assist US companies and governments that seek to develop LCAs for projects, the US Department of Energy's National Renewable Energy Laboratory created a life-cycle inventory (LCI) database that identifies and quantifies the flow of material and energy out of and into the environment for common industrial processes. A full LCA for a complex product requires the compilation of LCAs for the constituent elements of the product. The inventory can be used to assess the environmental impacts of a company, product, or technology and is made available to the public at the lab's website. Alternative projects can then be compared in terms of their life-cycle impacts, allowing the selection of options that minimize total impacts. Impact indicators could also be used to design interventions to reduce the magnitude and extent of the impacts.

Life-cycle assessments have an obvious appeal to environmentalists but they should also be attractive for advocates of free markets because they can produce prices that reflect the true cost of production and distribution. The great promise that markets make of producing efficient and rational outcomes is threatened by the problem of externalities such as air and water pollution and the failure of prices to reflect all of the relevant costs. Markets often require governmental intervention to ensure that true costs are identified and incorporated into prices so that the benefits of markets can be realized, and LCA is a systematic way to identify all of the costs associated with the production and distribution of goods and services. The daunting problem, however, is quantifying and monetizing all of the true costs so they can be accurately reflected in prices. LCA gets us part of the way but it does not address the fundamental paradox that well-functioning markets require the ability to identify and monetize factors that do not have market prices, but nevertheless must be included in order to produce efficient, true, full-cost prices.

There are other significant challenges to the widespread implementation of LCA. For example, LCA quantifies energy and raw materials used and waste generated at each stage of the life of a product but may not include indirect impacts such as those generated to create the production process itself. The energy that a company uses in its operations may not be part of the analysis but it often has a significant environmental impact. Similarly, the production of components purchased from others could include consequences that are not factored into the LCA (US Department of Energy, National Renewable Energy Laboratory 2009). For these reasons, it is essential to require all major producers of goods and services to perform LCAs, a difficult and controversial task in itself.

Another challenge is deciding what constitutes the cradle and the grave for products. Recycling, for example, may result in significantly reducing the resource and environmental impacts of a product over its life cycle when compared with the same product that is not recycled. Because steel and aluminum are recyclable for many times, there may not be a practical "grave" for these materials. With current technologies, paper can be recycled four or five times before finally being discarded. So how much recycling should be expected in calculating the life cycle of a product? Developing standard measures of impacts has become an essential part of the global effort to encourage LCA (US Department of Energy, National Renewable Energy Laboratory 2007).

Describing the life-cycle impacts requires subjective judgments about what to include in the calculations, but even more subjective are the assessments of those impacts. Analyses of similar products may be quite different because of alternative assumptions and formulas used in making estimates. The inventory identifies the resources used and waste produced but the assessment must then evaluate the significance of the impacts, such as how the effects of different pollutants released at different volumes compare. Which, for example, imposes a greater environmental burden: heavy energy demand or heavy water use? Or how should the use of nonrenewable mineral resources such as oil or gas (the ingredients of plastics) be compared with the production of soft woods for paper?

Although not ideal, life-cycle assessment offers an existing, somewhat familiar path toward greater policy integration. Policy makers already have some experience with the process, as do businesses, so it represents an incremental reform that could be more widely implemented now. Additional ways of extending the use of LCA and other tools are explored in the following section.

Broadening the Environmental Impact Assessment Process

Another way policy integration might be expanded is to require all major proposed projects to conduct life-cycle analyses before project developers apply for construction and other permits. The LCA could be patterned after the environmental impact statement (EIS) required under the US National Environmental Policy Act (NEPA) (42 U.S.C. 4321 et seq.). NEPA requires that all "major federal actions significantly affecting the quality of the human environment" be preceded by an environmental assessment (42 U.S.C. 4332(c)). The agency begins by identifying the alternative policies it believes would achieve its goal and then assesses the environmental impacts associated with each of these options. If the agency believes the impacts associated with its preferred alternative are not significant, it can issue a "finding of no significant impact" and then proceed with it plans. If, however, the impacts are significant, the agency must prepare or contract with others to prepare a full EIS that examines and compares the environmental, social, economic, and other impacts associated with each option (Salzman and Thompson 2003).

Environmental impact statements are widely used in federal agencies, in state and local government agencies that rely on federal funding or permits, and in states that have adopted their own NEPA laws. Requiring agencies to conduct an LCA as part of the environmental impact statement thus has the advantage of building on existing procedures and represents an incremental change rather than a wholesale transformation. Critics of the current NEPA process argue that the EIS is sometimes nothing more than a post hoc rationalization for a decision already made in the agency; for that not to occur, top agency decision makers must commit that the integrity of the process will be protected and that decisions will not be made until the analysis is complete. But critics go further, warning that NEPA only lays out procedural hoops agencies must jump through and only requires disclosure of information rather than providing substantive standards for minimizing environmental impacts.

NEPA's expansive substantive language, written in 1969, reflects contemporary ideas of ecological sustainability: "It is the continuing policy of the Federal Government . . . to use all practicable means and measures . . . to create and maintain conditions under which man and nature can exist in productive harmony, and fulfill the social, economic, and other requirements of present and future generations of Americans (42 U.S.C. 4331(a)). If the NEPA process of preparing impact assessments were combined with substantive values that decision makers were required to follow, it could be a powerful tool to vindicate and preserve those values. At minimum, a NEPA-like requirement for LCA could help sensitize decision makers to the environmental and resource consumption impacts of their decisions. Much as the disclosure of environmental impacts can result in pressure to reduce those adverse impacts, requiring the calculation of resource use and pollution production in an LCA can similarly pressure companies to reduce their impacts. The requirement could go beyond a disclosure provision to impose more substantial obligations on companies, such as requiring them to demonstrate through LCA that the overall environmental impact of proposed projects are the lowest possible that still allow them to achieve their goals with a reasonable rate of return. Such a standard would require a great deal of additional discussion about how exactly to structure the requirement but pilot projects and experiments could be pursued to explore ideas.

Integration through Institutional Innovation

As we have seen, the interconnectedness of climate change, unsustainable energy practices, and air pollution threats clashes with the fragmentation of the policy-making process. One possible, albeit currently unlikely, path to integrating those policies more effectively is through institutional integration and structural innovations in the federal government. The Obama administration took steps in this direction in 2009 by naming former Clinton EPA administrator Carol Browner to a new position as White House coordinator for energy and climate policy. Browner's primary responsibility was to help cabinet departments and agencies work together, despite traditional boundaries, to fashion a single national policy (Hirsh 2009). Although the creation of a climate and energy coordinator may ultimately contribute to policy integration, a much clearer signal would be sent through more formal institutional changes, such as the establishment of a cabinet-level EPA or authorizing legislation that would give it express authority to regulate GHGs and to integrate climate and air pollution programs. Those signals would ultimately have to come through political leadership, which is essential in making policy integration a priority and making sure that institutional innovations translate into actual changes in the policy-making process and in policy itself.

Such proposals are not new, of course, and the lack of consensus over basic environmental policy issues has prevented an update in its structure since the EPA was created in 1970. Walter Rosenbaum's (2008, 88) depiction of the agency as coming to "resemble a regulatory holding company, a conglomerate of offices, each focused narrowly on problems in a single environmental medium (such as air, land, or water) or on one kind of pollutant (such as toxic waste)" illustrates the challenges faced in integrating traditional environmental problems, let alone integrating energy and climate issues. To be sure, a cabinet-level EPA would not automatically resolve these issues because Congress and the White House would need to overcome decades of distrust to restructure the agency. But cabinet-level status for the EPA would be essential in helping to facilitate coordination among the Departments of Energy, Agriculture, and Transportation and other agencies that need to be able to work much more closely together and to integrate their efforts with land use and transportation planning, zoning, and other policy tools.

Even more ambitious would be to create an even larger cabinet department for energy and the environment. That would send a clear signal that the federal government is serious about addressing climate change and that it recognizes that energy policy options cannot be assessed without exploring their broader consequences for climate, air pollution, and related concerns. The creation of the Department of Homeland Security after the September 11, 2001, terrorist attacks illustrates the symbolic and practical impact of institutional change. Elevating security to a cabinet-level department and bringing together a variety of programs under one roof does not necessarily lead to more effective and integrated policy making but it does reduce some of the barriers. The Department of Energy does not have a strong track record in regulatory policy making, and environmental protection is not part of its mission. It has primarily focused on energy research and development, and decisions in those areas will need to be shaped by climate change goals. The two most important energy regulatory bodies, the Federal Energy Regulatory Commission, responsible for interstate energy shipments, and the Nuclear Regulatory Commission, will also need to be part of climate policy making. The EPA already has a regulatory agenda of toxic chemicals, hazardous wastes, and air and water pollution that greatly exceeds its institutional capacity. But creating a new agency with greater capacity is easier said than done, especially at a time when both parties are afraid of new spending initiatives and programs. It is hard to imagine a scenario in the near future when such a proposal would garner sufficient support.

There is always the option of legislative reorganization as well; Congress could restructure the committee system to rationalize and integrate policy making for climate change. Altering committee jurisdictions is always problematic, even under the best of circumstances, and the political costs of doing so may outweigh immediate benefits. Committee and subcommittee chairs zealously defend their jurisdictions and do not cede responsibility easily. If the immediate task, however, is to produce more effective, integrated policies, part of the long-term agenda should be to improve the design of policy-making institutions. The best case for reorganization would likely be in the Senate, where the Environment and Public Works Committee overlaps in significant ways with the Energy and Natural Resources Committee. The House Energy and Commerce Committee's jurisdiction is quite broad and committee chairs have been very effective protectors of their committees' expansive reach. In both chambers, climate policy will be pursued to a great extent through tax subsidies and expenditures, and that will make tax-writing committees central players. Efforts to reorganize Congress in more rational ways to develop an integrated approach to climate change are inevitable but will likely not be worth the bloodletting that will occur, at least for now. In the interim, it seems much more prudent to try to secure legislative changes within the current committee framework than to take on the task of reorganizing congressional committees.

Vertical Integration and the Challenge of Federalism

State and local action on climate policy is, in part, a result of the federal government's failure to take decisive action, but it is also a traditional way in which the United States has developed policies for emerging problems. As it has done in the area of air pollution, California is leading state efforts to establish binding targets for GHG emission reductions, regulating power plant emissions directly and indirectly by setting environmental standards for power imported from other states, and requiring emission reductions from new motor vehicles sold in state. Regional efforts to develop cap-and-trade and other regulatory programs for GHGs further complicate the policy terrain. Enterprising state attorneys general and environmental organizations are taking large companies to court and seeking injunctions that will force the sources to reduce emissions. All these efforts are important in generating support for an integrated, coordinated federal climate policy that will rationalize conflicting programs and regulations and enhance the efficiency and effectiveness of policy efforts.

The institutional fragmentation so characteristic of the US political system should be dramatically refashioned to ensure that these kinds of policy integration actually occur. Vertical integration seeks to guarantee that climate policies are part of every relevant discussion of policy making in other areas, such as energy, transportation, agriculture, and clean air policies. Although difficult to enact in the current environment, institutional changes such as creating a cabinet-level EPA or reorganizing the congressional committee structure could make that easier. Ultimately, climate change must be viewed throughout government as more fundamental to national well-being than economic growth, and a newly empowered EPA would be uniquely positioned to negotiate with the dominant economic and budgetary policy-making actors. Horizontal integration seeks to ensure that climate policy commitments permeate policy implementation. In the United States, that raises difficult issues of federalism. The typical pattern in environmental and other policy areas has been to develop federal standards but to allow states to implement them with some flexibility and adaptability to regional and local concerns. Is that the appropriate model for climate policy? Should existing state policy innovations be insulated from federal preemption, such as California's efforts to impose carbon emission standards for vehicles sold in the state? States in the east and west have explored regional cap-and-trade programs, and it is essential that they are eventually integrated into a national scheme. It is critical that state and federal policy-making efforts be integrated to ensure that emissions do not increase in areas with less regulation and that regional differences in the availability of renewable energy sources are taken into account.

Given the lack of federal action and extensive state climate policies developed since 2000, integrating federal and state policies is essential. Rabe (2008a, 2008b) argues there are three primary options for federal policy makers as they begin to design national policies: federal preemption of state policy making, continued state-level policy making, and collaborative federalism. Federal preemption often occurs when states have taken the initiative to regulate problems, industries warn of having to comply with fifty different standards, and Congress creates a national program. States that have taken the lead in devising policies lobby against federal preemption in order to preserve the benefits they gained as early actors, but if regulated industries come to favor a new federal regulatory policy, it creates considerable political momentum. In the case of climate change, a national cap-and-trade program will likely preempt regional efforts in order to increase coverage and reduce leakage or unregulated emissions and maximize the size of the trades. Given the momentum for federal action, continued bottom-up climate policy making is unlikely to continue.

The third option, collaborative federalism, is the most attractive because it ensures that federal policy makers learn from state innovations, and states are free to customize policy making in ways consistent with local opportunities and benefits. As is the case in other areas of regulation, the federal government can establish national standards and states can go beyond them if they find benefits in doing so. States could be rewarded for taking early actions to reduce emissions and pursuing low-cost emission opportunities that are unique to them. All this requires a significant shift in the way in which Congress and the White House think about national policy and a commitment to engage with states in finding creative partnerships. However, there are few examples of this kind of collaboration in environmental and energy policy making in the past decades and little interest in Congress in learning from state climate policy innovation as it designs national policy options (Rabe 2008b).

In contrast to the US experience, the European Union has grappled with the challenge of balancing central authority and national autonomy; US policy makers can learn from the experience of others. Creative intergovernmental or vertical policy integration is difficult and climate policy is already so complex that national policy makers will be tempted to try to simplify the task as much as possible. But if they do so, they lose the opportunity to build on the important policy innovations of states and threaten to ignore much valuable policy learning and experimentation.

Policy and Political Benefits of Policy Integration

Despite success in some areas, policy deadlock best describes environmental policy making in Congress (Klyza and Sousa 2008). In the face of overwhelming evidence that air pollution is a major public health threat and responsible for thousands of premature deaths a year, many areas continue to exceed national air-quality standards, and legislation aimed at speeding up the achievement of these standards languishes in Congress. Similarly, despite strong scientific agreement and clear signs of the seriousness of the threat of disruptive climate change, the United States lags behind the rest of the world in formulating an effective regulatory program to reduce emissions. Political leaders also seem unmoved by the precariousness of US dependence on imported oil, the way in which that dependency threatens national security, and the growing agreement among petroleum geologists and engineers that the era of cheap oil is drawing to a close. As a result, Congress and the White House have continued to produce energy bills that do little to address the fundamental challenge of beginning to wean the country from its dependence on fossil fuels. In fact, although most energy experts agree that more ambitious actions are essential, energy policy making has rarely gone beyond subsidies for fossil fuels and nuclear power and modest investments in renewable energy research and development.

Policy integration offers a path out of the wilderness. The policy benefits that can come as a result of integrated efforts are clear and compelling; the political benefits are less certain but tantalizing. Although no one issue has been able to generate sufficient political support to produce an effective policy response, a broad coalition of interests might be more likely to produce major policy change, aided by external events such as dramatic climate change–driven damages or major disruptions in energy supply. Because energy policy typically enjoys higher agenda status than air pollution and other issues with environmental implications, such as agriculture or transportation, it tends to be highly partisan and conflictual. Breakthroughs in policy, then, might be more likely in the less polarized arenas (Eckerberg et al. 2009). Although the debate over integration and institutions continues, the difficult task of formulating climate, energy, air pollution, agriculture, and other related policies is the subject of the next chapters.

3

US Climate Policy

Climate change requires a global policy response but US climate policy plays a critical international role for several reasons. The United States has been the major emitter of GHGs and its cumulative emissions tower over those of other nations. If the United States does not curtail its emissions, other countries will resist taking action, fearing that it will do little good. The pressure, then, is on the United States to take the necessary actions now to begin to cut emissions through dramatic investments in energy efficiency, conservation, and existing renewable energy technologies. The policy challenges represented by the threat of climate change are unprecedented and require a tremendous commitment of resources, political will, policy-making creativity, technological innovation, and policy integration and coordination.

The chapter begins with an overview of US greenhouse gas emissions and trends and then examines the evolution of the climate policy debate. The chapter then turns to a discussion of carbon taxes and cap-and-trade programs, the two climate policy options that in the United States have received the most serious consideration.

US Greenhouse Gas Emissions

In 2009, total US emissions of greenhouse gases were 6,633 teragrams of carbon dioxide equivalent (Tg CO_2 Eq.). Emissions increased by 7.3 percent between 1990 and 2009 but actually fell in 2008 and 2009. Lower emissions in those years were the result of decreased energy consumption from the deep recession that began in 2008 and a decrease in the carbon intensity of fuels used to generate electricity; higher coal prices and lower natural gas prices led utilities to switch fuels (US EPA 2011e). Emission trends between 1990 and 2009 are illustrated in figure 3.1.

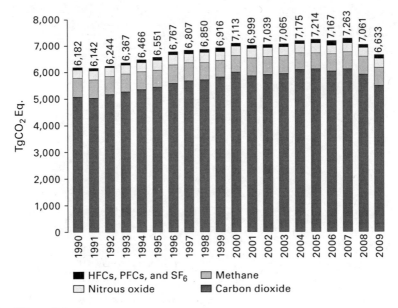

Figure 3.1
US Greenhouse Emissions by Gas, 1990–2009
Source: US EPA 2011e, ES-4.

Figure 3.2 illustrates the contribution of the primary greenhouse gases to total US emissions. Carbon dioxide currently accounts for 83 percent of total US GHGs. Methane, emanating primarily from natural gas production, livestock, and the decomposition of waste in landfills, is responsible for 10.3 percent of total emissions. Nitrous oxide emissions, primarily from agricultural practices and motor vehicles, now account for 4.5 percent of the total; since 1990, though, nitrous oxide emissions have declined more than 6 percent. Emissions of hydrochlorofluoro-carbons (HFCs), perfluorocarbons (PFCs), and sulfur hexafluoride (SF$_6$) represent 2.2 percent of total emissions. HFCs, which are substitutes for ozone-depleting substances, are the primary component of fluori-nated gas emissions, and have increased by 240 percent since 1990. PFCs are a consequence of semiconductor manufacturing and aluminum production, and SF$_6$ releases occur primarily through electrical distribu-tion and transmission systems. These last three substances, although emitted in relatively small quantities, have extremely high global warming potential and, in some cases, long atmospheric lifetimes, which magnifies their impact. Global warming potential (GWP) compares the ability of

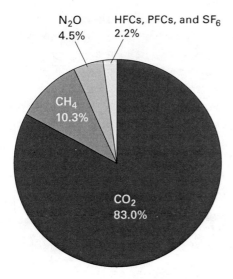

Figure 3.2
Greenhouse Gas Emissions by Gas (percents based on Tg CO_2 Eq.).
Source: US EPA 2011e, ES-7.

Table 3.1
Global Warming Potentials of Greenhouse Gases

Gas	Global warming potential (100-year time horizon)
CO_2	1
CH_4	21
N_2O	310
HFCs	140–11,700
PFCs	6,500–9,200
SF_6	23,900

Source: US EPA 2011e, ES-7.

each greenhouse gas to trap heat in the atmosphere relative to another gas. Table 3.1 shows the global warming potential of the major greenhouse gases.

Carbon Dioxide Emissions
As noted, CO_2 emissions comprise the bulk of US GHG emissions and are thus a key target in climate policy. Fossil fuel combustion was

responsible for nearly 95 percent of carbon dioxide emissions in 2009, with the bulk of emissions coming from the electricity generation, transportation, industrial, residential, and commercial sectors (see figure 3.3). In 2009, electricity generation accounted for 41 percent of the CO_2 emissions from fossil fuel combustion. The type of fuel used to produce electricity largely determines the level of CO_2 emissions and, although some US electricity is generated with low-carbon fuel sources such as nuclear, hydro, or wind, most electricity comes from burning coal or natural gas. When CO_2 emissions from electricity generation are distributed to the other four "end-use" sectors, transportation activities account for nearly a third from fossil fuel combustion, virtually all from petroleum. Emissions from industrial sources are the third largest source (26 percent) of CO_2 emissions from fossil fuel combustion; the fuels used in this sector are primarily natural gas and oil. About half of these emissions come directly from fossil fuels used to produce steam or heat for industrial processes; the other half comes from the generation of electricity used to power motors, lighting, and other equipment. The residential and commercial sectors were responsible for 22 and 19 percent, respectively, of carbon dioxide emissions from fossil fuel combustion. These emissions are largely from natural gas, although home heating oil continues to play a significant role in residential CO_2 production (US EPA 2011e). Finally, these emissions are partly offset by the carbon sequestration that occurs in forests, urban trees, soils, and other forms of plant life. In 2009, biological sequestration offset 15 percent of total GHG emissions (US EPA 2011e).

Methane Emissions
As noted, methane has a significantly higher global-warming potential than carbon dioxide. As figure 3.4 illustrates, the largest anthropogenic sources of methane are natural gas systems, enteric fermentation (digestion) in livestock, landfills, coal mining, and manure management. Emissions from natural gas systems have increased nearly 17 percent since 1990 and are expected to rise as natural gas development expands. Methane emissions have also increased from coal mining, enteric fermentation, and manure management; the increase in the last is due largely to the increased size of swine and cattle operations and the increasing use of liquid systems, which produce greater methane emissions. Emissions from landfills, however, have decreased since 1990 because more landfill gas is collected and burned (US EPA 2011e).

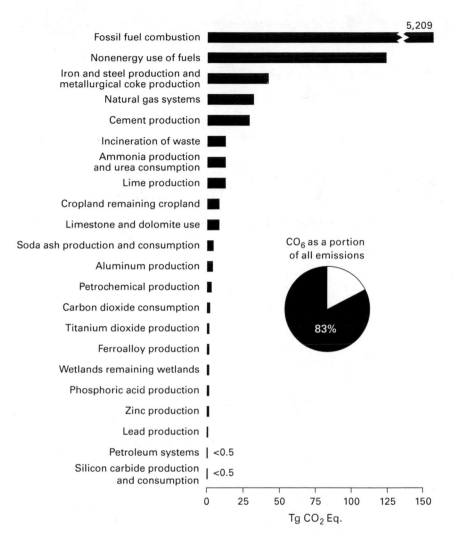

Figure 3.3
Sources of CO_2 Emissions, 2009.
Source: US EPA 2011e, ES-8.

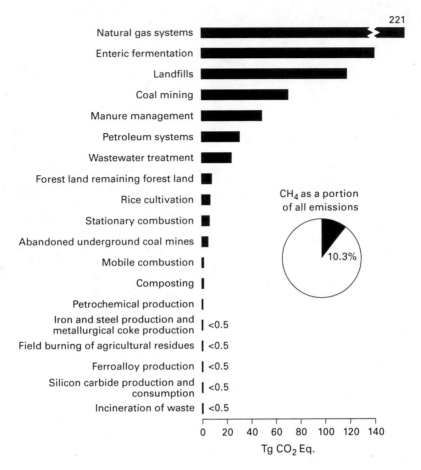

Figure 3.4
Sources of Methane Emissions, 2009.
Source: US EPA 2011e, ES-11.

Nitrous Oxide Emissions

Nitrous oxide accounts for only 4.5 percent of all GHG emissions but it is three hundred times more powerful than carbon dioxide in trapping heat in the atmosphere. The primary sources of nitrous oxide emissions are agricultural soil management, gasoline combustion in motor vehicles, manure management, nitric acid production, and stationary fuel combustion, largely in power plants. Agricultural soils account for nearly 70 percent of nitrous oxide emissions in the United States and total emissions from this source have remained stable since the 1990s. Since 1990, NO_x emissions from motor vehicles have declined nearly 46 percent as a result of improved control technologies (US EPA 2011a).

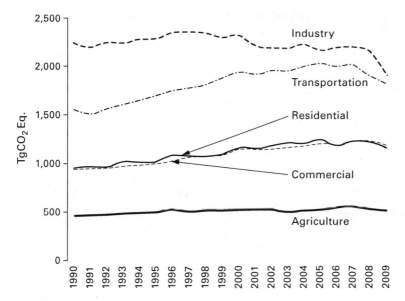

Figure 3.5
GHG Emissions Allocated to Economic Sectors, 1990–2009.
Note: Does not include US territories.
Source: US EPA 2011e, ES-19.

Figure 3.5 illustrates overall GHG emissions by economic sector. As with CO_2, electricity generation is the largest source, responsible for 33 percent of US emissions in 2009, followed by transportation (27 percent), industrial activities (20 percent), agriculture (7 percent), commercial (6 percent), and residential (5 percent). Emissions have decreased in several sectors, with the long-term decline in the industrial sector the result of fuel switching, energy efficiency, and to structural changes in the US economy, notably the shift from manufacturing to services. Emissions are largely carbon dioxide in all of the sectors except agriculture, where methane and nitrous oxide emissions predominate (US EPA 2011e). Given their total emissions, the greatest opportunities for GHG reductions are in electric generation, transportation, and industrial uses of electricity.

The Evolution of Climate Change Policy

The federal government's failure to develop an effective climate policy is not a great political puzzle but the reasons for the failure help explain why future policy action will be difficult as well. US scientists and political leaders initially played a leading role in the evolution of efforts to identify climate change as a global environmental threat. In speeches and hearings in 1987 and 1988, Senators Al Gore (D-TN), Tim Wirth (D-CO), and John Chafee (R-RI) were among the first politicians to draw attention to the threat of global warming and disruptive climate change. Research by US scientists played a role in laying the foundation for the first global climate change meeting in 1988, where scientists called for a 20 percent reduction in carbon dioxide and other GHGs by 2005.

In 1988, at the end of the Reagan administration's second term, then vice president George H. W. Bush, seeking to distance himself from controversial and unpopular Reagan environmental policies, expressed some support for efforts to reduce the threat of climate change. He promised those who were worried about the greenhouse effect that, if elected, he would unleash the "White House effect" to solve the problem. In 1989, Secretary of State James Baker suggested that the United States pursue a "no-regrets" policy—taking prudent steps such as investing in energy efficiency and reducing emissions of air pollutants "that are already justified on grounds other than climate change" and would produce significant benefits even if the threat of global warming turned out not to be serious (Bryner 2000, 112–113).

By 1990, however, support for a legally binding commitment to reducing GHG emissions was waning as the Bush administration focused on the nation's economic woes. Senior administration officials warned that reducing emissions would threaten the US economy and the United States aggressively opposed efforts during the 1992 United Nations Conference on Environment and Development in Rio to negotiate a binding agreement to reduce GHG emissions. The United States and some 180 other nations eventually agreed to the Framework Convention on Climate Change, which entered into force in 1994. Under the accord, the signatories committed to a voluntary, nonbinding agreement to stabilize greenhouse gas emissions "at a level that would prevent dangerous anthropogenic interference with the climate systems" and to "take precautionary measures to anticipate, prevent, or minimize the causes of climate change and mitigate its adverse effects" (United Nations 2002, Articles 2 and 3).

The Clinton administration's (1993–2001) climate change policies, formulated as part of the United States' obligation under the Framework Convention, were largely a set of voluntary measures aimed at industries, commercial establishments, and consumers. The administration did not pursue mandatory emission reductions such as higher fuel efficiency standards or increased energy taxes because of their political unpopularity and because it did not want to jeopardize economic growth. Its opportunity to push through bold initiatives lasted only two years; in 1994, Republicans took control of Congress and promised to reduce regulatory burdens and free industry from government interference (Kraft 2006). By 1997, opposition to climate change policies was so strong in Congress that the Senate voted 95 to 0 to pass a resolution opposing US participation in protocols to the climate accord that did not include binding limits on developing nations (Senate Resolution 98, July 25, 1997). The Clinton administration signed the Kyoto Protocol in 1998 but also indicated that it would not submit the treaty for ratification until the accord required meaningful participation by the developing countries and flexibility measures, such as emissions trading, to ease compliance costs (Pope 1998).

During the 2000 presidential election candidate George W. Bush, much like his father had done, promised to take on climate change. One of his campaign promises was to support a regulatory effort to clean up coal-fired power plants and reduce their emissions of four pollutants: sulfur dioxide, nitrogen oxides, mercury, and carbon dioxide. Shortly after taking office, however, President Bush reversed his position on CO_2 controls, announced that his administration was withdrawing from the Kyoto Protocol, and promised to provide its own plan for reducing the threat of climate change. The administration eventually released its climate initiative, a voluntary program to encourage emissions reductions and a business-as-usual commitment to continue the nation's improvement in energy efficiency, called *energy intensity*, which measures the amount of energy used per unit of economic output.[1] It also began to engage China and other major emitters in the Asian Pacific Partnership to encourage the use of clean energy in economic development. The Bush administration steadfastly opposed a binding GHG reduction, first because it argued more research was needed and later because it simply opposed mandatory programs that would raise energy costs. After Democrats took control of Congress in the 2006 midterm elections, a host of climate bills were introduced, but none passed.

The election of Barack Obama as president in 2008 seemed to herald the transformation of US climate policy. During the campaign, Obama had championed action on climate issues and the new administration and congressional leaders moved quickly to propose new climate and energy policies. In April 2009 they issued a finding under the CAA that GHGs endangered health and safety, thus allowing the EPA to begin to prepare to issue emission limits on mobile and stationary sources (US EPA 2009). This finding was politically important because it formalized the shift in policy that had already occurred between the Bush and Obama administrations. It also increased pressure on Congress to act by raising the prospect of EPA regulation under the CAA; the thinking was that Congress would prefer a congressionally designed cap-and-trade scheme that would give sources more flexibility. Industry groups preferred a legislative approach for the same reason, fearing that a regulatory approach would lead to mandatory cuts in greenhouse gas tailpipe emissions, expensive retrofits for old power plants, and mandates for additional renewable energy production (Weisman and Hughes 2009).

In 2009, the House took the lead in climate policy when Henry Waxman (D-CA), chair of the Energy and Commerce Committee, and climate subcommittee chair Ed Markey (D-MA) introduced the American Clean Energy and Security Act (ACES). After months of negotiation and compromise, the House passed the measure by a narrow 219 to 212 margin. The final bill established a cap-and-trade program for several greenhouse gases and required a 17 percent reduction in GHG emissions below 2005 levels by 2020, a 42 percent reduction by 2030, and an 83 percent reduction by 2050. The bill also provided allowances, regulated by the Federal Energy Regulatory Commission, to help minimize the costs for consumers and businesses. Initially 75 percent of allowances would be distributed for free; over time, though, up to 40 percent would be auctioned. The bill also provided for up to two billion tons (one billon domestic and one billion international) in offsets through emission reduction or sequestration projects. In addition, the bill preempted state cap-and-trade programs but allowed states to enact other, more stringent climate regulations.

In the end, the Senate failed to act on climate legislation, which was hardly surprising because votes earlier in the year had signaled how little support there was for an effective climate policy. For example, the fiscal year 2010 budget resolution included an amendment stipulating that no climate change bill should raise energy or gasoline prices. It is hard to imagine an effective carbon policy that does not somehow result in higher energy prices. Another successful amendment sought to ensure that a cap-and-trade program not be authorized as part of a budget reconciliation vote because those measures only require fifty-one votes to pass rather than the sixty votes required to overcome a filibuster that could be used to oppose a climate bill arising under regular lawmaking rules (Danish 2009).

In the end, climate policy was derailed by the recession and economic stimulus policies. The administration did, however, work with Congress to create a ten-year $150 billion spending program for energy efficiency and renewable energy (see chapter 5 for details). The recession provided the primary impetus for the enactment of energy legislation and the transition to cleaner energy. Energy and climate change, however, were still not integrated into a coherent whole. Democrats and Republicans were wary of any energy policy initiative that would raise energy prices or have other short-term adverse economic impacts, and demands for cheap energy prices continued to dominate energy politics (Gingrich 2009).

The Politics of Climate Change

The development of a host of state and regional initiatives for a problem that, because of its scope, clearly requires national and international policy responses is striking. The broad agreement among scientists about the need for massive GIIG reductions has reached many state capitols even as Washington continues to deny there is a problem. When compared with the public health implications of air pollution and the national security costs of fossil fuel addiction, climate change is a more challenging issue for politicians to address. Public policies that impose costs on current voters in order to secure benefits for future generation, such as climate change mitigation actions, are notoriously difficult to enact. The complexity of climate change itself is also part of the explanation for federal inaction; it is rife with uncertainties about when, how fast, and in what ways climate changes might occur, and the scientific debates have been difficult for the public to understand. Some of the consequences of climate change lie well into the future and, as a result, do not generate the kinds of demands for political action that other environmental problems posing immediate health threats and risks typically do (Gelbspan 2004; Kolbert 2006).

In addition, a concerted campaign by Republicans and industry officials to sow doubt about climate science contributes to the difficulty of generating support for climate policies. For many Republicans, the climate science consensus represented by the National Academy of Sciences and the Intergovernmental Panel on Climate Change is not enough to offset their ideological opposition to climate change policy because it means more government regulation. Strong opposition to environmental politics from businesses that oppose new regulatory burdens in general and climate policy in particular has also been a factor. Companies such as Exxon and Koch Industries have invested in advocacy groups that have raised questions about climate science, and Republicans have used these doubts to block action on climate initiatives (Kraus 2007; Begley 2007). Because of the major role of fossil fuels in GHG emissions, climate policy is also energy policy, and efforts to transform energy production from fossil fuels to cleaner alternatives is imperiled by the political influence of oil, gas, and coal interests (Layzer 2006).

During the first era of US environmental policy making, in the 1960s and 1970s, environmental protection was a bipartisan issue, with Republicans and Democrats playing leadership roles. The aggressiveness of environmental laws, such as the 1970 CAA's mandate to the EPA to establish national ambient air-quality standards that would protect public health "with an adequate margin of safety" (42 U.S.C. 7409) and consequently without consideration of costs, and the 1972 Clean Water Act's goal of eliminating *all* discharges of pollutants into the nation's waterways by 1985, reflect the result of competition between the parties over who could be most environmentally friendly. Both sides clamored to make moral statements about how bad pollution was and how important it was for the nation to set ambitious goals to force the development of new technologies and not allow government agencies to backslide (Salzman and Thompson 2003).

The fracture in bipartisan environmentalism was primarily the result of Ronald Reagan's hostility toward the federal government in general and his appointments to the EPA, Department of Interior, and other agencies that believed that some of the laws under their jurisdiction were unconstitutional (Andrews 2006). Ideological commitments replaced bipartisanship and consensus in environmental policy making. Congressional Democrats fought pitched battles with administrators hostile to the laws that Congress had passed the decade before. Broader political forces have also polarized the United States and made it much more difficult for those seeking policy change. Gone is the era of bipartisan cooperation in protecting environmental quality and environmental advocates now face a more hostile political climate. Richard N. L. Andrews (2006, 350–351) calls this the "era of base politics," where strident ideological and partisan conflict has replaced bipartisanship and political parties routinely use environmental conflict as a means of mobilizing their base. Environmentalism appears to have entered a new phase, one that differs fundamentally from the consensus that dominated early environmental policy making.

State and Local Climate Initiatives

The paralyzing partisanship and entrenched ideological polarization that characterizes national climate policy has been much weaker at the state and local levels; indeed, state and local governments have been active on the issue for some time (Betsill and Bulkeley 2003; Rabe 2004; Klyza and Sousa 2008). Early in 2005, the mayors of 132 cities formed a bipartisan coalition and agreed to reduce their emissions in line with Kyoto Protocol targets; by October 2011, more than one thousand mayors had embraced that goal and committed to lobby Congress to enact greenhouse gas–reducing legislation (US Conference of Mayors 2011). Even more ambitious are the goals states are setting for reducing GHG emissions. By 2011, twenty-one US states have established GHG emissions reduction goals; twelve of them have committed to reducing emissions by 75 to 80 percent by 2050. Although these long-term goals are not yet codified into law in most states, and many are largely concentrated in the Northeast and West Coast, areas that are traditionally greener than the rest of the nation, it is striking that so many states have accepted the need to significantly curtail their GHG emissions. Indeed, most states have developed or are in the process of developing climate action plans; forty-one states participate in the Climate Registry's plan to develop a consistent methodology for reporting GHG emissions (Royden-Bloom 2009). In short, states have been active in setting emissions targets but there is a broad range of targets and deadlines, illustrating the challenge in integrating state and national climate policies.

Regional efforts in New England and the West to set GHG-reduction goals are particularly important. The Northeast's Regional Greenhouse Gas Initiative (RGGI) was the first regional program to create binding emission limits; the governors of seven states have committed to a cap-and-trade system that would impose a target for reducing carbon dioxide emissions from power plants, allocate emission allowances to each source, and allow them to find the cheapest way to reduce emissions and meet their targets by trading allowances. Their goal is to stabilize emissions at current levels from 2009 by 15 percent and then reduce them by 10 percent by 2019. In July 2007, the governors of California, Oregon, Washington, Arizona, New Mexico, and Utah formed a western climate initiative to develop a greenhouse gas registry (building on California's pioneering work in this area) and agreed to develop plans to reduce emissions by 15 percent by 2020. It is striking that so many states have accepted the idea of a 75 to 80 percent reduction goal. The magnitude of that goal also depends on what baseline is used: a 75 percent reduction in emissions from a 1990 baseline versus a 2005 to 2006 baseline is large, and although most states are using the 1990 baseline, some are using the current level of emissions.

Transforming the Politics of Climate Policy

Unless there are major breakthroughs in clean energy technologies or engineering innovations to counter global warming, the transformation to a stable climate will require a massive restructuring of economic life, which results in a dramatic reduction in energy use. Suburban sprawl, single-occupant vehicles, energy-consuming recreation and entertainment, food shipped around the world, and goods and services produced with intensive energy will have to be dramatically curtailed. Food production itself will either decline or replace the production of other goods that people will no longer be able to afford. Governments and societies will be unable to afford much besides adapting to the disruptive consequences of climate change.

The challenge posed by such a dramatic transformation in the way the world produces and consumes energy far outstrips the capacity of our political system. Carbon dioxide is an inevitable by-product of fossil fuel consumption, and the primary way to significantly reduce the threat of climate change is to reduce the use of fossil fuels. But burning fossil fuels has become central to human life. As societies get richer, they are able to reduce some environmental ills, such as traditional air and water pollutants, but their carbon emissions steadily grow. Bill McKibben (2007, 24) argues that environmental organizations are well suited to take on specific environmental problems, such as protecting the Arctic national Wildlife Refuge, but are overwhelmed by the challenge of taking on energy production and use, the major driver of modern life: "Well armed for small battles with insurgent polluters, we suddenly find ourselves needing to fight World War II," but "this is a war that environmentalism as currently constituted simply can't win." The magnitude of the problem of fossil fuel use requires a broad political movement, a social transformation that pressures politicians to take a strong position on climate policy and, similar to other broad social movements, changes the nation's basic political architecture.

Environmental organizations enjoy considerable resources and can play a significant role in the transformation to a new environmental politics to reduce the threat of climate change. Because Republican opposition to climate policy is designed to maintain its base of electoral support, if major segments of that base were to shift and support action to reduce CO_2 emissions, it could destabilize the party and lead to policy action. Some environmental organizations, such as the Sierra Club, are working through the National Religious Partnership for the Environment to educate and mobilize the religious community about the risks of climate change. If this effort attracts support among evangelicals and those that make up the "religious right," the political dynamics of climate change could shift. There are, however, few signs that such a shift is taking place (*Science* 2006; Eilperin 2007).

Business is the other significant portion of the Republican political base. Some utilities have expressed support for climate regulations because it provides them with greater certainty. If state regulation of CO_2 creates an inconvenient patchwork of regulations, utilities may seek national action (Cleaning Up 2007). Shareholders are increasingly concerned about the federal government's failure to address climate change because of its financial implications; shareholder climate-change resolutions have met with some success. If state attorneys general and others are successful in tort suits against auto and power companies seeking compensation for climate-related damages, companies could seek federal regulatory action as a form of protection (Bryner 2007a).

The only occasional success that environmental groups have enjoyed in working with industry demonstrates how difficult these efforts are. The Natural Resources Defense Council (NRDC) and Environmental Defense Fund (EDF) have been involved in a number of efforts to help companies develop cleaner fuels and become more energy efficient. In 2006, EDF challenged TXU Energy's plans to build eleven new coal-fired plants in Texas and waged a public battle with the firm over its GHG emissions. In February 2007, when the company was to be sold to two large private equity firms, the new owners negotiated an agreement with EDF, promising to scale back the new construction plans and to comply with a new set of environmental principles. EDF, later joined by NRDC, also demanded a commitment to reduce GHG emissions to 1990 levels by 2020 and a $400 million investment in energy efficiency (Sorkin 2007).

Climate Policy Options

The debate over climate policy options includes a wide array of issues, but two questions are central: what should be the goal or target for GHG reductions and how should those reductions be achieved? With respect to the first question, given the dynamic nature of climate science, the uncertainty over the timing and distribution of impacts and the inherent difficulties in making long-term policy commitments, the debate over targets might seem arbitrary. But it deserves attention because positions taken here reflect differing views about the seriousness of the climate-change threat and the priority it should be given. Some champion the 80 percent reduction goal by 2050 that many climate scientists argue is essential and others assume a more modest goal, either because of skepticism about the threat itself or because they place a higher priority on economic growth.

Although it is difficult to assess the array of options for establishing a GHG reduction target, the best estimate of consensus bodies of climate scientists about what is required to stabilize the climate is the place to begin. The United States and most every other country agreed to that goal in 1992 but it was not clear what magnitude of reductions was required to meet that commitment. The best science currently suggests the answer is an 80 percent reduction by midcentury from 1990 levels. As climate science evolves, of course, that target may change. But the sooner we begin to make reductions, the more options we will have. For example, if the United States had committed to hold emissions constant in 1990 while scientific research continued, we would have prevented the 16 percent increase in emissions that occurred between 1990 and 2005 (US EPA 2006).

Setting goals forty years into the future makes sense because of the lifetime of many of the energy-related investments we make. Similarly, having a clear goal is critical to ensuring that new power plants, buildings, and factories are designed so they can contribute to the ambitious GHG-reduction goal at midcentury. The sooner we make the commitment, the sooner there will be at least some measure of certainty for companies to rely on in making long-term plans. But the uncertainties about the future of climate change make it all the more important for planning to build in maximum flexibility so adjustments can be made as new scientific findings and technological breakthroughs occur.

Despite clear, long-term goals, there is always a risk that politicians will embrace the goals, claim credit for having addressed the issue, and then leave to their successors the need to make painful policy changes. The Bush administration's decision in 2008 to accept the G8's 50 percent reduction by 2050 is a good example; the decision earned global plaudits and helped erase frustration with the lack of participation by the administration in earlier negotiations but it was not accompanied by immediate (and probably unpopular or controversial) measures to begin reducing emissions. Much more important than the establishment of a specific goal is a commitment to reversing current trends and to begin taking steps to steadily reduce emissions.

The second key question facing policy makers is how should the reductions be achieved? Four primary approaches have dominated discussion in recent years: a carbon cap-and-trade program that sets a cap or ceiling on emissions required to produce the desired reductions; a carbon tax that raises the price of carbon dioxide emissions (and other GHGs through a carbon-equivalent tax) aimed at creating an incentive to reduce emissions; conventional regulations such as emissions standards that mandate cuts; and subsidies and tax incentives that encourage the development and deployment of clean energy practices and technologies that reduce emissions. The four approaches are not mutually exclusive and could all be employed but in the United States the debate has largely focused on the advantages of cap-and-trade versus carbon taxes, with cap and trade perceived as more politically feasible. Both cap-and-trade and carbon-tax options can be part of an integrated approach to policy making, and policy integration is a central concern in blending the overall strategy selected with the extensive regulations and subsidies that are already in place.

Strategies for Achieving the Emissions Reduction Target

As indicated previously, there are a number of ways we might try to reduce carbon emissions and their role in climate change. We could enact laws and implement policies that ban certain products that release high levels of carbon, as we did in enacting amendments to the CAA in 1990, which banned products that use certain chlorofluorocarbons (42 U.S.C. 7671). We can reduce carbon emissions by imposing efficiency standards on sources, such as the corporate average fuel economy (CAFE) standards for motor vehicle manufacturers; efficiency standards for appliances, industrial equipment, lighting, and buildings are also examples. We can subsidize low-carbon energy sources such as wind, solar, and hydropower and encourage people to use less energy or cleaner forms of energy through educational campaigns. We can require electricity producers to shift to cleaner burning fuels, such as natural gas, and to sequester carbon emissions rather than releasing them into the atmosphere. These options are explored in the following section.

We can also act to ensure that energy prices include all costs resulting from the carbon emissions from energy production and use. These approaches are not mutually exclusive, of course; a combination of approaches can and will needed to reduce carbon emissions. But in an economic system dominated by and fundamentally organized by markets, it makes a great deal of sense to focus on correcting those markets so they reflect the true costs of producing energy. Economic theory is simple, straightforward, and compelling here. Markets promise to yield decisions about production and consumption that reflect the interests of consumers while promoting the most economically efficient use of available resources. If markets reflect all the costs associated with goods and services, and if consumers have accurate information about the true costs and benefits of alternatives, then markets will be able to produce the benefits they promise. The policy-making task is to ensure that, as much as possible, true cost prices dominate and accurate information is available because producers also have an incentive to maximize their profits by externalizing as many costs as possible. What is clear in theory, however, is exceedingly difficult to achieve in practice. Because there are so many uncertainties concerning the impacts of the growing concentration of GHG gases in the atmosphere, calculating the true costs of preventing disruptive climate change is challenging.

As mentioned previously, the two most widely discussed ways of internalizing the costs of carbon into markets are carbon taxes and carbon cap-and-trade programs. Carbon taxes can take a variety of forms, from taxes on fuels, calculated based on their carbon content, to taxes imposed on those who consume energy and other goods and services implicated in carbon emissions. Cap-and-trade programs set a ceiling or cap on total allowable emissions, allocate allowances or permits to carbon sources that set a cap on their individual emissions, and then allow the sources to meet their cap by a combination of emissions reductions and buying excess allowances from other sources that have reduced their emissions beyond their cap.

Carbon Taxes
Despite the obvious political barriers to raising taxes, carbon taxes are an attractive policy option for reducing GHG emissions. Compared to cap-and-trade policies, carbon taxes are relatively simple to design and implement, easy to understand and explain, and can be put in place

more quickly. If they are sufficiently high, carbon taxes can also create clear incentives to reduce emissions. Unlike emission standards that, once met, provide no incentive for further innovations, taxes provide a continuous reason to find ways to reduce emissions. Carbon taxes could also raise revenue to finance investments in energy conservation, improved efficiency, and renewable energy sources and could help produce more efficient markets by ensuring that prices include more of the total costs of producing and using goods and services. Taxes can also be adjusted up or down if necessary to achieve environmental and economic goals.

Carbon taxes possess the important virtue of making more transparent the total costs of the goods and services we consume. A carbon tax raises prices proportionately to the amount of carbon that is generated at each step in the production of the goods and services. For example, if the growing, milling, mixing, baking, and transporting of a loaf of bread produces 0.01 ton of carbon, then a carbon tax of $30 per ton would raise the price by 30 cents, and, if the information is disclosed to consumers, they would be able to calculate their carbon footprint from eating bread and know the true cost of their consumption. More broadly, a carbon tax would provide information to consumers about the climate-related costs of the goods and services they consume so they could make choices armed with that information. Producers and investors could similarly make informed decisions (Nordhaus 2008). Although taxes of any kind are wildly unpopular with policy makers and the public, a carbon tax is consistent with efficient markets. Carbon taxes could be balanced by reducing taxes on other behavior, such as people's work, and thereby contribute to markets that work better and generate more of the benefits that markets promise, in theory, to produce.

Cap and Trade

Cap-and-trade approaches to reducing GHG emissions, similar to carbon taxes, have advantages and disadvantages. Perhaps the most important advantage, until recently, was that cap-and-trade programs did not suffer from the political opposition generated by calls to raise taxes, which is why most of the recent climate legislation considered by Congress embraced cap and trade rather than carbon taxes. But once President Obama endorsed it, most Republicans who had previously endorsed cap and trade rejected it as another example of excessive federal interference in the free market. Prior to Obama's support, though, many Republicans who supported cap and trade did so precisely because it was consistent with market principles, and it allowed sources the flexibility of deciding how best to reduce their emissions. Cap-and-trade programs were also thought to have the best chance of becoming law because they were familiar to policy makers; the acid rain program adopted in the 1990 CAA amendments used the approach.

In theory, cap-and-trade programs offer other benefits as well: allowances could be auctioned to raise revenue that, like a carbon tax, could be used to fund clean energy investments or rebates to taxpayers (making it more acceptable politically); if accurately set, the emissions cap could ensure that environmental protection goals are achieved at lower cost than under regulatory approaches; the market in allowances effectively sets the price of carbon and channels private sector resources more efficiently than government mandates.

However, designing and implementing cap-and-trade programs is no easy task. Such programs are complex, involving difficult choices such as at what level the cap should be set, to whom the allowances allocated under the cap should be given, whether allowances should be sold or distributed for free, and how long the allowances should last before they expire. The implementation of a program is just as daunting, requiring accurate monitoring and reporting of emissions, enforcement of allowance caps, and the imposition of sanctions for violations. Moreover, once allowances are allocated, they are difficult to retrieve if too many are distributed. Finally, compliance costs in cap-and-trade programs are uncertain and difficult to plan for in business and government decision making.

There are tremendous challenges involved in designing and implementing an effective cap-and-trade program, but if those challenges can be addressed, it can be an important part of efforts to reduce the threat of climate change. A cap-and-trade approach focuses on the key issue of what is required in order to secure a healthy environment. Although it is difficult to know exactly what the emissions cap should be, cap-and-trade approaches focus attention on the need to make policy decisions based on the best scientific evidence we have. Carbon tax advocates argue that we need policies with fixed economic costs and thus reject cap and trade because the costs are uncertain, but more important than setting a limit on the amount of money to be spent on climate stabilization, it makes more sense to give priority to trying to determine what is required to secure a stable climate. Cap-and-trade discussions begin with the right question, even if the answer is not always clear.

As is true of carbon taxes, cap-and-trade programs seek to ensure that markets reflect the true costs of products such as energy. A carbon tax that reflects the true cost of emitting carbon in producing goods and services would help achieve that purpose but it is difficult to know what level of taxation does that. If the tax is set too low, then sources will simply continue to release GHGs and pay the tax, so the problem will not be solved. As Monica Prasad (2008, 27) put it, "a carbon tax is a tax you want to impose but never collect." If carbon taxes are high enough that sources of GHGs would rather reduce their emissions than pay the tax, however, the climate goal is advanced. But if the purpose of the tax is to raise money for clean energy and other projects, a stringent tax will not deliver the hoped-for revenues.

Prices for goods and services containing carbon, for example, if they are determined in a market shaped by such a carbon cap, will reflect at least the climate change–related costs. One major problem here, of course, is that there is not an unambiguous cap for climate change. There is no point at which we shift from no climate change to climate change; rather, it is a matter of degree. Setting a cap to achieve an 80 percent GHG reduction, then auctioning allowances to all sources so that total emissions do not exceed the cap, allows markets to allocate scarcity in the most economically efficient manner and avoids the very difficult political challenge of allocating emission allowances. Again, this is an imprecise calculation, fraught with difficulties and uncertainties, but it focuses attention on securing environmental quality and then using markets to achieve that goal rather than putting an economic goal first. In the end, if a cap is designed well enough to achieve the environmental goal, it then establishes a market mechanism for determining true costs.

Industries typically favor trading programs rather than taxes because, in the United States, trading programs usually distribute allowances for free in order to minimize political opposition. Taxes represent clearly visible cost increases, and thus most politicians shy away from them. If a carbon tax could be uniformly applied to create a level playing field, it might be attractive to industries because it would make their compliance efforts much simpler to calculate than under a cap-and-trade scheme. But a carbon tax would reward some industries and fuels and penalize others, and the creation of winners and losers makes the politics of designing a carbon tax very dicey. In short, cap-and-trade and carbon-tax policies are difficult to design and implement in the face of powerful interests' ability to exert political pressure.

Carbon taxes and cap-and-trade schemes could also be combined. A hybrid cap-and-tax system, for example, could establish an emissions cap, allocate allowances to major sources, and also impose a carbon tax. In order to put a check on compliance costs, allowances could be sold at a price above that of the carbon tax so sources that faced high emission-reduction costs could purchase more allowances (Nordhaus 2008). Or a trading system could be created for some sources and a tax used to create incentives for sources outside the system to reduce their emissions.

Given the complexity of designing and implementing a cap-and-trade program, the difficulty in altering the distribution of allowances if necessary to make further cuts, and the lack of governing capacity in many countries to make such a complicated program work, a carbon tax seems a more attractive route. That may eventually be the case, but in recent years the policy debate has focused on creating a national cap-and-trade program. For this reason, it makes sense to ask what are the requirements for an effective carbon cap-and-trade program.

Requirements for an Effective Cap-and-Trade Program

One key component of effective trading programs is getting the cap right. As noted previously, the CAA of 1990 established a cap-and-trade system for sulfur dioxide to reduce acid rain–producing emissions from coal-fired power plants. The heart of the acid rain emissions trading system is the idea of a cap on total emissions projected, by the year 2010, to result in a reduction of sulfur dioxide emissions of ten million tons from 1980 levels. The targets of the acid rain program were met and at a much lower cost than would have been expected without the cap-and-trade program. The projected cost per ton of achieving the reductions was expected to be more than $350 per ton in the 1990s and rise to more than $500 a ton throughout the first decade of the twenty-first century. Instead, actual costs per ton have remained between $100 and $200 per ton (Environmental Defense 2008). Research suggests, however, that the problem of acid deposition is far from solved, and that many lakes, streams, and forests continue to suffer from the effects of sulfur dioxide emissions. The problem requires further study but it appears that the cap may have been set too low or that one national cap may not adequately take into account the variety in the susceptibility of different areas to the effects of acid rain. According to one study, acid rain is still a problem for Atlantic salmon populations in Nova Scotia, lakes in Canada and New York, streams in Virginia, fish diversity in northern Pennsylvania, and red spruce and sugar maples in the Northeast (Clean Air Task Force 2001). These problems highlight how critical it is to devise a cap that will ensure the environmental goal is achieved, and that is no small task for climate change, which involves several different gases.

Another issue is which GHGs to include in the program. A cap-and-trade system is complicated enough if it just includes carbon dioxide; adding the other GHGs may make it theoretically more efficient and may even facilitate greater reduction of GHG concentrations but it also raises difficult issues of comparing the carbon content of alternative gases and managing trading across very different kinds of activities. Until recently, most trading programs debated in Congress have only included CO_2.

A related question is whether there should be a national trading system or whether we should encourage regional programs. A national system is essential in developing an effort that engages the entire country, but in the absence of a federal program, regional programs provide opportunities to experiment with alternative approaches. A major problem with regional programs, though, is that they may reduce emissions within the participating states but emissions may increase outside of the boundaries. For example, if states agree to limit production of electricity from conventional coal-fired power plants, power from such plants might continue to be produced outside the system. If the regional program is designed to incorporate all of the states within an electricity transmission network, this problem of leakage can be minimized. More broadly, a national carbon-trading program can allow states to continue to experiment but careful coordination is required to ensure that regional systems develop common approaches that can eventually be integrated. This is part of a broader question of whether state or regional carbon programs that include regulatory standards such as emission limits on motor vehicles should be preempted by federal legislation. Most industry groups have lobbied hard for a national standard but state authority is critical in allowing states to continue to experiment with alternative approaches and to promote policy innovation.

Another key issue is the development of an accurate GHG inventory, which is critical in establishing a baseline from which emission reductions are calculated and in determining the allocation of allowances for trading. There are some positive signs here, as most states now participate in the Climate Registry, an effort aimed at developing a nationwide system for reporting GHG emissions. According to the World Business Council for Sustainable Development and the World Resources Institute's Greenhouse Gas Protocol Initiative, governments at all levels should follow certain principles to guide their GHG accounting and reporting. These include accounting for all GHG emission sources and activities within their boundaries, reporting consistently to allow meaningful comparisons of emissions over time, and ensuring that emissions are calculated and reported accurately (World Resources Institute 2004).

Another challenge to developing an accurate inventory is defining and verifying emissions throughout the life cycle of a product. Emissions can occur from the processing of raw materials purchased for manufacturing as a result of the production of the electricity used in manufacturing components and from the transportation, use, and disposal of products. These complex life-cycle calculations must be broad and inclusive to ensure emissions are not excluded (Pew Center on Global Climate Change 2001). Reporting and monitoring mechanisms need to be efficiently integrated with requirements under environmental laws in order to minimize the costs of participating in the program.

Determining the emissions-reduction benchmark is also difficult. The generation of GHG-reduction credits is based on the calculation of the level of GHGs that would have been emitted in the absence of a project. This is a hypothetical figure that is inherently difficult to calculate, and sources and nations have strong incentive to inflate their GHG inventory in order to be in a position to claim additional reduction credits. Governments may be hard pressed to be able to calculate accurate baselines and there will be strong incentives to establish generous baselines and credits. The calculation of credits requires certifying bodies to be able to ensure that reductions are permanent and additional.

Then there is the issue of whether allowances should be auctioned or distributed for free. Allowances allocated through auctions use market mechanisms to promote their efficient allocation. Sources that have reduced emissions voluntarily are not punished because they now need to purchase fewer allowances and those that have put off reductions have to buy more. The revenues from the auctions can be used to subsidize emissions-reducing activities, fund research and development, help meet adaptation costs, and other relevant purposes. Auctions can raise prices of high-emitting processes and facilities and encourage reductions. But auctions are strongly opposed by industries that naturally prefer their free distribution, and many carbon-trading programs anticipate an initial free distribution, with auctions to come later.

Offsets have been another challenge in designing cap-and-trade programs. Offsets are allowances or credits that regulated entities can purchase by investing in projects that emit fewer GHGs, such as electricity-generating windmills, or that sequester carbon, such as tree plantations. Offsets are attractive because sources may find it cheaper to pay for these programs rather than reducing their own emissions. From the perspective of economic efficiency, trading should be broad and open to as many parties as possible but trading also poses the problem of appearing to allow sources to buy credits from others rather than reducing their own emissions. One of the major problems with some emissions-trading programs is that offsets are often included in order to increase the number of available allowances, thus reducing their price. There are also concerns that trading will allow sources to invest in carbon-sequestration projects with uncertain or only temporary benefits rather than actual, long-term emissions reductions. Offsets are typically provided for in certificates for sale that show emissions have been avoided or sequestered, but this requires clear demonstration that certain emissions would have occurred were it not for the action taken, an admittedly difficult task (Fahrenthold 2009).

Projects aimed at reducing GHG emissions or increasing carbon sinks may create incentives for increased emissions and decreased sinks elsewhere. For example, if some sources shift away from using coal, it might deflate coal prices and stimulate increased use by others. Similarly, carbon sequestration may be pursued through investments in tree plantations that displace farmers and encourage them to move to other areas and cut down trees for croplands. There is evidence, for example, that ethanol subsidies have encouraged just this sort of behavior (Fargione et al. 2008).

Effective enforcement that creates incentives for compliance is critical to the success of carbon trading. But there are conflicting imperatives to be balanced. Simple rules, minimal transaction costs, and other factors lead to maximizing the volume of trading and the consequential benefits, and effective compliance and enforcement place limits and costs on the process. Sanctions for noncompliance must be developed but who should bear responsibility for nonfulfillment of conditions—the buyer? The seller? Government? It may be possible to devise insurance schemes, funded by charges imposed on each transaction, which can be used to purchase credits to meet shortfalls. The system could also include extra credits to be used for such a purpose. Sanctions for failure to comply with conditions could include a prohibition on future trading and reduction of subsequent allowances by the number of credits in dispute. Generators of credits may be required to demonstrate that real reductions have been produced before trading can occur, as is the case in other commodity markets, where producers must show that the product is available and certify its quality. This requires strong political will to sanction parties that fail to meet their obligations.

The daunting problems faced in designing and implementing an effective carbon-trading program are discouraging because so much of the climate policy debate is based on the premise that a trading program will be the core of a national climate policy. Supporters of carbon trading emphasize the importance of rigorous monitoring, auditing, and enforcement, and advocates argue that the acid rain program is evidence these requirements can be met and a carbon-trading program can be similarly successful (Chameides and Oppenheimer 2008; Schlesinger 2008). But the acid rain program experience suggests how difficult carbon trading will be in practice. Most important, reductions in sulfur dioxide emissions occurred primarily because eastern and midwestern companies had access to cheap, low-sulfur coal from the Powder River Basin in Montana and North Dakota; the companies that bought most of the allowances did so because they had no railroad connections to get Powder River coal. The key policy development was thus not cap and trade itself but rather the abolition of the Interstate Commerce Commission, the deregulation of interstate train commerce, and the ability of companies to buy cheap coal from the West. Power companies were able to cut costs, save money, and reduce emissions (Reitze 2009). It is difficult to envision how that scenario could unfold under a carbon-trading system.

Framing the Climate Debate

Setting a GHG emission reduction target is a critical first step in climate policy making because it sends a signal about how seriously one takes the threat of climate change. As argued previously, whether the goal is 50 or 80 percent is not as important as being within the range of reductions that reflects a commitment to fundamentally transform the way in which energy is produced and used. Such a goal recognizes that, based on the best science currently available, stabilizing the climate, as the United States and most every other country committed to do in 1992, has finally become a prime policy directive. It also reflects a commitment to pursue what the best scientific research available suggests is necessary rather than setting goals based on ideology or political feasibility.

The second policy task is to include the true cost of carbon emissions in the price of energy. Cap-and-trade and carbon-tax proposals are consistent with this goal. This is critical for several reasons. In a market-based economy, getting prices right so they reflect the true costs of producing goods and services is essential to producing rational decisions about energy use. If the true costs of energy production are included, fossil fuels are clearly more expensive than many forms of alternative fuels, and strong incentives can be created that will encourage conservation, efficiency, and alternative sources. It is essential that prices for energy remain sufficiently high to encourage long-term investments. One of the problems with previous energy policies is the boom-and-bust cycle of prices. Energy requires long-term investment decisions and long-term price projections. A combination of market prices, education, and political leadership is thus essential. People will need to become convinced that energy prices will have to be much higher than they have been in the past, and that will require strong leadership. As people come to embrace ideas of conservation, efficiency, and green power, they will for the most part still need price signals to reinforce their commitments. Behavioral economics provides convincing evidence that people are only partially economically rational beings, which suggests that they are open to educational efforts to get them to act in ways that are not simply a result of self-interested cost-benefit calculations.

Cap-and-trade and carbon-tax options recognize that well-functioning markets are never free from government intervention but require a wide range of public policies to ensure that markets work well and that, in particular, they reflect the real costs of producing goods and services. Markets are inescapably located in and constrained by the natural world. Economic activity is dependent on the resources of the natural world and its ability to process wastes, and only economic activity that is consistent with ecological conditions and limits is ultimately sustainable. Effective governance is required to rescue capitalism from unsustainable environmental and economic trends but part of the problem with free-market ideology is its commitment to weakening government, the very thing on which its future depends.

Discussions of politics and markets often focus on the differences between political and market allocation of scarce resources. Politics is denigrated as irrational, plagued by political calculations, pressures, and incentives that are aimed at currying favor with powerful industries.

The result is that industries are insulated and protected from competition, and policies are dominated by subsidies and pork barrel spending that are economically inefficient. Markets, by contrast, are depicted as paragons of virtue, designed to provoke innovation, reduce costs, and expand choices. Characterizing politics and markets as polar opposites is an attractive debating strategy for those who wish to curtail government and unleash private power but it fundamentally misstates the nature of markets. In reality, many markets fail to produce the benefits promised because they do not work as advertised; their prices do not reflect the true costs of goods and services because powerful interests that can externalize costs on third parties have a strong incentive to do so. Externalizing some costs increases profits and expands market share, shifting costs to those who are powerless to defend themselves. A more helpful approach looks at the intersection of politics and markets and admits that effective markets require strong and capable institutions to ensure that the benefits promised by markets are realized and are not sacrificed amid the relentless push to maximize profits.

Policy design and implementation are essential to ensure that carbon markets produce the benefits they promise. If effective markets can be constructed and maintained, they can play a major role in reducing the threat of climate change. But functioning markets are only part of the solution; regulation, subsidies, research, education, and other policies as needed as well. A commitment to making markets work can provide common ground among liberals and conservatives. If such common ground can indeed be found, it could create political momentum for dealing with a host of contentious issues concerning the details of climate policy that are discussed in the chapters that follow. And even if well-functioning markets are established, additional policies will be required to deal with the distributional consequences of markets. Policies will need to address the impacts of climate change and help those who suffer its disruptions adapt. In short, well-functioning markets are part, but only part, of the broad set of actions humankind will likely need to pursue throughout the century as it seeks to find ways to stabilize the climate.

Finally, both a carbon tax and a carbon-trading regime can contribute to policy integration. Either can serve as an overall strategy for forcing emission reductions that also includes regulatory measures such as energy efficiency and renewable energy mandates and subsidies and incentives to develop and deploy cleaner technologies. But the task of integration, because it is so complicated, suggests that simplicity is essential whenever possible. Despite the significant political obstacles, a carbon tax on fossil fuel is simpler and less susceptible to manipulation. Given the complexity of climate policy making and the pervasiveness of unintended consequences (and even intended consequences that are the result of manipulating policies to benefit narrow interests), the simpler some elements can be, the greater the likelihood we will be able to design and implement an effective climate policy.

4

Reducing Greenhouse Gas Emissions from Generating Electricity

Despite the considerable progress made in improving the energy efficiency of the US economy, emissions from generating electricity continue to be a major contributor to GHG levels. Although the economic downturn that began in 2008 has reduced the overall growth rate, electricity demand is projected to rise by just over 30 percent over the next quarter century (US Department of Energy, Energy Information Administration, 2011c). Rising demand for electricity is a problem because coal is the dominant fuel for generating electricity in the United States, and it is dirty. In fact, coal is the single largest source of GHG emissions and is also a major source of conventional air pollutants, including fine particulates, that are most harmful to public health.

Coal is king because it is an efficient and plentiful fuel and domestic supplies make it very attractive amid the debate over energy security. Shifting to alternative fuels will be expensive because of the investment reflected in the coal-fired plants currently operating and because burning coal in these plants is still the cheapest way to produce electricity on a large scale. Despite its low cost, however, beginning the transition away from coal is essential because coal combustion produces more GHG emissions per unit of energy generated than any other fuel. Coal is responsible for the lion's share of CO_2 emissions from electricity, accounting for more than 81 percent. Natural gas produces 17.3 percent, and petroleum is responsible for about 1 percent (US EPA 2011e).

Because burning coal also produces pollutants that contribute to acid rain, urban air pollution that threatens public health, and toxic mercury emissions, there are significant co-benefits that would follow from either clean air or climate policies. And because many of the same processes produce CO_2 and conventional pollutants, clean air policies can also reduce GHG levels. But there are also perplexing trade-offs: control equipment aimed at reducing particulates, responsible for the most serious public health threats from air pollution, also reduces the efficiency of power plants, thus requiring that more fuel be used and leading to higher CO_2 emissions.

Although coal has clear environmental disadvantages, there is currently no clear alternative to replace it immediately. Lower prices and a dramatic increase in supply due to hydraulic fracturing (also known as *fracking*) have made natural gas an option but the chemicals used in fracking have raised concerns about contamination of drinking water. Nuclear power is also an option, given the generating capacity of large nuclear units, but that would require a massive investment in new plants and would only magnify the problem of waste storage and safety concerns. Renewables such as wind, hydro, and solar are certainly cleaner than coal and natural gas, but they are either not yet economically competitive or available on a wide-enough scale to displace fossil fuels. Coal also has powerful allies in Washington, making it difficult to chip away at policies that support its use. Perhaps most important, power from coal is cheap and proponents support its continued use in order to keep energy prices as low as possible.

For all these reasons, reducing emissions from coal is an immediate climate policy priority even as policies chart the long-term transition from coal to cleaner fuels. There are three primary ways of reducing GHG and other emissions from coal-fired power plants: (1) changing the way in which coal is used to produce electricity, (2) improving the efficiency of the production and use of power so that less electricity needs to be generated, and (3) shifting to cleaner, alternative fuels. If we are going to make significant progress in reducing emissions, we will need to pursue all three.

This chapter begins with a brief discussion of GHG emissions from electricity generation, particularly carbon dioxide, and then examines options for reducing our reliance on coal in order to pursue climate change, air pollution, and other related policy goals. Throughout this chapter, the underlying issue is how integrating energy, climate, and air pollution policies helps frame the policy issues and choices.

An Overview of US GHG Emissions from Electricity

Electricity generation, transmission, and distribution were responsible for the largest share of greenhouse gas emissions (33 percent) in the United States in 2009, followed by transportation (27 percent) and industry (20 percent) (US EPA 2011e). If electricity emissions are distrib-

	Coal	Petroleum liquids	Petroleum coke	Natural gas	Other gases	Nuclear	Hydro	Renew- ables	Hydro pumped storage	Other	Total generation (million kWh)
2000	51.7%	2.7%	0.2%	15.8%	0.4%	19.8%	7.2%	2.1%	−0.1%	0.1%	3,802,521
2001	50.9%	3.1%	0.3%	17.1%	0.2%	20.6%	5.8%	1.9%	−0.2%	0.3%	3,737,052
2002	50.1%	2.0%	0.4%	17.9%	0.3%	20.2%	6.8%	2.1%	−0.2%	0.4%	3,858,919
2003	50.8%	2.6%	0.4%	16.7%	0.4%	19.7%	7.1%	2.1%	−0.2%	0.4%	3,883,783
2004	49.8%	2.5%	0.5%	17.9%	0.4%	19.9%	6.8%	2.1%	−0.2%	0.4%	3,970,782
2005	49.6%	2.5%	0.6%	18.8%	0.3%	19.3%	6.7%	2.2%	−0.2%	0.3%	4,056,199
2006	49.0%	1.1%	0.5%	20.1%	0.3%	19.4%	7.1%	2.4%	−0.2%	0.3%	4,065,762
2007	48.5%	1.2%	0.4%	21.6%	0.3%	19.4%	6.0%	2.6%	−0.2%	0.3%	4,158,267
2008	48.2%	0.8%	0.3%	21.4%	0.3%	19.6%	6.2%	3.1%	−0.2%	0.3%	4,121,184
2009	44.6%	0.7%	0.3%	23.3%	0.3%	20.2%	6.9%	3.6%	−0.1%	0.3%	3,953,898

Figure 4.1
US Electric Generation by Source, 2000–2009.
Source: US Department of Energy, Energy Efficiency and Renewable Energy 2010, 12.

uted across these sectors to reflect how they use electricity, then industry and transportation account for the largest share of GHG emissions, each responsible for about 28 percent of the total (US EPA 2011e). Overall GHG emissions from electricity generation have increased 17 percent since 1990, although they declined in 2008 and 2009 because of lower economic output, reduced demand for electricity, and a decline in the carbon intensity of the fuels used to produce electricity. Carbon intensity declined because the price of coal increased and natural gas prices dropped, so utilities switched to natural gas and other sources, including renewables (US EPA 2011e).

As shown in figure 4.1, coal is by far the largest source of electricity in the United States, accounting for approximately 45 percent of the total, followed by natural gas (23 percent), nuclear (20 percent), and hydro (7 percent); a variety of sources provide the remaining 5 percent (US Department of Energy, Energy Information Administration 2011a). Coal fueled much of the growth in transportation and industry in the United States throughout the nineteenth century and well into the twentieth century and provided three-fourths of all the energy used each year until after World War I. Figure 4.2 illustrates starting in the 1950s, with

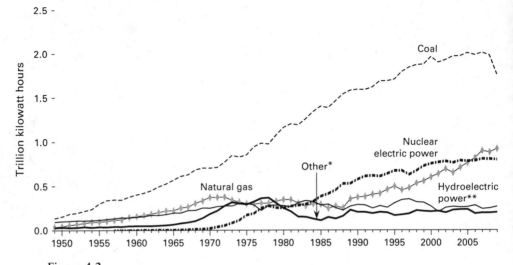

Figure 4.2
Total Electricity Net Generation by Source, 1949–2009.
Notes: *Wind, petroleum, wood, waste, geothermal, other gases, solar thermal and photovoltaic, batteries, chemicals, hydrogen, pitch, purchased steam, sulfur, miscellaneous technologies, and nonrenewable waste (municipal solid waste from nonbiogenic sources, and tire-derived fuels). **Conventional hydroelectric power and pumped storage.
A note on measures: A kilowatt or a thousand watts (Kw) is a measure of instantaneous power; it is enough to power a window-mounted air conditioner or electric fan heater. A megawatt (MW) or a million watts is the amount of power a typical Walmart store uses. A gigawatt is the output of a large power plant.
Source: US Department of Energy, Energy Information Administration 2010a, 228.

the growth of motor vehicle ownership, oil and natural gas provided much more total energy than did coal but coal use continued to grow as demand for electricity increased. Nuclear power was added to the US energy mix in 1957 and grew steadily between 1970 and 2000. As discussed in chapter 5, renewable energy has begun to play a more significant role since the turn of the twenty-first century.

Although fossil fuel combustion is by far the largest source of greenhouse gas emissions from generating electricity, it is not the only one. Coal mining, for example, also emits methane, with underground mining contributing the largest share of emissions. Even after mines are closed, they continue to emit methane to the atmosphere. Although it burns cleaner than coal, natural gas production is a significant source of GHGs too, and the total has increased 17 percent since 1990 (US EPA 2011e).

Significant levels of methane and CO_2 are released from wells, pipelines, and storage tanks during field production, processing, transmission and storage, and distribution, with the bulk of emissions coming during the first two stages. A recent study estimated that 4 to 8 percent of methane from shale gas formations escaped into the atmosphere, a much higher amount than previously thought. And because methane is a more powerful greenhouse gas than carbon dioxide, it raises questions about whether natural gas is a good substitute for coal, even in the short term. Robert Howarth and colleagues concluded that "the large greenhouse gas footprint of shale gas undercuts the logic of its use as a bridging fuel over coming decades, if the goal is to reduce global warming. The full footprint should be used in planning for alternative energy futures that adequately consider global climate change" (Howarth, Santoro, and Ingraffea 2011, 688).

Clean Air Politics

For nearly four decades, clean air politics and policy making has followed a well-developed pattern that helps explain why air-quality goals have been so elusive. Environmental groups have been effective in framing clean air regulation as a public health imperative that demands ambitious goals. Industries affected by clean air regulation, including some of the largest and most influential corporations and trade associations, have a long history of issuing dire warnings about the adverse economic consequences of new rules, but those warnings typically fail to deter Congress from formulating ambitious clean air goals. In response to strong public interest in clean air and lobbying by environmental organizations, members of Congress draft legislation that sets ambitious goals that promise to solve the problem and ensure that everyone breathes clean air. This allows members to claim credit for addressing an issue of great importance to the public. Business groups, even if united, are unable to block legislation that enjoys broad public support (Smith 2000; Bryner 2007b).

At the same time, though, industry warnings about job loss, higher prices, and other economic consequences of regulation resonate strongly in Congress. These are the most potent arguments business can offer, and although they do not deter members of Congress from embracing clear goals, they prompt members to ensure that the path to achieving those goals is shaped by industry concerns. Industry groups regularly warn that clean air goals are unrealistic and inconsistent with available technologies and practices and lobby Congress to extend deadlines far into the future. The justification is plausible—businesses need time to develop new pollution control technologies and processes. Yet pollution control equipment usually turns out be less expensive than industry warnings indicate and, once companies have an incentive to invent new control technologies, actual costs end up significantly lower (Easterbrook 1995).

Although aggressive lobbying by regulated industries shapes legislation at the margins, industry officials play a dominant role in the implementation of clean air laws. Once laws are enacted, business and environmental groups challenge most major regulations the EPA proposes and litigation regularly delays implementation (and thus the compliance costs) even when business is unsuccessful in challenging agency rules. In this way, equilibrium is reached. The public sees strong laws on the books, industry rewards members of Congress for their responsiveness to business needs, and incumbents are reelected (Schoenbrod 2005). Some environmental progress also occurs but clean air goals remain largely unrealized (US EPA 2005).

Clean air policy has been shaped not only by environmental laws but also by other laws aimed at changing the processes by which regulations are formulated and implemented. A key compromise in Congress over the years has been to limit the resources granted to the EPA, which helps ensure that business can effectively intervene in administrative and judicial proceedings (Bryner 1987; Smith 2005). Since about 2000, members of Congress, prompted by industry demands for less regulation, have found additional ways to slow regulatory activity without directly amending environmental laws. They do so by imposing generic requirements on the EPA and other regulatory agencies, such as cost-benefit analysis and paperwork-reduction requirements. Recent presidents have issued a series of executive orders aimed at specifying when and how agencies are to consider costs and requiring them to balance the costs and benefits of the actions they propose. These efforts have been motivated by a variety of goals, such as reducing the cost of complying with regulations in order to foster economic growth, increasing the cost effectiveness of rules so that benefits are maximized, and ensuring that agency actions are consistent with administration policy objectives.

Passage of the Clean Air and Clean Water acts and other environmental legislation in the 1970s demonstrate that environmental initiatives have been strongest and industry influence weakest when political leaders from both political parties have competed for leadership on environmental issues. The partisan competition for strong environmental protection policy soon gave way to regulation as a wedge issue in the 1980s and beyond. Democrats and Republicans now differ dramatically in their views on the need for more aggressive environmental policies. Still, Republican control of Congress or the White House is not by itself a guarantee of business success. Senate Democrats and Republicans from the Northeast have blocked proposals they believed went too far in weakening environmental protections. Conversely, Democratic control of government has not guaranteed action on environmental issues. Democrats controlled both chambers of Congress in the 1980s, for example, but were deadlocked among themselves over how to amend the CAA. Democrats representing high-sulfur coal–producing states and states with old coal-burning power plants often locked horns over clean air legislation with their counterparts who favored strict emission controls. The Clinton administration did not issue many of its most important environmental and natural resource initiatives until its final days, evidence that it was wary of imposing new regulatory requirements on business (Vig and Kraft 2006).

The last time the CAA was updated in 1990 was when the first Bush administration helped break the deadlock in Congress over how to reduce acid rain, and Congress developed a new set of regulatory programs to push the EPA to reduce emissions more effectively. Despite widespread agreement that the law has failed to achieve many of its goals, it has not been reauthorized because Washington has been deadlocked over how to amend it. The profound differences in policy priorities and the lack of trust among all involved have produced insurmountable barriers to action. The broad support for clean air has not translated into an effective political call for more aggressive and effective policies. In part this is because the emergence of energy security and climate change as issues has complicated clean air policy making because policy makers give higher priority to securing a stable supply of cheap energy than to other policy goals. As an example, the Bush administration's focus on a national energy policy that emphasized production required some sacrifice of cleaner air goals. And as oil prices stay high, it is hard to imagine, under current political conditions, how commitments to clean air will not suffer.

Protecting public health has typically been the most effective environmental protection message but it has always fallen short in challenging the imperatives of economic growth and protecting jobs, and high energy prices and fear of shortages will only make clean air rules more vulnerable. Much of the progress in clean air is due to economic modernization and the gradual replacement of facilities with newer, more efficient and cleaner equipment. It is difficult to sort out the comparative contributions of public policies and market forces. One study found, for example, that the CAA's system of nonattainment designations had, at best, only a modest impact on sulfur dioxide levels (Bennear and Coglianese 2005). Golkany (1999) argues that air pollution levels were falling before national policy efforts as a result of technological advances and state efforts. The act's emphasis on creating new incentives for technological development and deployment reinforce, if not shape, market competition that can stimulate new technologies. But some pressures, such as those in the electricity market, have led to prolonged use of old, dirty, coal-fired power plants that continue to operate long beyond their design span because they are among the cheapest ways of producing electricity.

The CAA appears to have been most effective when Congress provides specific mandates such as emissions limits on motor vehicle emissions and eliminating lead from gasoline. Industry groups, however, have generally opposed congressional mandates, favoring instead delegation to EPA and administrative rule making, where it enjoys great influence (Schoenbrod 2005). The clean air compromise is rooted in the idea that long-term goals make sense: because the most effective way to clear the air is through preventing or reducing emissions through new technologies, it is important to give businesses sufficient time to design and deploy those technologies in the next generation of facilities. Long-term goals are also politically popular because they allow elected officials to claim victory, declare the problem solved, and turn over to their successors the responsibility for managing costs and making sure that goals are met. As deadlines approach, industry reports that new technologies are unavailable and threaten plant closures if standards are enforced, and Congress and the White House negotiate new goals or carve out exemptions.

Although the clean air compromise has worked politically in Congress, it has not been successful in reducing air pollution to safe and healthy levels. The EPA has been caught in the vise of competing pressures, set up for frequent policy failure because it has been unable to satisfy the expectations created by environmental laws. As noted previously, the most significant reductions in pollution have largely followed from the few times when Congress was willing to mandate specific emissions reduction targets rather than giving the EPA broad grants of power.

Congressional willingness to delegate responsibility to the EPA to make the hard choices required to reduce pollution has come at a price. Thousands of Americans continue to die prematurely from air pollution and millions suffer adverse health effects.

As a result of national policy gridlock in clean air and other environmental issues, there is growing interest in local, state, and regional regulatory innovation. Many air pollution problems cross political boundaries and will require some creative ways to bring these subnational actors together. But the breakthroughs in national policy making required to address persistent air pollution problems as well as the next generation of environmental problems await a number of political developments, such as new leadership (Mazmanian and Kraft 2009). Clean air would also benefit from a coalition that went beyond traditional environmental groups to include labor, civil rights, and other progressive organizations, as well as governors pressuring the national government to act and industry to lobby to preempt growing state regulations with national standards. Perhaps most important, a policy breakthrough will also require a sense of urgency that carbon dioxide emissions from power plants must be regulated as part of a broader effort to reduce the threat of disruptive climate change. In the end, this may require the development of a new public ethic that demands a more cautious, protective stewardship of the earth so that succeeding generations will be able to live in a hospitable world.

Cleaning Up Coal

The challenge of reducing carbon emissions from coal use is rooted in its abundance. The United States has 27 percent of the world's reserves, and if production levels remain at current levels, the reserves would last for more than two hundred years. Federal energy policy has historically sought to maintain low prices, which has lead to policies aimed at facilitating the use of fossil fuels. According to one study, the federal government spent $644 billion between 1950 and 2003 (in 2003 dollars) to promote and support the development of energy resources; nearly 44 percent of the total was spent on tax incentives for development. Although oil was the largest recipient of federal subsidies between 1950 and 2003, coal was a close second, receiving more than $80 billion in subsidies and an additional $4 billion in research and development funding (Bezdek and Wendling 2006). The largest coal subsidy has been the $2 billion-a-year synfuels tax credit, enacted in 1978, to encourage the production of new types of fuel from coal. The tax credit, however, has largely supported the general use of coal: the fifty-seven plants that received subsidies used coal the same way unsubsidized coal was used and the tax credit expired at the end of 2007. A much smaller subsidy of 50 cents per liter was created in 2005 for the production of liquid fuels from gas. More recent laws have also supported the continued use of coal; the 2005 Energy Policy Act, for example, authorized $1.8 billion in loans, loan guarantees, and grants and $1.3 billion in tax credits over nine years to encourage the development of coal gasification and other advanced coal projects (International Energy Agency 2008).

Coal continues to be central to the energy plans of the United States and many other nations. There are more than eight thousand coal-fired plants operating in the United States. In 2007, plans for more than fifty conventional coal-fired plants were canceled or delayed in the United States because of concerns about their carbon consequences. Virtually every new coal-fired power plant proposed in recent years has been challenged by environmental organizations or state government officials who were concerned with emissions and with the viability of conventional power plants in a carbon-constrained world.

The United States is not alone. Because it is the cheapest way to produce electricity, countries around the world are rapidly increasing their use of coal in electricity generation. There are massive coal reserves around the world that represent hundreds of gigatons of potential carbon emissions (Martelle 2009). Whereas China and India are global leaders in new coal-fired power plant construction, the allure of coal has even seduced Europeans. Since 2003, European nations have announced plans to build more than fifty new coal-fired plants, a stunning reversal in European leadership on climate change (Rosenthal 2008).

Proponents of new coal-fired plants are optimistic about the potential for *clean coal,* a term coined by the industry decades ago to signal its commitment to reducing particulates, sulfur dioxide, and nitrogen oxide emissions from coal combustion. Coal is, in fact, much cleaner now than in the past because of the widespread use of control technologies in industrial countries. Nevertheless, coal-fired power plants, even under optimal conditions, release twice as much CO_2 as gas-fired plants; in developing countries, where plants use lower-quality coal and less-efficient equipment, carbon emissions are even higher (Rosenthal 2008).

Much of the so-called clean coal effort has been aimed at trying to devise carbon capture and sequestration processes that collect CO_2

before it is released, compress the gas for transporting in pipelines or other systems, and then inject it into underground storage reservoirs. Carbon sequestration and storage (CSS) demonstration projects are underway in Europe and the United States but because the task is complex, CSS has been compared to putting a person on the moon. Plants with carbon capture cost 10 to 20 percent more to build and are less efficient than plants without it because they require additional energy to separate the CO_2 from the emissions stream. The task of storing the CO_2 is equally daunting because reservoirs must store the CO_2 safely and avoid leaks. Moreover, the cost of retrofitting existing plants would be enormous. All this will take considerable time and money, and if CSS is a challenging task in the United States, it will be even more so in China and India if they are to develop clean coal technologies.

The search for clean coal has been a critical element of the industry's political strategy in recent years. This is perhaps best illustrated by the FutureGen program, initiated in 2003 as part of the Clean Coal Power Initiative developed by the Department of Energy (DOE), which centered on a plan to construct a coal-fired power plant that would gasify coal and produce a hydrogen-rich synthetic gas that could be used to generate electricity and provide fuel for fuel-cell vehicles. The plan was to produce electricity and hydrogen and eliminate virtually all air pollutants, including SO_2, NO_x, particulates, and mercury, and cut CO_2 emissions by 90 percent. The plant would capture its carbon emissions and sequester them through underground injection. FutureGen included thirteen partners from around the world, including China, Germany, Britain, and Australia. States competed vigorously to host the project, and Mattoon, Illinois, was selected for the pilot project. By 2008, the federal government had spent $40 million and its partners another $10 million but the estimated cost of the project had ballooned to $1.8 billion, almost double the original estimate, because of rising prices for labor and materials. In 2008 DOE announced it was pulling the plug on FutureGen and would instead create a new plan that would use the conventional technology of pulverizing coal, but would still capture CO_2 and sequester it as in the initial plan.

The collapse of FutureGen was a major blow to coal-fired power plants, and industry representatives quickly focused their efforts on convincing Congress and the Obama administration to revive the plans for the pilot plant. In August 2010, Energy Secretary Chu announced that the project, renamed FutureGen 2.0, would go ahead in a revised form. The private sector partners would now retrofit an old 200-megawatt coal plant with new technology that would capture 90 percent of the CO_2; the captured carbon would be stored at a separate facility in Illinois (US Department of Energy 2010).

The promise of zero carbon–emission coal-fired plants such as Future-Gen has been a central element in the goal of reducing CO_2 emissions by 80 percent from 1990 levels by 2050. If we are to achieve that goal while continuing to burn coal to generate electricity, then hundreds of these CSS plants will have to be operating within the next few decades. One sobering lesson from FutureGen, though, is how difficult it is to translate innovative energy ideas to commercially viable projects (Smith and Power 2008).

Nearly half of the energy-related funding in the American Recovery and Reinvestment Act (ARRA) of 2009 was for CSS demonstration projects. The Department of Energy's Clean Coal Power Initiative received an additional $800 million of government cofinancing for new clean coal technology projects. The law also provided $1.5 billion for CSS projects from large industrial sources and approximately $70 million for research into geologic sequestration sites.

Power plants typically have a thirty- to fifty-year service lifetime so decisions made now about what kind of fuel they use are critical for climate policy. It is true that power plants could be abandoned before their design lifetime has ended but that would make alternatives all the more expensive and controversial. One option is a moratorium on new coal-fired plants, at least until CCS technologies are developed. In this vein, in 2009 the United Kingdom began requiring that new coal plants include CSS technology and capture at least 25 percent of their CO_2 emissions (100 percent by 2025) (Enviro News 2009). A similar policy in the United States would be one of the most potent measures we could take to reduce GHG emissions but it is unlikely that Congress will move in that direction.

A 2007 study of coal by MIT scientists argued that unless public policies were enacted that restricted its use, coal would continue to grow as the primary fuel source for generating electricity. Coal could rise from providing 52 percent of electrical power in 2000 to 68 percent by mid-century and 75 percent by 2100, an increase of 2.3 percent a year. Given its plentiful supplies, coal consumption is constrained by the price of carbon, the price of natural gas (the main competitor for coal in generating electricity), the cost of carbon capture and sequestration technologies, and the relationship between coal and natural gas technologies in dispatching (distributing) power. The report assumed that although low carbon-emitting electricity generation will grow, it would still represent only small share of the total by midcentury.

The study also estimated the impact on coal use if carbon emissions were taxed and concluded that the use of coal would decline but it would remain a viable option for generating electricity in Europe and the United States. If carbon were priced at $340 per ton by 2050, the study concluded that coal use would decline 50 percent from the business-as-usual projection; at a carbon price scenario of $170 per ton, coal use would fall by 37 percent (McFarland, Herzog, and Jacoby 2007).

Given the likelihood that coal will continue to play a major role in electricity generation, a key question then becomes, what should be the CO_2-related performance requirements for new coal-fired power plants? The MIT authors suggest that the components of CCS are commercially available and that CCS systems are not currently in place because it is simply much cheaper for utilities to emit CO_2 than to capture and store it. Pulverized coal plants and integrated gasification combined cycle (IGCC) facilities can separate out and recover CO_2 from plant emissions but decisions about what kind of facility to build are significantly shaped by public policies. For example, if air quality policies further limit emissions of SO_2, NO_x, and mercury and if carbon emissions are taxed or regulated, then IGCC appears to be the most rational way to proceed. But if plant operators seek the ability to use lower-cost coals, develop short-run opportunities for greater efficiency, and adjust operations in response to changing conditions in the grid, then conventional pulverized coal makes the most sense. The MIT report suggests that the choice be left to utility companies and recommends only that "new coal units should be built with the highest efficiency that is economically justifiable" (Massachusetts Institute of Technology 2007, xiv). That, of course, does not provide a clear environmental standard and suggests that CO_2 emissions are still fundamentally a function of economic calculations, which is how the problem was created in the first place.

One action that could be taken immediately is to develop the regulatory structure for monitoring and permitting CCS. This is, in part, a chicken-and-egg situation: companies do not want to begin constructing CCS systems until they know what the regulatory requirements are, but there are no commercial-scale facilities that can inform the writing of regulations. Another similar policy dilemma is whether to proceed with a series of demonstration projects for the various components of CCS or to start building power plants with carbon sequestration, transfer, and storage as part of the design (Hawkins and Peridas 2007).

Natural Gas

Natural gas burns cleaner than coal, is relatively abundant in the United States, and has dropped in price in recent years. Figure 4.2 shows that natural gas is now the second largest source of electricity and its share has steadily increased over time, especially since 1995. The industrial sector uses more natural gas (32 percent) than any other, followed by electricity (30 percent), residential (21 percent), commercial (14 percent), and transportation (3 percent). Natural gas is also the largest fuel source for space heating in the United States, heating 51 percent of homes in 2007 compared to 33 percent for electricity (US Department of Energy, Energy Information Administration 2010a).

As figure 4.3 shows, natural gas production and consumption were in balance through 1986, but then consumption outpaced production and imports increased. As of 2009, production was 21 trillion cubic feet (Tcf) and consumption was 22.8 Tcf (US Department of Energy, Energy Information Administration 2010a). In just the last few years the use of directional (horizontal) drilling and hydraulic fracturing (fracking) in shale formations has greatly expanded natural gas production. Fracking involves a process in which water, sand, and a mix of chemicals are

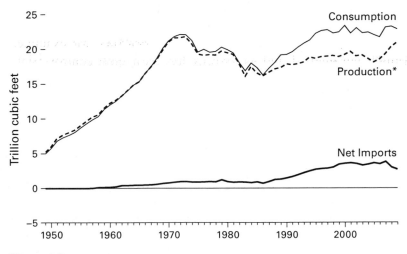

Figure 4.3
Natural Gas Production and Consumption, 1950–2009.
Note: *Dry gas.
Source: US Department of Energy, Energy Information Administration 2010a, 186.

pumped into gas wells at high pressure to open cracks in the shale rock, thereby allowing gas to flow from the shale into the wells. According to the Energy Information Administration, Energy Information Administration (2010a), dry shale gas production has expanded from 1 Tcf in 2006 to 4.8 Tcf in 2010.

Geologists have long known that large quantities of gas were often trapped in shale formations but until the advent of horizontal drilling and fracking it had been uneconomical to produce. The most recent Energy Information Administration estimates are that the United States has 2,543 Tcf of potential natural gas resources, enough for one hundred years at current usage rates; with shale gas totaling 862 Tcf, double the previous year's estimate (US Department of Energy, Energy Information Administration 2010a). As with all such estimates, there is a great deal of uncertainty over the size of shale resources. Many of the shale wells are relatively new so we do not have an extensive track record of their production rates over time. In addition, production thus far has been in "sweet spots" (areas with the highest production rates for the gas play), so if production rates for those areas are extrapolated for the entire play, it probably overstates the amount of gas that might be found. Similarly, only small portions of the plays have been explored to date and it is not clear how productive other areas of the play might be.

Natural gas development and extraction also raises host of environmental issues (C. Davis 2011; Urbina 2011). Fracking, for example, is virtually unregulated and its growth has been quite controversial. Fracking requires huge amounts of water and raises concerns about depletion of groundwater supplies and aquifers (Pless 2010). Fracking fluids also contain chemical contaminants that can affect groundwater and drinking water supplies, and spills of fracking chemicals have harmed rivers and streams. There are also concerns that abandoned gas wells may provide a path for contaminants to reach drinking water supplies. Fracking also produces a lot of waste water, which is contaminated with the fracking compounds, and most treatment plants are not equipped to treat the produced water properly (US EPA 2010b). Air quality is also a serious problem in areas with significant gas development (Associated Press 2011).

Natural gas is currently the primary alternative to coal for generating electricity and its use is expected to increase. Indeed, it has long been seen as a possible bridge from coal to cleaner renewable fuels, and its abundance in the United States makes it an attractive hedge against supply disruptions from abroad. To be sure, natural gas burns cleaner than coal and thus emits less CO_2 but the controversy over fracking shows that an increased reliance on natural gas raises its own set of environmental concerns, further complicating efforts to integrate energy, air, and climate policies. As noted previously, in addition to the air- and water-quality issues, natural gas production is a significant source of methane, a potent greenhouse gas. Methane emissions from gas production have increased since the 1990s, and unless technology and regulatory requirements change, they will continue to climb along with gas production. Natural gas, then, is not a panacea to the nation's air pollution, energy, and climate problems.

Nuclear Energy

Even before the accidents at the Fukushima reactors in Japan, nuclear power was arguably the most controversial alternative to fossil fuels for generating electricity. The United States has more nuclear power plants than any other nation, with 104 units operating in thirty-one states, producing nearly 20 percent of the nation's electricity. The average capacity of these plants has increased from 70 percent in the 1990s to more than 90 percent in the first years of the twenty-first century, which has allowed nuclear power to maintain its share of total electricity production as demand has risen, even though the number of reactors has not increased since 1996. Skyrocketing construction costs and public concerns with reactor safety and waste disposal thrust the industry into a more than thirty-year slump: the last US nuclear plant started was thirty-five years ago, and every one proposed since then, until recently, was canceled.

Despite public concerns, the federal government has continued to support the industry with subsidies and legislation designed to facilitate the construction of new plants. The Energy Policy Act of 1991, for example, granted a long-time industry wish by streamlining the approval process for new plants. Utilities may now file a combined construction and operating license (COL) application; in the past, separate construction and operation licenses were required and companies ran the risk of failing to receive an operating license after construction had been approved and even commenced. In recent years the Nuclear Regulatory Commission, the federal agency responsible for regulating nuclear power, has granted twenty-year extensions to the forty-year design lifetime of nearly fifty units and is expected to approve another thirty-five units moving forward. In another move to aid the nuclear industry, the 2005 Energy Policy Act provides tax credits, loan guarantees, and an extension of liability limits for nuclear power plants in the case of accidents (the Price-Anderson Act). In its aftermath, utilities proposed more than thirty new reactors, but the recession, reduced demand for electricity, and low natural gas prices lead many to delay or cancel their projects.

But a nuclear renaissance faces many well-known obstacles (Duffy 2011). The two nuclear power plant accidents, at Three Mile Island in Pennsylvania in 1979 and the Chernobyl meltdown in 1986 that contaminated large parts of Europe, damaged nuclear power for a generation. The prospect of climate change allowed advocates to position nuclear power as a solution, and opinion surveys suggested that the public was becoming more receptive to the technology. Then came the disaster in Fukushima, which lead the Nuclear Regulatory Commission to initiate a comprehensive review of reactor safety. Although it is too early to gauge the long-term effects of the accident on the industry, the NRC later approved the construction of four reactors, despite concerns over cost overruns and safety issues (Wald 2012).

In addition to the difficulty of siting new plants is the challenge of storing waste. US nuclear plants produce about two thousand tons of nuclear fuel waste each year. The high-level waste is currently stored at power plant sites in water-filled pools or dry casks, awaiting shipment to a final repository. The 1982 Nuclear Waste Policy Act orders the federal government to find a site where it can manage used fuel and high-level waste. Storage costs are to be funded by a one-tenth of a cent-per-kilowatt-hour (kWh) fee on nuclear electricity generated. In 2002, the DOE recommended Yucca Mountain, Nevada, as the storage site, which was approved by Congress and the president. Construction was planned to begin in 2011 but there is strong opposition to the site and the Obama administration has attempted to terminate the Yucca program and explore alternative waste disposal options.

Cost remains the major obstacle to nuclear power. Construction costs for nuclear plants were prohibitively high even before Fukushima and increasing by 15 percent annually (Cambridge Energy Research Associates 2009). Furthermore, nuclear power is not competitive without government subsidies. According to the Congressional Budget Office (US Congress 2008) the subsidies provided in the Energy Policy Act of 2005 are critical to a nuclear revival and "by themselves could make advanced nuclear reactors a competitive technology for limited additions to base-load capacity" (2). Electricity from nuclear plants would be approximately 35 percent more expensive than coal without the incentives and 30 percent more expensive than natural gas.

The Congressional Budget Office also concluded, however, that in the long run a carbon tax would increase the competitiveness of nuclear power and "could make it the least expensive source of new base-load capacity." Carbon charges of about $45 per metric ton "would probably make nuclear generation competitive with conventional fossil-fuel technologies as a source of new capacity, even without EPAct incentives. At charges below that level, conventional gas technology would probably be a more economic choice" (US Congress, Congressional Budget Office 2008, 2). The CBO estimated that a carbon tax of between $20 and $45 per metric ton would give nuclear generation an economic edge over coal but not natural gas. The CBO suggested that utilities would likely decide to keep existing coal plants open until carbon charges reached about $45 per ton (US Congress, Congressional Budget Office 2008). In short, only a sizable carbon tax would induce utilities to substitute nuclear for coal plants, but one is not in the offing. Until then, we should not expect that nuclear power will provide a solution to the climate problem.

Integrating Climate Change and Clean Air Regulatory Programs

The CAA predates concern with climate change but creates opportunities to reduce GHG emissions from power plants as well as more conventional air pollutants, especially if clean air and climate programs are better integrated. Aggressive clean air regulations, for example, could lead to greater reductions in GHGs and GHG restrictions could help put pressure on old coal-fired power plants that have been grandfathered or protected from the air pollution standards required for new sources under the CAA. To cite another area of overlap, some power plants have met the law's acid rain emission–reduction targets by investing in clean energy. In short, there are many reasons why decisions on new power plants should take clean air and climate impacts into account. This sort of integration has not happened yet, in large part because the act's provisions are complex and implementation has been difficult. In addition, rule making under the law is complicated by the fact that programs overlap; particulates, ozone, SO_2, and NO_x, for example, are subject to multiple rules (US EPA 2007b). Perhaps most important, rule making under the law has been a political flashpoint for decades. As a result, the CAA has not produced the desired reductions in emissions from power plants and legislative action is needed to ensure progress toward both goals. Given the political impasse on climate and environmental policy, though, such action is unlikely in the near term because neither side is willing to risk revisiting the law and providing their opponents with an opportunity to rewrite the law. The overlapping, fragmented, and contentious nature of some clean air programs that must be integrated with climate and energy policies are discussed in the following section.

Regulating CO_2

The landmark 2007 Supreme Court decision in *Massachusetts* v. *EPA* has the potential, over the long term, to greatly reduce carbon dioxide emissions from power plants and other sources. That decision, subsequently reaffirmed by the court in 2011, opened the door to EPA regulation of greenhouse gases under the CAA.

During the 2008 campaign Barack Obama pledged that, if elected president, he would act to curtail GHG emissions. Following up on that pledge, in April 2009 the EPA determined that carbon dioxide and five other gases (methane, nitrous oxide, hydrofluorocarbons, perfluorocarbons, and sulfur hexafluoride) endangered public health. This "endangerment finding" was the first step toward regulating CO_2 and other GHGs. In announcing its ruling, the EPA found that there was compelling evidence that the gases contributed to increased drought, more frequent and heavier rainfall and flooding, and more heat waves and wildfires (Broder 2009).

The following year, when it became clear that Congress was not going to adopt a climate change law, the agency committed to setting CO_2 standards for power plants and oil refineries, the two largest sources in the United States. The first rules, which took effect in January 2011, applied only to those utilities planning large, new facilities and those making major modification to existing facilities. The EPA said it was acting cautiously and trying to minimize economic costs and estimated that the rules would affect only about four hundred plants in each of the first few years (Broder 2010b). In March 2012, the EPA proposed the first standards for carbon pollutants from new power plants. The proposed rule, which limits new plants to no more than 1,000 pounds of CO_2 per megawatt-hour generated, would make it much harder to build conventional coal plants, which emit upward of 1,700 pounds per megawatt-hour. Most natural gas plants, on the other hand, already meet the standard. The new rule applies only to new generating facilities and not to existing plants or to those slated to begin construction in the next year (Plumer 2012).

The prospect of regulating CO_2 clearly has enormous implications. Short of a carbon tax or other mechanism to price carbon, it would be hard to devise a policy that could do more to curtail GHG emissions, combat climate change, and reduce air pollution. At the same time, it would be difficult to imagine a more controversial course of action. The economic consequences would be profound, affecting vast swaths of the US economy. The political fallout would be enormous as well and so the Obama administration has been exceedingly cautious, delaying rules while seeking ways to minimize their economic consequences. Opponents of regulating CO_2 have portrayed the rules as job-killers, a powerful argument at a time of high unemployment, especially in states in the Midwest, which are crucial to Obama's reelection. The new Republican majority in the House has also launched a legislative onslaught against the EPA, passing bills that seek to block the agency from regulating CO_2, which would overturn the agency's endangerment finding that global warming threatens public health and which would preempt states from setting their own GHG standards. The House has also considered other measures aimed at preventing the agency from expending any funds on climate rules.

Faced with a Republican House, nervous and wavering Democrats, and a fragile economy, the Obama administration has tried to walk a fine line, articulating ambitious policy goals while delaying several critical rules in an effort to mollify opponents. That effort is likely to fail because the White House and the EPA will be criticized whether the rules are issued or not, and environmental and public health advocates will be disappointed by the administration's failure to do more. At this point, the administrative path is the most likely route to limiting CO_2 emissions—Congress was unable to enact a climate bill when Democrats had large majorities in both chambers—and it is virtually impossible that climate legislation would go very far in the current Congress. The Obama administration, though, has shown little willingness to aggressively assert its executive powers, at least before the president's reelection campaign.

Acid Rain

Power plants emit four primary pollutants that significantly affect human health: nitrogen oxides (NO_x), sulfur dioxide (SO_2), fine particulates ($PM_{2.5}$), and mercury. NO_x emissions come from combustion of oil, coal, natural gas, and other fossil fuels and contribute to lung damage and respiratory illnesses. They are also an ingredient of acid deposition that damages trees and lakes, and acid aerosols can reduce visibility and corrode stone used in buildings, statues, and monuments. SO_2 emissions are a product of fossil-fuel combustion, especially high-sulfur coal from the eastern United States, and are a major cause of respiratory problems. SO_2 emissions are also an ingredient of acid deposition. Fine particles or particulates include a wide set of substances, ranging from dust from agricultural activities and road traffic, often measured as PM_{10}, to the more dangerous fine particles ($PM_{2.5}$) that are the result of the combustion of wood, diesel and other fuels, and other materials. Fine particles are the most dangerous form of pollutants because they are able to bypass natural defense mechanisms and become lodged deeply into lung tissue and are associated with premature mortality as well as nose and throat irritation, lung damage, and increased respiratory disease symptoms. Coal-fired power plants are also the primary source of mercury, a hazardous air pollutant. Mercury emissions are deposited onto soil or into lakes and streams, where they persist and bioaccumulate in the environment, affecting food chains and posing significant risks to those who rely on fish as a major part of their diets.[1]

The acid rain program enacted by Congress as Title IV of the CAA of 1990 established the goal of reducing sulfur dioxide emissions from fossil fuel–fired plants by ten million tons below 1980 levels by the year 2000 (US EPA 2008a). Phase I began in 1995 and regulated emissions from 263 units in eastern and midwestern states; an additional 182 units later joined the system. Phase II added smaller plants and lowered the cap on total emissions to 8.95 million tons. There are now more than two thousand units covered, including all generators with a capacity of more than 25 megawatts and all new units. Based on their historic fuel consumption and a formula governing an acceptable emissions rate, each unit was given a fixed number of allowances for SO_2 emissions; each allowance permitted one ton of SO_2 a year. Allowances may be bought, sold, or banked for future use. At the end of each year, the EPA compares the number of allowances units hold with their actual emissions and gives owners sixty days to reconcile their account. Other sources of SO_2 may voluntarily enter the system; they can reduce their emissions and sell extra allowances to the utilities.

The 1990 law also set a goal of reducing NO_x emissions by two million tons from 1980 levels in a two-phase process but did not establish a cap-and-trade program. The program imposes emissions limits on coal-fired electric utility boilers. Units are to achieve a rate, expressed in pounds of NO_x per million Btu of heat input, and can meet the target either by ensuring that all boilers comply or that the average of all boilers meet the target (so that individuals boilers can exceed the limit). This gives utilities some flexibility in meeting the standards in the most cost-effective way. If a utility installs the correct equipment and operates it as required and still cannot meet the emissions cap, it can apply for an alternative emission limitation (AEL) that matches the level it is capable of achieving.

Emissions of SO_2, NO_x, and CO_2 are reported in real time to state regulatory agencies through the continuous emissions monitors all units are required to have. If emissions of SO_2 or NO_x exceed allowances, companies must pay a fine of $2,000 per ton, adjusted for inflation. These requirements, along with other clean air obligations, are included in an operating permit each plant must have (US EPA 2008a). Companies can cut their emissions by using cleaner fuels, shifting production from dirtier to cleaner units, or reducing generation through conservation or efficiency programs. The EPA reported that the program saved as much as $3 billion a year in compliance costs compared with a typical command-and-control approach.[2]

Studies confirm, though, that much of the cost savings (and emissions reductions) were a result of switching to low-sulfur coal and not efficiency or even cleaner fuels. Six states in which the power plants regulated under phase I of the program are located have regulatory programs that favor scrubbing as a compliance option, as a way to protect their local coal industries. Fourteen facilities operating in these six states opted for scrubbing as a result of regulatory pressures. Installation of scrubbers was also encouraged by the awarding of bonus allowances for utilities that met their emission-reduction targets through scrubbing. The cost of scrubbing also fell in response to competition from other means of reducing emissions, such as fuel switching. Overall, low-sulfur fuel was responsible for about 50 percent of the emissions reductions achieved in phase I. The costs of cleaner coal were lower than projected because of the deregulation of the railroad industry, the development of fuel-mixing technologies that allowed high- and low-sulfur coal to be mixed together to reduce emissions, and the surprising decline in low-sulfur coal prices even as demand increased. Although the cost savings have been significant, the success of the acid rain program in achieving its environmental goals is in doubt. Companies have been less interested in trading to reduce compliance costs than they have been in banking allowances for use in phase II of the program, when requirements are more stringent. Scrubbing may become more necessary to comply with the more stringent phase II requirements and one of the major effects of the trading program may be to delay the installation of scrubber and other controls (Bohi and Burtraw 1997). In the end, then, the acid rain program has cut emissions but it has fallen short of the type of reductions that are necessary to achieve clean air and climate goals.

National Ambient Air-Quality Standards

The CAA requires the US Environmental Protection Agency to regulate diverse forms of air pollution that endanger public health and welfare. The EPA has issued national ambient air-quality standards (NAAQS) for the six criteria pollutants: ozone, particulate matter (ranging in size from tiny or fine particles ($PM_{2.5}$)) to larger particles (PM_{10}), carbon monoxide, sulfur dioxide, nitrogen oxide, and lead. In order to attain the NAAQS, states develop state implementation plans (SIPs) that contain control measures such as limits on emissions from stationary sources (such as factories), area sources (small, diffuse sources such as residential fireplaces), and motor vehicles (inspection and maintenance programs to ensure vehicles continue to meet EPA-established emission standards). States and EPA address pollution that crosses state boundaries through SIP requirements and interstate agreements, such as the northeastern states' Ozone Transport Commission; coal-fired power plants are a major source of these pollutants.

One of the most difficult and contentious issues has been how to regulate interstate pollution because the CAA relies on state-level cleanup plans. State implementation plans, for example, must include provisions requiring state air-quality officials to notify neighboring states before the construction of new sources of pollution that might affect these states. No state may authorize the construction of a new source of pollution that would contribute to another state's failure to comply with the national standards. The act also permits the creation of interstate agreements to combat air pollution but the framework it provides is complex, particularly because it is superimposed on the rest of the act, which is built on direct relations between EPA and individual state regulatory agencies. Interstate compacts can be an important means of facilitating interstate collaboration, and the law authorizes the EPA administrator to establish interstate transport regions whenever he or she "has reason to believe that the interstate transport of air pollutants from one or more States contributes significantly to a violation of a national ambient air quality standard in one or more other States" (42 U.S.C. 7492). Governors of affected states may also petition the EPA for the creation of a transport region commission.

Rule making under the law has been plagued by delay and inconsistency. As an illustration, in December 2003 the Bush administration proposed two rules to control power plant emissions—one for nitrogen oxides and sulfur dioxide and another for mercury. NO_x and SO_2 are precursors of fine particulate and ozone pollution and the Clean Air Interstate Rule (CAIR) was aimed at helping states meet the new standards by reducing regional emissions from power plants. According to the EPA, power plants are responsible for 50 percent of the nation's mercury emissions, 50 percent of the acid gas emissions, and 25 percent of all toxic metals emissions. Moreover, coal-fired plants are the largest human-generated source of mercury in the United States and account for 99 percent of all mercury emissions from power plants (US EPA 2011c). Mercury in the atmosphere falls to Earth through rain and snow and as dry deposition. In lakes, rivers, and estuaries, it is transformed into methylmercury, where it builds up in fish tissue. Eating contaminated fish is particularly dangerous for women of childbearing age because developing fetuses are the most sensitive to the toxin and exposure adversely affects the neural health of children (US EPA 2008b).

The Clean Air Interstate Rule promised to reduce SO_2 emissions in the eastern and northeastern states by more than 70 percent and NO_x emissions by more than 60 percent from 2003 levels. EPA analyses found that the reductions would produce $85 billion to $100 billion in health benefits, "substantially reduce premature mortality in the eastern United States, and result in almost $2 billion in visibility benefits" each year in southeastern national parks such as Great Smoky and Shenandoah by 2015 (US EPA 2007c). CAIR created a cap-and-trade system for both pollutants and promised to reduce SO_2 emissions by 5.4 million tons (57 percent) by 2015. When fully implemented, the reductions were expected to reach 73 percent below 2003 levels. The new rule also promised to reduce NO_x emissions by two million tons, a 61 percent reduction from 2003 levels, by 2015. Under the proposal, the EPA was to issue NO_x allowances to each state and states, in turn, would allocate them to specific sources. The sources could achieve their cap by installing pollution control equipment, switching fuels, or buying excess allowances from other sources that have reduced their emissions (US EPA 2007c).

The CAIR rule was challenged in court and in 2008 the District Court instructed the EPA to issue a new rule, which it did in July 2011. The new rule, known as the Cross State Air Pollution Rule, replaced CAIR and required twenty-seven states in the eastern United States to reduce power plant emissions of SO_2 and NO_x that cross state lines and contribute to ground level ozone and fine-particle pollution in other states. The reductions were to take place in two phases beginning in January 2012 and were expected to result in a 73 percent reduction (from 2005 levels) of SO_2 emission from power plants and a 54 percent drop in NO_x emissions (US EPA 2011b).

The Clean Air Mercury Rule sought to limit mercury emissions from new and existing coal-fired power plants in two phases. The first phase imposed a thirty-eight-ton cap per year on emissions; these reductions would occur as a co-benefit from reducing SO_2 and NO_x under CAIR. The second phase, to begin in 2018, would eventually shrink the cap to fifteen tons. New coal-fired plants (defined as those where construction began after January 30, 2004) were also required to comply with the emissions cap and to meet new source performance standards as well. The standards are required by the act to reflect maximum achievable control technologies, which are based on the performance of specific control technologies, but, unlike a cap that declines over time, do not provide a continuous incentive for innovations (US EPA 2008b).

The proposed rules followed the well-trod pattern of imposing new cleanup standards and extended compliance dates but it reflected acceptance of less ambitious goals than included in the CAA and was a significant retreat in clean air policy. The mercury rules were particularly controversial because in at least three different instances, passages in the proposal mirrored almost word for word portions of memos written by industry lobbyists (Eilperin 2004). They were also controversial because they proposed using a cap-and-trade approach, which raised the prospect of mercury "hot spots" near power plants, and because the EPA sought to remove coal- and oil-fired power plants from the list of regulated sources under the CAA. A final rule was issued in 2005 and companies began installing pollution-control equipment. The rules were immediately challenged in court, though, and in summer 2008, the Court of Appeals for the District of Columbia rejected them, concluding that the EPA did not have the statutory authority to remove coal and oil plants from the list of sources of hazardous pollutants in the CAA, and remanded the rule back to the EPA. The Supreme Court declined to hear the appeal in February 2009, allowing the lower court ruling to stand. What followed was predictable. States had been relying on the CAIR rule to help them meet the next round of air-quality standards for ozone and fine particles and had to seek other ways to reduce emissions from power plants. The absence of a clear federal rule meant that each state was on its own to figure out how to reduce power plant and other emissions, and an opportunity to reduce GHG emissions from power plants was lost, at least temporarily (Bachman and Wierman 2008; Weiss and Kinsman 2008). In March 2011, the EPA proposed a more stringent final rule to reduce air toxics (including mercury) from power plants and revised the new source performance standards (NSPS) for fossil fuel plants for PM, SO_2, and NO_x. According to the agency, the new rule would cut mercury and acid gas emissions from power plants by 91 percent, fine particle emissions by 30 percent, and SO_2 emissions by 53 percent (US EPA 2011c).

Not surprisingly, the utility industry opposed the new rule, arguing that it would drive up the cost of energy and jeopardize jobs. Some suggested that the new rules could prompt a significant shift away from coal to natural gas as a source of electricity but the EPA estimated that just 2 percent of coal capacity would be retired as a result of the rule by 2015 (Power 2011).

Legislative action is required in other areas as well to address chronic problems with the process for issuing and implementing national air-quality standards. In 2006 and 2008, the EPA issued new standards for particulate matter and ozone even before the 1997 standards had been implemented and, as typically happens, the actions were challenged in court. In 2009, the Court of Appeals in Washington, DC, remanded the standards to the agency to show why the level of protection it had chosen was "requisite to protect the public health" with an "adequate margin of safety" as required by the CAA (NRDC v. EPA, 571 F.3d 1245 (D.C. Cir. 2009). The court, typically willing to defer to agency interpretation of the science underlying its actions, noted that the agency's final rules were inconsistent with the recommendations of EPA staff members and its Clean Air Scientific Advisory Committee (Bachman 2009). In 2010, after months of delay, the EPA announced a draft proposal to strengthen the NAAQS for ground level ozone, lowering the standard from 75 parts per billion to 60 to 70 parts per billion but backed away from the move in September 2011, when the White House requested it be withdrawn (US EPA 2010a). The Obama administration capitulated to industry lobbying, fearful that the rule would be attacked by opponents as a job killer and another example of excessive federal regulation. Public health and environmental advocates were furious at the administration's backtracking on such a critical issue and threatened to challenge the decision in court (Broder 2011). The decision illustrates the continued chaos of the regulatory landscape on this issue and further postpones needed action (Langworthy 2009).

New Source Review

The CAA requires new major stationary sources and major modifications of existing sources to obtain permits, perform air-quality analysis, and install more stringent controls than are required for existing sources. The EPA must issue NSPS for categories of stationary sources that are to be constructed or modified in nonattainment areas. These standards require sources to produce emissions that are achievable through the best system of emission reduction (the lowest achievable emission rate or LAER). NSPS are technology-based standards that must be met by every new source within specified categories of industry if the source is constructed after the EPA has proposed an NSPS for its industry. Modifications to existing sources are also subject to NSPS if the modification results in the emission of any new pollutant or the increased emission of any existing pollutant. The EPA exempts routine maintenance actions from triggering the NSPS requirements.

In the 1980s, electric utility industries began spending money to keep plants operating longer rather than retiring them and building new ones. As a result, these old, grandfathered plants dominate emissions of SO_2, NO_x, and other pollutants. Industry officials have claimed that these investments are routine maintenance but evidence describes these projects as going beyond that to actually increasing capacity. The EPA's rules governing new source reviews for power generators define routine maintenance to exclude any project that increases a facility's ability, either technically or economically, to generate electricity above the capacity existing before the investment. These rules are quite generous to sources and allow them to use the maximum polluting hour and the average of the two highest polluting years in determining the limits that they must stay within when making routine maintenance investments. The EPA has argued that determining whether or not a project is routine maintenance is a highly fact-specific decision, and for thirty years it has issued "applicability determination" letters to resolve questions about whether specific projects can or cannot count as maintenance (Hawkins 2000).

In 1998, the EPA announced an initiative to target violations of the new source review (NSR) programs. In its first major enforcement effort under this initiative, the agency issued complaints against seven electric utility companies in 1999, charging that they had made major modifications at their facilities without meeting the NSR requirements (Poffenberger 2000). The Bush administration reversed this policy initiative, although it continued to pursue some enforcement cases (Barcott 2004; Shogren 2004). In 2007, the EPA issued revised NSR rules that made it easier for old power plants to continue operating without investing in new emissions control equipment and scaled back its enforcement efforts. The new rules reflected a major policy victory by industry and effectively ended some of the enforcement actions started in the Clinton administration. The rules allowed utilities to undertake maintenance and other projects that cost up to 20 percent of the total cost of the plant without triggering requirements that they install the stringent emission controls required of new sources. They would also make it easier for older plants to increase their output without installing new control equipment by changing the way emissions were calculated (counting the hourly rater of emissions rather than annual emissions) (Hughes 2008). Unless these rules are reversed in the Obama administration, these old coal-fired plants will continue to pollute at high levels.

Fuel Switching and Better Efficiency

Although conventional air pollutants can be removed from stationary source emissions through control devices such as baghouses and electrostatic precipitators for particulates, scrubbers (flue gas desulfurization devices) for SO_2, and selective catalytic reduction for NO_x, removing CO_2 is expensive and energy intensive because it is not an impurity or by-product of combustion. For now, with current technologies, the only ways to reduce CO_2 are fuel switching and improved efficiency, actions that have the added benefit of significantly reducing emissions of other pollutants as well.

Shifting from coal to natural gas and other low-carbon fuels in electric power plants has produced major environmental improvements. Natural gas-fired combined-cycle plants, for example, when combined with using the excess heat produced in a heat recovery generator, are about 50 percent efficient compared to the 33 percent efficiency of coal-fired power plants. According to one estimate, the combined impact of switching to a cleaner fuel and improved efficiency reduces CO_2 emissions by 66 percent and virtually eliminates NO_x and SO_2 emissions. Similarly, in combined heat and power (CHP) processes, electricity and useful heat are produced together, increasing overall plant efficiency by as much as 40 to 50 percent while reducing fuel consumption and all related emissions as well. Reducing the use of fossil fuels is critical because "once GHGs have been formed as the product of fuel combustion, they cannot effectively be reduced without expending the use of a level of energy that approaches or exceeds the energy production that formed the GHG emissions in the first place" (State and Territorial Air Pollution Program Administrators and Association of Local Air Pollution Control Officials [National Association of Clean Air Agencies] 1999, 3).

One way to create an incentive for energy efficiency is to convert emission standards to the amount of pollutant emitted per unit of energy produced, such as pounds of pollution per megawatt hour for CO_2, NO_x, and SO_2. This would make it easier for cleaner, efficient plants to meet the standards and more difficult for more polluting plants to comply. This approach would also encourage owners to shut down older, inefficient units, exactly the kind of incentive that is essential in reducing emissions but has been missing from clean air regulations to date.

A recent report by the National Association of Clean Air Agencies (2008) reemphasized the importance of a multipollutant approach to air pollution to ensure that efforts to reduce emissions of one kind of pollutant do not lead to increased emissions of another pollutant. Policies aimed at cutting GHG emissions can help reduce other emissions from old coal-fired power plants that have been grandfathered or protected from the air pollution standards required for new sources. One of the biggest failures of the CAA has been its inability to create sufficient incentives to close down those highly polluting plants—the big dirties— and replace them with newer, cleaner, more efficient plants. Because they have so few pollution controls, these plants are cheaper to operate than competing modes of generating electricity and continue to operate despite their environmental costs. GHG standards can also help states and localities achieve their targets for energy efficiency and renewable energy, as discussed in chapter 5.

Clean Air, Clean Coal, and Climate Change

For decades, coal-fired power plants have been the target of clean air policy making and, as a result, new plants are much cleaner than old ones. In one sense, then, the CAA has been a success. But because old plants have so few pollution controls, these "big dirties" plants are cheaper to operate than competing modes of generating electricity, giving their owners incentive to keep the plants open long after their design life. In that sense, the CAA has been a failure.

A host of studies on the health effects of air pollution have linked power plant emissions with premature death and other health effects. Epidemiological research by C. Arden Pope III and others has concluded that "fine particulate matter and associated combustion-related air pollutants" are "largely responsible" for the respiratory and cardiovascular disease associated with the health effects of air pollution. The exposure-response relationships for fine particles, in terms of short- and long-term exposure, "are nearly linear, with no discernible safe thresholds within relevant ranges of exposure." Although air pollution is only one of several risk factors contributing to pulmonary and cardiovascular disease, "it is one that can be modified" (Pope and Arden 2004, 1132–1133). Pope and Douglas W. Dockery (2006, 731) summarized research on the health effects of fine particulates, examining studies of long-term exposure as well as those evaluating daily levels of exposure, and found "reasonably consistent associations between cardiopulmonary mortality and daily changes in PM [particulate matter]." Whereas short-term exposure studies reflect some of the health effects from inhaling fine particulates, "long-term repeated exposures have larger, more persistent cumulative effects than short-term transient exposure."

Tens of thousands of lives could be saved if emissions from the old, dirty coal plants were cleaned up but Congress, the White House, and the EPA have been deadlocked for years. The EPA estimated that the benefit of the acid rain program in 2010 would be $122 billion and costs would only be about $3 billion, a 40:1 benefit-cost ratio. The benefits largely came from the avoided health effects of reducing fine particulate pollution (US EPA 2007a).

If such dramatic benefits to public health cannot prompt effective policy making, it is easy to see why the threat of climate change has also been unable to compel action. Protecting public health is typically the most potent weapon in the environmental protection arsenal, often able to generate public support even when compliance costs are high. But it does not always work in the face of powerful lobbies that fiercely protect their interests and a widespread view that energy costs must be kept as low as possible.

5

Increasing Energy Efficiency and the Use of Alternative Energy

Improving energy efficiency is a compelling climate and energy priority because it reduces air pollution, cuts spending on energy, avoids the need for siting new facilities, and eliminates the economic and environmental costs of building new sources of energy. Developing alternative energy sources is also a critical element of climate policy but virtually every option includes difficult costs, trade-offs, or problems. From the perspective of policy integration, energy efficiency is the clear winner, and compared to the cost of developing alternative energy sources energy efficiency investments are usually a bargain. Many options for reducing CO_2 emissions through energy efficiency cost \$10 to \$30 a ton of CO_2 avoided compared with alternative energy projects such as wind power that cost in the \$60 to \$70 per ton range and beyond (Quirk 2008).

Renewable energy has a long history in the United States. Until the mid-nineteenth century, most of the nation's energy came from renewable energy sources. Some renewable technologies, such as windmills and pump water, have been used for centuries, and hydropower continues to play a significant role in some regions. The rise of coal and then oil, however, with their great advantages of portability and efficient power production, quickly overwhelmed renewable sources. Nevertheless, alternative energy sources such as nuclear power, solar, and wind have considerable climate-related advantages because they are largely free of GHG emissions and are central to the production of electricity in a carbon-constrained world. At the same time, though, there are significant environmental impacts associated with some alternative fuels and, perhaps most important, costs are almost always higher than fossil fuels whose prices fail to reflect the true price of producing and using energy. Energy efficiency and renewables are central to integrating energy and climate policy. This chapter focuses first on energy efficiency policy options and then shifts to consideration of alternative energy sources.

Improving Energy Efficiency

The clear-cut, unambiguous advantages of energy efficiency are unusual in energy policy and, as a result, improving efficiency and conservation should be a top priority for energy policy making. The energy intensity (the amount of energy used per unit of economic output) of the US economy has steadily improved over the past three decades, declining at an annual rate of 1.6 percent from 1990 to 2007 (International Energy Agency 2009). Since 2000, federal and state policies have encouraged greater efficiency and use of renewables but it is difficult to know how much of that improvement can be attributed to public policies because investments to modernize products and processes independent of policy actions also contributed to these trends. Improving energy intensity, however, has not significantly reduced either total energy production or GHG emissions because economic growth has produced emissions that have overwhelmed any gains from improved efficiency. And although the United States has become more energy efficient and spends more on renewable energy research and development than any other nation, more can be done to reduce GHG emissions from energy production and use (International Energy Agency 2009). This section reviews the challenges of increasing energy efficiency, examines some of the relevant policies in place and how well they are working, and explores options for increasing energy efficiency.

Evolution of US Energy Efficiency and Renewables Policies

The Energy Tax Act of 1978 was the first major law aimed at encouraging efficiency and renewables: it provided tax credits for businesses and households that installed solar and wind energy equipment (homeowners, for example, could receive a credit for 30 percent of the first $2,000 they spent on solar and wind energy equipment and 20 percent for the next $8,000 they purchased, and businesses received a 10 percent tax credit for investment in conservation or alternatives). The tax credits were increased in 1980 to 40 percent of the first $10,000 homeowners spent; businesses could deduct up to 15 percent of their spending on conservation or renewables as part of the Crude Oil Windfall Profits Tax Act of 1980. Congress also established national efficiency standards for appliances and equipment in 1978 and updated them in 1988, 1992, 2005, and 2007.

Concerns over energy security prompted the passage of the Energy Policy Act of 2005 (P.L. 109–58, 119 STAT. 609), which authorized a research and development program covering energy efficiency and a broad array of renewables. The law also provided tax credits to encourage the deployment of energy efficiency and renewable technologies, including, for the first time, a tax credit for residential solar energy systems; set new goals for improved energy efficiency for federal agencies; established a new renewable fuels standard (RFS) to encourage use of ethanol, biodiesel, and other renewable fuels; and created a new set of consumer tax credits for purchasing energy-efficient hybrid, clean-diesel, and fuel-cell vehicles.

The Energy Tax Incentives Act of 2005, passed as part of the Energy Policy Act, also established a number of incentives for renewable energy: the renewable electricity production credit, clean renewable energy bonds, a business solar investment tax credit, a business fuel cell credit, and a residential energy efficiency property credit. These tax credits, worth an estimated $3.6 billion through 2015, were a significant part of the more than $14 billion in benefits provided in the 2005 law. Renewable energy facilities eligible for the 1.8 cents per kWh of electricity produced credit include wind energy, closed- and open-loop biomass, solar, small irrigation power, landfill gas, trash combustion that had already received subsidies under previous laws, and added hydropower, fuel cells, Indian coal, "refined coal," and wave, current, tidal, and ocean thermal energy. The tax incentives in the law had very limited time frames for eligibility to ensure that credits were only available for new investments.

Continued congressional concern with energy security led to the 2007 Energy Independence and Security Act (P.L. 110–140, 121 STAT. 1492), which tightened energy efficiency standards for home appliances, provided for new standards for the design of energy-efficient windows and equipment of commercial buildings, and required the federal government to make all of its buildings carbon neutral by 2030 (US Department of Energy, Energy Efficiency and Renewable Energy 2011). Specific provisions included new or revised standards for light bulbs, clothes washers, dishwashers, dehumidifiers, motors, commercial refrigerators and freezers, and external power suppliers for electronic products. The law also required federal agencies to reduce their energy consumption by 30 percent by 2015 and directed that they also reduce the use of energy produced from fossil fuels in federal buildings by 55 percent in 2010 and 100 percent in 2030. The law also expanded and extended the renewable fuel standard, requiring that thirty-six billion gallons of biofuels be used in the United States annually by 2022 (US Department of Energy, Energy Information Administration 2011f).

Many of the energy efficiency tax incentives enacted in 2005 were scheduled to expire in 2008 but the economic meltdown and credit crisis that fall led Congress to enact $17 billion in tax credits for clean energy as part of a $700 billion rescue package. Among the specific incentives Congress extended were the commercial buildings tax deduction, the residential energy efficiency property credit, and the tax credit for efficient furnaces, boilers, air conditioners, and water heaters, and insulation and window upgrades to existing homes. Congress also extended a bonding program for green buildings and sustainable design and established a new energy conservation bond program that would help local and state governments to fund energy conservation efforts.[1]

The American Recovery and Reinvest Act (ARRA) (P.L. 111–5, 123 STAT. 115), adopted early in 2009, authorized more than $27 billion in spending aimed at expanding increasing efficiency and renewables as well as new jobs. Among the key items were $6 billion in loan guarantees for renewable energy and electric transmission technologies and $2 billion for advanced car battery technologies. ARRA also set aside more than $3.2 billion for energy efficiency and a conservation block grant program for states, local, and tribal governments for efficiency programs in the building and transportation sectors. The state energy program received $3.1 billion in grants to establish state energy offices and to upgrade state and local government buildings. States and communities could also use the funds for rebates to homeowners for energy audits and efficiency improvements in residential buildings. ARRA also extended the federal renewable energy production tax credit of 2.2 cents per kWh for all wind facilities in operation by the end of 2012 and closed-loop biomass facilities in operation by the end of 2013. Spending provisions in the Recovery Act helped boost the renewable share of total DOE research and development spending to 31 percent in 2010 (US Department of Energy, Energy Information Administration 2011f).

There has been significant policy activity at the state level as well. Thirty-two states, for example, subsidize the installation of renewable energy equipment through grants, rebates, or tax credits, and thirty-seven states and the District of Columbia have enacted renewable portfolio standards (RPSs) (US Department of Energy, Energy Information Administration 2011f). Renewable portfolio standards are designed to increase the generation of electricity from renewable fuels. They can be mandatory or voluntary and typically require or encourage electricity providers to provide a specified minimum share of electricity from renewable sources. Typically, RPSs specify which renewable fuels qualify, which varies from state to state. According to the Energy Information Administration the standards are responsible for significant increases in renewable-generating capacity and have displaced coal and some nuclear and natural gas generation (US Department of Energy, Energy Information Administration 2011f).

There has been a considerable amount of policy activity since 2000 aimed at improving the nation's energy efficiency and its use of renewable energy. Many of the laws enacted during that period enjoyed bipartisan support, with the 2007 law passing during a time of divided government. That was not the case with ARRA, however, which passed the House with no Republican votes and just three in the Senate. Republicans objected to the size and substance of the law, arguing that it was too expensive and represented a major expansion of federal involvement in the market. The debate over the Recovery Act marked the beginning of Republican opposition to all things Obama, an approach that proved politically astute as Republicans won control of the House in the 2010 elections and gained seats in the Senate. Since then, Congress has shown no appetite for additional spending, focusing instead on cutting spending levels for many programs, including efficiency and renewables.

Challenges in Increasing Energy Efficiency
Despite a steady improvement in the efficiency of the US economy in using energy, the United States continues to lag behind many other industrial countries in promoting energy efficiency. Table 5.1 compares energy use in the United States with that of other large economies. In terms of the amount of energy used to produce each unit of economic output, Western European countries and Japan are more energy efficient than the United States. Comparative data mask important differences between countries, such as the significantly higher costs of transporting energy (and goods and services) across the much longer distances required in the United States than in Western Europe, but also reflect different levels of commitment to promoting efficiency. Denmark and the other Scandinavian nations, for example, have made energy efficiency a public priority. In the United States, however, efficiency has simply not been an energy policy priority and it has been much less important than finding new sources of energy, whether produced domestically or abroad.

Why is energy efficiency lagging in the United States? One challenge is that many people associate efficiency and conservation with using less, having less, and consuming less. But energy efficiency need not significantly reduce the level of comfort or consumption. Air conditioners still

Table 5.1
World Energy Intensity by Region, Reference Case, 2006–2035 (Thousand Btu per 2005 Dollar of GDP)

Region	History			Projections					Average annual percent change, 2008–2035
	2006	2007	2008	2015	2020	2025	2030	2035	
OECD									
OECD Americas	7.8	7.7	7.6	6.7	6.1	5.5	5.0	4.6	-1.9
United States*	7.7	7.7	7.6	6.7	6.0	5.4	4.9	4.4	-2.0
Canada	11.7	11.7	11.6	10.4	10.0	9.4	9.1	8.7	-1.1
Mexico/Chile	5.4	5.1	5.1	4.7	4.2	3.8	3.6	3.4	-1.5
OECD Europe	5.7	5.5	5.5	5.1	4.8	4.4	4.1	3.9	-1.3
OECD Asia	6.9	6.7	6.7	6.2	6.0	5.8	5.6	5.4	-.08
Japan	5.9	5.7	5.6	5.2	5.3	5.3	5.2	5.2	-.04
South Korea	10.1	9.9	9.9	8.7	7.7	7.1	6.7	6.3	-1.7
Australia/New Zealand	8.0	7.8	7.8	7.0	6.5	5.9	5.5	5.1	-1.6
Total OECD	6.8	6.7	6.6	6.0	5.6	5.1	4.8	4.4	-1.5
Non-OECD									
Non-OECD Europe and Eurasia	15.4	14.5	14.0	12.3	10.8	9.7	8.7	8.0	-2.2
Russia	15.8	15.0	14.6	13.1	11.7	10.6	9.4	8.5	-2.1
Other	14.9	13.7	13.1	11.2	9.7	8.7	7.9	7.3	-2.3

Non-OECD Asia	9.1	8.7	8.7	7.4	6.3	5.7	5.1	4.7	-2.3
China	12.0	11.3	11.2	9.3	7.7	6.8	6.1	5.6	-2.6
India	6.8	6.6	6.6	5.3	4.6	4.3	3.9	3.6	-2.0
Other	6.5	6.3	6.2	5.2	4.7	4.3	3.9	3.6	-2.0
Middle East	11.0	10.4	10.6	9.6	8.6	8.0	7.4	6.9	-1.5
Africa	6.6	6.5	6.5	5.5	5.0	4.6	4.3	4.0	-1.7
Central and South America	7.1	6.8	6.8	5.8	5.3	4.9	4.6	4.3	-1.7
Brazil	7.2	7.1	7.1	6.3	5.6	5.2	4.8	4.5	-1.7
Other	7.1	6.6	6.5	5.4	5.0	4.6	4.3	4.1	-1.8
Total non-OECD	9.5	9.1	9.1	7.7	6.6	6.0	5.4	5.0	-2.2
Total World	7.9	7.7	7.7	6.8	6.1	5.6	5.2	4.8	-1.8

Note: *Includes the fifty states and the District of Columbia. Totals may not equal sum of components due to independent rounding.

Sources: United States: US Department of Energy, Energy Information Administration, Annual Energy Outlook 2011a.

cool, cars still run, and TV screens still shine. There are some sacrifices, though: the car's acceleration is not as fast and performance is compromised, and the air conditioner blows less powerfully. So one critical challenge will be changing perceptions about the connections between energy usage, on the one hand, and economic growth and progress, on the other.

A second challenge is that although the benefits of energy efficiency improvements usually outweigh the costs, the distribution of the costs and benefits often fail to create clear incentives for action. To cite one example, apartment owners whose renters pay for utilities may not be interested in investing in efficiency measures so that their renters pay less for gas and electricity. Furthermore, renters will not likely invest in efficiency because they are likely to move before they can recapture the cost of their investment. Thus another challenge is that if benefits do not accrue to those who paid the costs, the incentive for investing in efficiency disappears.

Third, the cost of efficiency retrofits, lack of information about the availability of efficiency options and their benefits, and inertia and competition from the wide range of concerns that compete for our attention also contribute to suboptimal investments in efficiency. Perhaps most vexing is the fact that efficiency may work too well—consumers save money when their energy use falls, which may encourage them to purchase new devices that use electricity, thus leading to an overall increase in energy consumption. Reducing the energy intensity of consumer products is no guarantee that total energy usage and the associated emissions will decline as well. In order to reduce the threat of climate change, combat air pollution, and use fewer resources, efficiency measures must be combined with conservation programs to curtail energy use.

Energy Efficiency Policy Options

Because energy production and use is the primary driver of climate change, it is critical that energy policy reflect the linkages among air pollution, climate, and energy security. Improved energy efficiency is the most cost-effective way to deal with all three problems—it prevents pollution as it cuts energy use and improves economic competitiveness as energy costs fall. US EPA data on energy-efficiency programs demonstrate that they usually cost less than producing additional electricity from power plants; these programs save energy at a cost of about 3 cents per kWh, about 50 to 75 percent of the cost of electricity from new sources and less than one-half the average retail price of electricity. CHP systems, power plants that produce electricity as well as heat that can be used to warm buildings, achieve efficiency as high as 60 to 75 percent above the average efficiency of separately produced power and heat. Implementing existing efficiency technologies that are currently economically and technologically feasible could reduce total electricity demand nationwide by about 25 percent by 2025, which represents a 50 percent reduction in electricity demand growth (US EPA 2007c).

The United States thus requires a massive investment in deploying existing energy-efficiency technologies in order to reduce demand and an equally large research and development investment in new energy-efficiency technologies. Reducing demand is far superior to increasing supply because efficiency improvements almost always reduce environmental impacts (Vine 2003). As suggested previously, with a $10 trillion dollar energy infrastructure, and energy facilities such as power plants that typically have a forty-year life span, we need to invest trillions of dollars during the next decade in order to transform our energy production and distribution system (Holdren 2001; Congressional Quarterly 2006). Some of that investment can come in the form of government assistance to help pay for new energy investments; market-based incentives such as a carbon tax and government procurement and efficiency standards can also stimulate private sector initiatives.

Innovative industries have already demonstrated that improved efficiency can save money. A wide range of US and multinational companies have concluded that precautionary action to reduce the threat of climate change is in their self-interest and have developed voluntary programs to cap and reduce greenhouse gas emissions. In September 1998, British Petroleum pledged that by the year 2010 it would reduce its emissions of greenhouse gases by 10 percent from 1990 levels. The company met its goal in October 2001, more than eight years ahead of schedule and saved some $650 million in the process (Griscom 2002). Many other large firms made similar commitments, including Shell, Dupont, Johnson & Johnson, IBM, Nike, and Lafarge (Griscom 2002; Carey 2004). Michael Northrop, cofounder of the Climate Group, a coalition of companies and governments committed to reducing GHG emissions, said, "It's impossible to find a company that has acted and has not found benefits" (Carey 2004, 69). "Proactive action on climate change," argued another, "presents opportunities for new and expanded business activity, reduced costs, and increased shareholder value that will produce a net economic benefit" (Carbontrader 2002).[2]

The major target for conservation and efficiency should be energy use in buildings because more than half of all energy used in the United States goes to heat, cool, ventilate, light, and otherwise operate industrial, commercial, government, and residential structures, and to produce and transport materials to construct those buildings. The Energy Independence and Security Act of 2007 and the American Recovery and Reinvestment Act of 2009 were steps in the right direction. The 2007 law sought to reduce electricity use through more efficient lighting and appliances. Lighting is responsible for 5 to 10 percent of residential energy use, and phasing out the use of incandescent light bulbs promises to save more than $600 million in annual energy costs. Under the law, light bulbs emitting the equivalent of 100 watts must use no more than 72 watts; by 2014, 40, 60, and 75 watt bulbs will be required to meet proportional reduction targets; by 2020, the required savings will be about 7 percent of current electricity use. The Alliance to Save Energy, an advocacy group, estimated that the new lighting standards would reduce consumer's electricity bills by $13 billion in 2020, eliminate the need to build sixty new midsized power plants and lower expected CO_2 emissions by one hundred million tons (Associated Press 2007).

The compact fluorescent bulb (CFB) has been the primary means of making lighting more efficient. Other kinds of lights, including light emitting diodes (LEDs), which are twice as efficient as CFBs (Mufson 2008), are being developed to satisfy the standard, in part because of the disadvantages of the fluorescent bulbs, which contain mercury. CFBs have also faced consumer resistance because of their high cost, relative to incandescent bulbs, despite the energy savings over the life of the bulb, which General Electric projects to be $36. The reluctance to buy the more expensive bulbs illustrates the importance of educational campaigns, rebates, and other promotional incentives that will be required to change consumer behavior in ways that are in their economic self-interest (*Columbia Daily Tribune* 2008; International Energy Agency 2011b).

The 2007 law also tightened energy efficiency standards for home appliances by making average standards minimum requirements and provided new standards for the design of energy efficient windows and equipment in commercial buildings. The law also required the federal government to make all of its buildings carbon neutral by 2030.

Another way to understand the prospects for reducing energy use and promoting efficiency is to look at what homeowners can do. Households and individuals, at home, and not counting their nonbusiness travel, use more energy than any other sector, 38 percent of all energy used. Industry uses 32.5 percent, commercial users make up 17.8 percent, and non-household transportation, 11.7 percent. In addition, the share of energy used by households is increasing: in 2000, it was only 32.4 percent of the total energy use. Gardner and Stern (2008, 13, 16) argue that, "by changing their selection of use of household and motor vehicle technologies, without waiting for new technologies to appear, making major economic sacrifices, or losing a sense of well-being, households can reduce energy consumption by almost 30 percent—about 11 percent of total U.S. consumption."

Considerable progress has been made in the United States in reducing energy use through conservation and efficiency. The US Energy Information Agency measures the nation's annual energy use in quads; one quad equals one quadrillion (10^{15}) Btus. Each year, we use about one hundred quads of energy. The Alliance to Save Energy estimates that energy efficiency improvements since 1973 saved forty-nine quads in 2006 alone (Loper 2009). In other words, absent any improvement in efficiency or conservation, our energy use would be nearly 50 percent higher than actual levels. There are a number of policy options states are pursuing that, if more widely diffused or pursued as national policies, could help move the United States beyond current energy efficiency efforts. Government entities can establish voluntary or mandatory efficiency improvement targets, which could be applied to government operations or to all major energy users. All major energy users could be encouraged or required to report their energy use and related GHG emissions. Disclosure requirements can ensure companies identify their energy use and emissions and create an incentive for them to improve efficiency and improve their green reputation and marketing opportunities.

Another option would be to create government bonds to finance residential and commercial energy efficiency and renewable energy investments, thereby overcoming the problem of how to fund the upfront costs of these efforts. The governing body of Berkeley, California, developed a municipal bonding program that allows homeowners to borrow money for energy improvements and repay the loans through a property tax assessment. The governing body in Boulder, Colorado, developed a smart grid initiative that promises to reduce residential peak energy demand by providing consumers with real-time price and environmental information and advanced in-home technologies (Wilson 2008). Other states impose a tax or surcharge on energy users and use the revenues to fund energy efficiency and renewable energy projects. An energy efficiency

fund (EEF), for example, requires energy providers to generate a specified portion of their energy to consumers through energy efficiency
measures.

A public benefit fund (PBF) is a method of funding energy efficiency
programs by means of a small charge on a consumer's electricity bill.
These forms of demand side management (DSM) are typically designed
to overcome barriers to investment in energy efficiency and renewable
energy programs. Once implemented, funds can be allocated to the DSM
programs from a public benefit fund. Indeed, some states require utilities
to use their own funds for the development of efficiency and RPS programs; California, for example, requires its utilities to allocate their own
procurement funds to their EEFs. Although the specific details vary, a
PBF typically requires state legislation and an oversight committee to
guarantee effective implementation. In all three of these DSM programs,
though, utilities also play a key role in implementation, processing
charges, and collecting results data (US EPA 2007c).

Clean energy programs can also help states achieve their clean air
goals because the programs result in lower energy production and emissions of traditional pollutants. States can use clean energy investments
as emission reduction measures in air-quality plans under the CAA. For
example, in 2004 and 2005, the EPA identified and designated $PM_{2.5}$
areas that had not attained the requisite level and completed the review
of designations in January 2006. In September 2005, the EPA issued a
proposed rule to implement the $PM_{2.5}$ NAAQS; the rule calls for states
to submit (within three years of an area being designated as a nonattainment area) implementation plans for achieving the new standard. If states
were to quickly implement the new air pollution standards for fine particulate pollution, they would almost certainly invest in energy efficiency
measures as one of the most cost-effective ways to reduce air pollution.
Table 5.2 provides other examples of how air pollution and energy policies can be integrated.

The US EPA also provides technical assistance to help states develop
and implement clean energy–environment state action plans. The goal is
to "improve air quality, decrease energy use, reduce greenhouse gas emissions, and enhance economic development." In exchange for the assistance, states sign a memorandum of understanding that lays out their
commitments to identify and analyze a range of options for improving
air quality and clean energy, establish at least one clean energy–air-
quality goal, provide resources for implementing the plan, and convene
a committee of state officials and key stakeholders to provide advice and

Table 5.2
Integrating Energy Efficiency and Renewables into Clean Air Plans

States seek to achieve national air-quality standards by designing and implementing SIPs that impose control requirements on large stationary sources, smaller area sources, and mobile sources. Plans could include a variety of clean energy options:

• SIPs include baseline electricity demand projections based on past trends and current public policies that must be taken into account in achieving and maintaining air-quality goals; if a decline in expected growth can be shown to be a result of energy policies that are real, permanent, and verifiable, then growth projections can be adjusted downward, reducing the amount of emission cuts state officials will need to mandate in their plan.

• SIPs can include energy efficiency actions as emission-reduction measures; for example, a Texas SIP used new building energy efficiency standards to claim credit for reducing NO_x emissions.

• SIPs can include credits for voluntary actions by stationary sources to cut emissions as long as these reductions are quantifiable, verifiable, surplus (the reductions are not used to satisfy some other regulatory requirement), permanent, and enforceable (action can be taken against the state to ensure that reductions occur). However, because of limited EPA experience with this and problems of enforcement, reductions claimed here can be no more than 3 percent of the total emission cuts required in the SIP.

• The EPA's program to reduce NO_x emissions and their contribution to forming ground-level ozone required twenty-two eastern states and Washington, DC, to submit revised SIPs that addressed the regional movement of ground-level ozone. The US Department of Energy and state energy offices worked with the EPA and state air-quality agencies to develop a compliance strategy that included integrating energy-efficiency efforts into SIPs. The federal program created a pool of allowances that are taken from states' NO_x emissions budget and awarded for clean energy projects. States can choose whether or not to participate in the energy efficiency and renewable energy set-aside program as they formulate plans to reduce NO_x emissions.

• The regional haze rule requires states to set goals for reducing emissions that impair visibility in the nation's 156 national parks and wilderness areas through a new set of SIPs. Nine western states are authorized to implement a regional approach. SIPs must include air pollution prevention and energy efficiency renewable energy, and economic development measures.

Note: A 2003 review of these options found that they were largely an "untapped mechanism for encouraging energy efficiency" because they were not well known or lacked aggregating mechanisms to make them a significant factor in decision making.
Source: Vine 2003, 31–32.

support. The agency estimates that if every state implemented a clean energy–air-quality plan along the lines of what some states have already done, the projected growth in demand for electricity could be cut in half by 2025, saving $70 billion and 900 billion kWh by 2025, eliminating the need for three hundred new power plants, and reducing GHG emissions equivalent to eighty million of today's motor vehicles. Economic benefits include lower energy costs for consumers who install energy-efficiency measures, lower total energy costs for all energy consumers on the grid, and job creation (US EPA 2005, 4).

Dramatically improving energy efficiency will not be enough by itself to stabilize the climate but it can go a long way to put the US economy on the path to that end. The co-benefits of efficiency are clear and compelling, and choices here are much easier than for other energy policy issues. But thus far these choices have not translated into actions that have produced a fundamental shift in the nation's GHG emissions from energy production and use.

Expanding Electricity Generation from Alternative Energy Sources

Provisions aimed at increasing energy efficiency and developing alternative energy sources have been part of energy policy for decades but Congress has largely failed to develop a consistent, long-term strategy for encouraging renewables. Despite this, renewable energy capacity has more than tripled since 2000 and now accounts for just over 8 percent of the nation's total energy demand and 10 percent of electricity generation. In 2009, renewables comprised more than 55 percent of all new electricity capacity installed in the United States, which now trails only China in electricity produced from renewable sources. Furthermore, renewables are projected to provide 17 percent of the nation's electricity in 2035 (US Department of Energy, Energy Information Administration 2011a). The dramatic increase in renewable energy is the result of many factors, most notably federal tax credits, loan guarantees, and state policies. For example, thirty-seven states and the District of Columbia now have renewable portfolio standards.

As figure 5.1 illustrates, biomass accounts for a majority (53 percent) of renewable consumption, followed by hydroelectric (31 percent), wind (11 percent), geothermal (3 percent), and solar (1 percent). Wind capacity more than tripled between 2006 and 2010, driven mainly by RPSs at the state level and the federal production tax credit of 2.2 cents per kWh (US Department of Energy, Energy Information Administration 2011b).

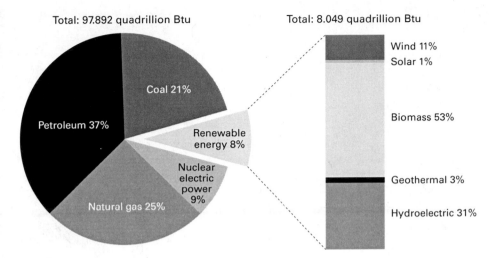

Figure 5.1
Renewable Energy Consumption in the US Energy Supply, 2010.
Source: US Department of Energy, Energy Information Administration 2011d, 1.

This is a clear example of how subsidies can help level the playing field with fossil fuels.

Figure 5.2 traces the production of fossil and renewable energy sources since 1950. Total renewable energy consumption generally tracks hydroelectric power output, which was the largest component of the total for most of the years shown. Hydropower is variable from year to year, though, moving up or down in response to snowpack and rainfall levels (Reuters 2002). Wind and solar photovoltaic are the fastest-growing renewable energy sectors; in fact, installed wind capacity increased more than fourteen times between 2000 and 2009. In 2009, wind accounted for more than 90 percent of installed nonhydro-renewable electricity capacity in 2009. Solar has experienced significant growth as well, especially in states with aggressive incentives, such as Colorado, Nevada, and California. (US Department of Energy, Energy Information Administration 2010a).

Figure 5.3 shows the use of renewable energy by sectors. Most renewable energy is consumed by the electric power sector to generate electricity. As early as 1958, the industrial sector became the second largest consuming sector of renewables, and consumption in the transportation sector more than doubled from 2006 to 2010 due to increased use of biofuels, primarily ethanol. Renewable use lags in the residential

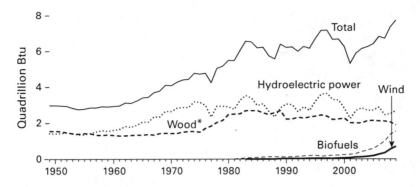

Figure 5.2
Renewable Energy Total Consumption and Major Sources, 1950–2009.
Note: *Wood and wood-derived fuels.
Source: US Department of Energy, Energy Information Administration 2010a,
xxxiii.

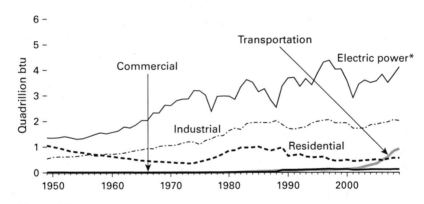

Figure 5.3
Renewable Energy Consumption by Sector, 1950–2009.
Note: *Through 1988, electric utilities only; after 1988, also includes indepen-
dent power producers.
Source: US Department of Energy, Energy Information Administration 2010a,
xxxiii.

and commercial sectors (US Department of Energy, Energy Information Administration 2011d).

Congress continues to struggle with the question of how to encourage alternative energy development. The tax incentives in the law have very limited time frames for eligibility to ensure that credits only apply to new investments. The short time frame for subsidies, though, provides another example of the trade-offs Congress has grappled with, contributing to an uncertain future and failing to create clear incentives for long-term investments.

Challenges in Expanding Alternative Energy

Until quite recently, the amount of renewable energy produced in the United States has not grown appreciably. In fact, the percentage of the total energy produced in the United States between 1990 and 2005 from renewable resources actually fell from 5.1 to 4.7 percent because cheaper fossil fuels were used to meet growing demand. It began to climb in 2004 in response to several factors that illustrate the complex environment in which energy policy making takes place. As the price of fossil fuels rose, renewables became more cost competitive and policies were implemented to encourage cleaner energy. Hydroelectric power, the primary renewable source of electricity, declined during drought years early in the century, then rebounded with higher rainfall and snowpack. State policies to encourage the use of renewables also expanded during the first years of the new century, as did federal tax credits that encouraged solar and wind power. Solar energy (photovoltaic and thermal) and wind energy each contribute about 1 percent of total renewable energy. Geothermal sources began producing a measurable amount of energy in 1960 and now account for about 3 percent of total renewable energy production.

Figure 5.4 shows trends in the installation of renewable electric-generating capacity and demonstrates a dramatic increase in wind and solar photovoltaic capacity since 2001. Although the trend line is moving in the right direction, a key policy question is how to dramatically increase production from renewable energy so that it becomes the primary energy source by midcentury. If policies do not fundamentally change and petroleum supplies remain abundant, our use of fossil fuels will increase dramatically through the first third of the century, and there will be only a minor increase in nonhydroelectric renewable energy. In short, energy security, air pollution, and climate change will continue to be problems.

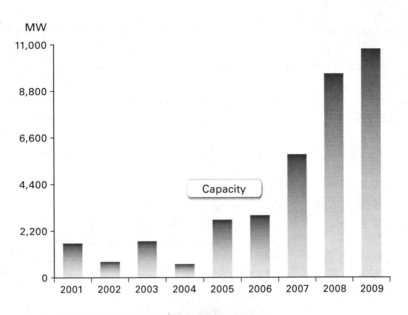

	Compounded annual growth rate (2000–2009)
Wind	33.7%
Solar PV	39.3%
CSP	2.2%
Biomass	2.0%
Geothermal	1.1%
Renewables (excluding hydro)	13.9%

Figure 5.4
Annual Installed Renewable Electric Capacity Growth (Excluding Hydro), 2001–2009.
Note: PV = photovoltaic.
Source: US Department of Energy, Energy Efficiency and Renewable Energy 2010, 25.

Existing renewable technologies provide only a small amount of total supply, and production from them needs to increase by orders of magnitude in order to replace fossil fuel–generated electrical power. Such an increase is possible but faces constraints of cost, geography, and politics. Renewable energy sources are typically more expensive than coal or natural gas, although some renewables, such as wood, municipal and agricultural solid waste, used tires, and landfill gas are decidedly low tech and relatively cheap. These renewable fuels also lack the high-tech allure of other options, such as solar panels.

Geography is also a challenge. Renewable resources are not uniformly distributed throughout the country, making national policy making more difficult because the burdens and benefits of locating facilities vary so widely. Some renewable resources, such as wind and solar, are often most plentiful in areas where there are few people, and electricity must be transported over long distances. In some places, such as the Northwest, hydropower has been a major power source but dams have significant environmental impacts as they destroy habitats, reduce biodiversity, and displace human communities. And similar to conventional fossil plants, alternative energy projects are often locally unwanted land uses and the process of siting them can be slow and contentious.

The hyperpartisan state of contemporary US politics has also complicated renewable policy making, as even research and development (R&D) spending has become a point of contention. Shortly after gaining control of the majority, House Republicans in 2011 proposed slashing renewable and efficiency spending by nearly $900 million (Lehmann 2011). The move was part of a larger effort by Republicans to curtail federal spending and rein in deficits and effectively established the terms of the debate for much of the year. In doing so, it appears that the boom-and-bust cycle typical of federal efforts on renewable energy will continue.

In order to dramatically increase renewable power, state and local governments will play a key role because of the challenges in siting new facilities. The federal government could do several things to encourage this, such as imposing a carbon tax or cap-and-trade program, providing tax credits and other subsidies to encourage the deployment of existing renewable technologies, and performing the difficult task of facilitating the construction of new transmission lines. The first two are currently highly unlikely, therefore, much of the difficult policy work will be done at the state and local levels where government leaders, renewable energy entrepreneurs, conservationists, and community members will need to find better ways to decide where to locate locally unwanted land uses.

Federal policy has been central to the development of the next generation of technologies. In order to dramatically reduce and eventually eliminate carbon emissions from electricity, we will need to radically transform energy production. Figuring out how to encourage energy technology innovation now is critical in meeting the climate challenge. For now, expanding renewable energy production poses daunting problems, reinforcing the importance of improving energy efficiency.

Costs of Alternatives

The primary challenge in expanding renewables is higher production costs. Electricity from solar and wind power, two of the most promising forms of renewable energy sources, is more expensive than that produced from coal and natural gas. Although technological advances have reduced the cost of renewable power, advances have also helped keep fossil fuel prices low. Some renewable technologies are already able to compete with conventional power generation. Wind power is typically the cheapest form of new renewable energy power source but solar power costs have been dropping as well. What may be most important is the price of oil and gas. The 2008 financial crisis hit funding of alternative energy companies particularly hard, and shares of those companies fell more sharply than the stock market as a whole because falling oil and gas prices dampened interest in alternatives. Venture capital for some advanced solar projects, for example, became scarce in fall 2008 and at least two wind companies had to delay projects because of capital shortages. The economic crisis that began in 2008 may result in a repeat of the history of the 1970s, when high fossil fuel prices led to increased investment in alternatives. When fossil fuel prices fell in the 1980s, however, so did interest in renewable energy (Kraus 2008). Economic downturns result in reduced energy use and accompanying GHG emissions but it is essential that energy prices remain high enough to maintain interest in renewables. To this end, energy taxes can play a key role in keeping energy prices high enough that renewables remain competitively priced, although they are not politically attractive. Table 5.3 compares the cost of renewable and fossil fuel energy sources, with conventional natural gas and coal plants, the cheapest options. As long as carbon emissions are not taxed or otherwise priced, fossil fuels have an advantage.

Hydroelectric power has been the largest source of renewable energy and currently provides just under half of the renewable total. Wood was the next largest source of renewable energy, followed by waste,

Table 5.3
US Average Levelized Costs for Plants Entering Service in 2016

Plant type	Capacity factor (%)	Levelized capital cost	Fixed operations and maintenance	Variable operations and maintenance	Transmission investment	Total levelized cost
Conventional coal	85	65.3	3.9	24.3	1.2	94.8
Advanced coal	85	74.6	7.9	25.7	1.2	109.4
Advanced coal with CCS	85	92.7	9.2	33.1	1.2	136.2
Natural gas conventional CC	87	17.5	1.9	45.6	1.2	66.1
Natural gas advanced CC	87	17.9	1.9	42.1	1.2	63.1
Natural gas advanced CC with CCS	87	34.6	3.9	49.6	1.2	89.3
Advanced nuclear	90	90.1	11.1	11.7	1.0	113.9
Wind	34	83.9	9.6	0.0	3.5	97.0
Wind-offshore	34	209.3	28.1	0.0	5.9	243.2
Solar PV	25	194.6	12.1	0.0	4.0	210.7
Solar thermal	18	259.4	46.6	0.0	5.8	311.8
Geothermal	91	79.34	11.9	9.5	1.0	101.7
Biomass	83	55.3	13.7	42.3	1.3	112.5
Hydro	53	74.5	4.0	6.3	1.9	86.4

Note: Costs are expressed in 2009 dollars per megawatt hour. CC = combined cycle. CCS = carbon capture and storage.
Source: Adapted from Department of Energy, Energy Information Administration 2010b.

geothermal, alcohol fuels, wind, and solar. Hydro remains an attractive alternative energy source but the most promising sites have already been exploited. Part of their costs must include environmental values such as protecting instream flows for fish habitat and the loss of terrestrial habitat when reservoirs are inundated. If climate change produces longer and more severe droughts, it will reduce the ability of hydro facilities to produce electricity.

Wind is the fastest-growing source of alternative electricity generation, although it still provides only a tiny fraction of the total supply. Several factors contribute to its expanded role in generating electricity. Research and development in the United States and other countries have helped improve technology and reduced costs. In 1980, wind power was selling at 8 cents per kWh (measured in current dollars); by 2008, the price had fallen to half that amount. Availability of the federal wind production tax credit has helped shape production: during years when the tax credit lapsed, rates of construction of new wind power dropped sharply. It has grown rapidly because wind prices, about 5 cents per kWh, are competitive with new coal-fired and natural gas power plants.

Policy Integration and Renewable Energy

Policy integration is a critical element of renewable energy policy. In order to increase the use of alternative energy sources, the price of traditional fossil fuels must be increased, either through a carbon tax or pressure from carbon trading. In addition, the environmental costs of developing and deploying renewable energy sources must be determined through life-cycle analyses so the true costs and benefits of alternatives can be compared. In addition to working through the challenges facing the development of each kind of renewable energy source, there are some crosscutting issues that must also be integrated. Two brief examples— securing sufficient capacity in transmission lines and energy technology research and development—illustrate some of these challenges.

Transmission Lines
One of the key challenges in making renewables work is that it is often difficult to get the power to markets because the best generation sites are often far removed from areas of significant demand. In addition, electricity generation is expanding at a rate four times faster than the transmission system needed to deliver it. The transmission system is also large and fragmented, with some two hundred thousand miles of power

lines controlled by five hundred owners and operators including private and public utilities and independent system operators. These networks are not able to accommodate significant increases in power and expanded lines are needed. Estimates of the amount of new high-power transmission lines needed range from twelve thousand to nineteen thousand miles, at a cost of from $3 billion to $6.4 billion. The new miles of lines needed represent about one-third of the nearly forty-seven thousand miles of the US interstate highway system. The cost of the new lines may not be as daunting a challenge as the process required to obtain permits and rights-of-way, which can require agreement among several states and companies (S. Davis 2011).

Alternative Energy R&D

Federal funding for advanced energy technologies has been inconsistent, rising and falling dramatically since the 1980s. According to a study by the US Government Accountability Office (2008), in 1978, federal spending on energy R&D, which includes renewable, fossil, and nuclear energy, reached a peak of $6 billion, measured in real terms, adjusted to 2008 dollars. Funding had grown rapidly after the 1973 oil crisis. However, as oil supplies expanded in the 1980s and 1990s, and prices fell, R&D spending plunged in real terms by 92 percent between 1978 and 1998, to $505 million. By 2008, spending had grown to $1.4 billion (Klein 2006).

The Government Accountability Office (GAO) report found that the nearly $58 billion spent on energy R&D since 1980 has not "dramatically changed" the nation's energy portfolio (US Government Accountability Office 2008, 1). In 1973, fossil fuel provided 93 percent of the nation's energy; nuclear energy (1 percent) and renewable energy (6 percent) made up the balance. By 2006, nuclear power had grown to 8 percent of the total, renewable energy sources provided 7 percent, and fossil fuels still accounted for 85 percent (US GAO 2008). That conclusion is not surprising, and is consistent with events subsequent to the GAO report; as figure 5.5 shows, most of the Energy Department's R&D funding has been for fossil energy and nuclear power. The amount of money appropriated is only a tiny fraction of the $15 trillion economy and only a tiny slice of the $10 trillion US energy infrastructure (Holdren 2001).

In seeking to remake our energy infrastructure, it is true that we cannot afford to abandon the existing energy infrastructure and simply lose the value of trillions of dollars of investment. At the same time,

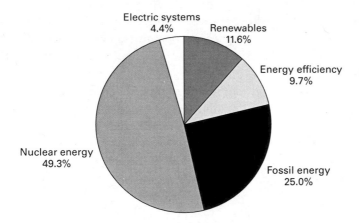

Figure 5.5
Department of Energy R&D Funding Shares, Fiscal Year (FY) 1948 to FY 2010.
Source: Sissine 2012.

though, waiting until old plants become too inefficient to operate and have to be replaced by more efficient plants locks us into decades of emissions that could be avoided. The programs and spending included in recent energy laws aimed at promoting the deployment of efficiency and renewable technologies as well as R&D spending are laudable but they represent only a tiny fraction of the nation's energy infrastructure. Despite years of energy reports, plans, programs, and legislation, US energy policy continues to fall short of developing a sustainable plan for managing and meeting energy needs. All too frequently, the desire to maintain the short-term benefit of cheap energy through fossil fuels overwhelms the long-term benefits of shifting to renewable energy sources.

Policy Integration and Renewable Energy Portfolios

One of the most powerful tools for governments to stimulate new markets in renewables are the RPSs, which require utilities to provide a specified percentage of their energy output from renewable energy sources, typically expressed as a percentage of total energy produced or actual megawatts of power generated by a certain date. Iowa was the first state to create RPSs, setting a goal in 1991 of requiring power companies to produce 105 megawatts of renewable power. Currently, thirty-seven states and the District of Columbia have RPS requirements for utilities, although in six states the targets are not mandatory (US Department of Energy, Energy Information Administration 2011e).

Although RPSs have been supported as a way to reduce greenhouse gas emissions, conventional air pollution, and the need to manage nuclear waste, the primary motivation has been promoting economic development by diversifying electricity supply and increasing reliability (Rabe 2006). For example, the RPS approved by the voters in a 2004 ballot measure in Colorado was the first citizen-initiated RPS enacted into law. Rather than frame it as a climate change measure, the sponsors of Amendment 37 argued that greater use of renewable energy resources would save consumers money, attract new businesses to the state, develop rural economies, reduce the volatility of energy prices, and protect the state's environment (Union of Concerned Scientists 2004).

The measure set a target for utilities serving more than forty thousand customers to supply 6 percent of electricity from renewable sources by 2011 and 10 percent by 2015. Renewables were defined to include solar, wind, geothermal, and biomass. Hydropower was also included, but in order to protect river flows, the construction of new dams was discouraged; only new, small hydroelectric plants (with a capacity of ten megawatts or less) or plants up to thirty megawatts in operation on January 1, 2005, were eligible to count toward the target. Preference was given to renewable energy produced within the state: every such kilowatt hour produced counted as 1.25 kilowatt hours in meeting the target. Four percent of the original target was to be supplied by solar and half of that amount was to come from distributed generation—installations on customers' property and structures. Customers that installed solar electricity generation could receive rebates of $2 per watt, and net metering was provided for so that consumers' surplus electricity was credited against their future bills (International Energy Agency 2008).

Utilities were on track to achieve the targets and in 2007, the state legislature expanded the program to require all retail providers of electricity with more than forty thousand customers to participate, and set a new target of 15 percent by 2015–19 and 20 percent by 2020 for investor-owned companies. The detailed provisions of the Colorado approach reflect the important policy choices that are embedded in the relatively simply context of an RPS. Different kinds of renewables can be favored and encouraged and different targets can be set for different kinds of utilities in order to reduce opposition. Targets can be phased in over time in order to have benchmarks to measure progress and to give utilities time to plan and build new power plants. Perhaps most important from a political perspective, in-state sources can be privileged in order to stimulate creation of local jobs.

The Colorado RPS is all the more remarkable because it shows how quickly policy change can occur—just two years earlier, the state had been firmly committed to continuing its reliance on fossil fuels. The 2006 election of Governor Bill Ritter, who ran on a platform of green energy, was a critical factor in turning the state 180 degrees, as was Democratic control of the state legislature. Xcel Energy, the state's largest utility, also came to embrace the measure.

The failure to include a renewable portfolio standard in recent federal energy legislation has been a major setback to the goal of encouraging new renewable energy technologies. Efforts to do so have been doomed by opposition from congressional delegations from regions, like the South, where coal use is greatest and where alternatives, such as cheap wind energy, are least plentiful. Opponents have argued that a federal RPS would increase electricity rates and succeeded in getting such provisions dropped from the bills (Fialka and Hitt 2007; Wald 2007). One indicator of how the cost of the shift to clean energy varies across the nation is to compare per capita emissions of carbon, which average about twenty metric tons per person annually nationwide. But the disparity between states is significant, from a high of 125 in Wyoming to a low of 10 in Vermont. States with above average per capita emissions include North Dakota (80), Alaska (69), West Virginia (63), Louisiana (40), Indiana (38), Kentucky (35), and Texas (30). The lowest emitting states are Connecticut, Rhode Island, Vermont, California, Idaho, New York, Oregon, Massachusetts, and Washington, and their emissions range from ten to thirteen tons per person per year (Johnston 2008). The differences help account for the political obstacles RPS provisions face in Congress.

A national RPS could be a relatively simple instrument that mandates a goal and then leaves it to the market to develop the needed technologies. A national standard could also facilitate interstate trading of renewable certificates in ensuring that the most cost-effective forms of renewable energy are developed, in the most productive settings, and that there are standard accounting protocols used by states. It could also be combined with tax incentives and subsidies to facilitate the transition to cleaner energy, guarantees that governments will purchase renewable power, and other policy instruments. Green power purchasing programs, for example, offer customers the opportunity to buy electricity generated from renewable resources such as wind, geothermal, biomass, and hydro (US EPA 2005).

The Alternative Energy Challenge

About 90 percent of the energy Americans use comes from fossil fuels and just 10 percent from renewables. In order to reduce CO_2 emissions by 70 to 80 percent by 2050, therefore, we need to roughly reverse the numbers and set as a goal procuring 70 to 90 percent of our energy from renewables and the balance from fossil fuels. This is admittedly a daunting challenge. Dramatic increases in all existing technologies are needed, shaped by efforts to minimize their adverse environmental impacts. Research and development into new forms of renewable energy should also be greatly expanded but the environmental consequences of fossil fuels are so significant that we cannot afford to wait until those new technologies are in place. Requiring government-industry partnerships can help create incentives for research, development, and demonstration projects that are sufficiently promising to attract private funding, and using public resources now can help ensure that resulting technologies are widely available. The law of accelerating returns suggests that technological advances in energy and other areas are exponential rather than linear. Although it may seem that we are making little progress, each breakthrough enables the next one to occur more rapidly. For example, the Human Genome project set out to sequence the entire genome in fifteen years. By the end of the first year, scientists had transcribed one ten-thousandth of the genome; after seven years, only 1 percent had been completed. But the rate of progress was doubling every year and the project was completed in 2003, two years ahead of schedule. If similar progress is made in areas such as solar nanotechnology and other renewable energy technologies, our energy infrastructure could be transformed within decades (Lyons 2009). The race is on between the development of new energy technologies and the accumulation of GHGs from fossil fuels, and the key question is whether the former will occur fast enough to slow the latter sufficiently to make climate change manageable.

Transforming Transportation

Nowhere is the case for policy integration clearer and more compelling than for reducing greenhouse gas emissions from transportation. Transportation sources are responsible for 27 percent of total US carbon emissions and 33 percent of all CO_2 emissions from fossil fuel combustion (US EPA 2011e). Passenger cars and light-duty trucks emit about 60 percent of the total, with trucks and buses emitting just under 20 percent, and the balance coming from other forms of transportation. Furthermore, transportation emissions increased by 16 percent from 1990 to 2009 as a result of population growth, economic growth, urban sprawl, low gas prices, and a significant increase in the number of vehicle miles traveled (US EPA 2011e).

Motor vehicle emissions are also a major source of conventional air pollutants, especially particulates, nitrogen oxides, carbon monoxide, and hydrocarbons that transform in the atmosphere into urban ozone pollution. All are threats to human health. Reducing GHG emissions from motor vehicles and other mobile sources is thus one of the key climate policy priorities, but it has been a vexing challenge because there are currently no control technologies to remove CO_2 from tailpipe emissions.

Our addiction to oil, mostly used for transportation, is another monumental challenge. In 2009, the world burned about eighty-four million barrels of oil a day, and the United States used one-fourth of the total. The International Energy Agency (2010) projects that demand will increase by fifteen million barrels per day by 2035 with nearly half of the increase coming from China, although the global recession triggered by the 2008 crisis in world financial and credit markets dramatically reduced demand for oil, and future demand is difficult to predict because of the uncertain global economy. Much of the world's oil comes from politically volatile regions where conflicts can disrupt supply and precipitate crises. As oil and transportation policy are linked to the broader issues of climate, energy, and national security policy, it is imperative that we develop policy responses that will effectively address all of these challenges. The political challenges, however, are daunting.

This chapter reviews the evolution of oil policies in the United States, including the ongoing political debate over whether the root problem is inadequate supply or excessive demand. The discussion then turns to integrated policies that seek to reduce emissions from motor vehicles through fuel switching, better fuel efficiency, and reducing vehicle use and the number of miles traveled. Transportation planning, land use and zoning decisions, and other policies also help shape emissions from motor vehicles and offer another example of the opportunities and challenges of integrating climate and energy-related policies. The necessary policies are a complex mix of federal, state, and local actions, making vertical policy integration all the more challenging.

Petroleum and Energy Policy

For nearly a century, the federal government has subsidized the development of oil reserves as a way to encourage the extraction of hard-to-reach resources and ensure a plentiful supply of cheap energy to fuel the nation's economic growth. Oil accounted for nearly half ($302 billion) of all federal energy subsidies between 1950 and 2003 (Bezdek and Wendling 2006). Nevertheless, despite ranking third in crude oil production the United States now consumes more than 19.1 million barrels a day (MMbd), almost half of which is imported (US Department of Energy, Energy Information Administration 2011b). Although a large percentage of imports continue to come from areas of political instability, including Saudi Arabia, Iran, Iraq, Venezuela, and Nigeria, the United States also imports a growing amount of oil from Canada and Mexico, which together provide 34 percent of all US imports. Figure 6.1 charts the rise of imported oil in recent decades.

Congress first enacted petroleum development tax provisions in 1916. Oil development companies could deduct their intangible drilling and development costs, including costs of drilling dry or unproductive holes. A depletion allowance policy allowed them to deduct 27.5 percent of the gross value of their annual production in recognition of the eventual exhaustion or depletion of the resource. These tax measures encouraged more rapid development of the resources than would have occurred under traditional accounting methods and also helped keep prices low, a top priority (US Congress, Library of Congress, Congressional Research Service 2002).

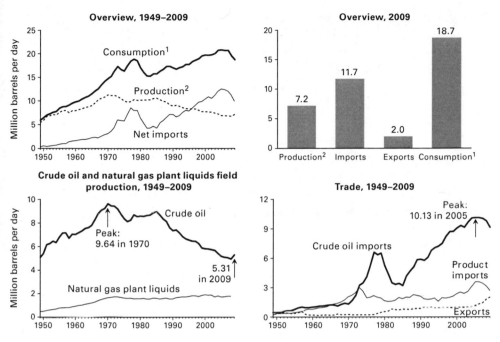

Figure 6.1
US Petroleum Consumption, Production, and Imports, 1950–2009.
Notes: 1. Petroleum products supplied is used as an approximation for consumption. 2. Crude oil and natural gas plant liquids production.
Source: US Department of Energy, Energy Information Administration 2010a, 128.

At the beginning of World War II, the United States was the world's leading oil-producing nation, and it supplied six billion of the seven billion barrels of oil consumed by the Allies. US leaders worried that domestic supplies of oil could be depleted by the war effort and the ensuing reconstruction, and fears of energy shortages stoked great anxiety in Washington. The Roosevelt administration in 1941 conducted the first study of the implications of declining domestic supply for US national security. By 1943, administration officials decided that the United States should adopt a broad policy to conserve US and other oil reserves in the western hemisphere and promote imports from the Middle East to supply growing demand (Brown 1999; Klare 2004).

Securing supplies from Persian Gulf oil fields was a major concern of the Cold War because the United States sought to protect access to oil from Iran, Saudi Arabia, and their neighbors from Soviet efforts to increase its influence in the region and from rising Arab nationalism.

US military assistance to Iran and Saudi Arabia dramatically expanded during the 1950s and 1960s as US oil imports increased and the US production-consumption gap began to grow. By 1973, the United States was importing 6.3 million barrels of oil and petroleum products each day. In October of that year, Arab countries that were members of the Organization of Petroleum Exporting Countries (OPEC) placed an embargo on exports to the United States in retaliation for US support of Israel in the Arab-Israeli war that had occurred earlier that year. Although the embargo lasted only a few months, it led to skyrocketing gasoline prices and thrust energy issues into public consciousness for the first time. A few years later, Iran's pro-American government was deposed by the revolutionary Islamic regime, which took US hostages from the US embassy in Tehran; the Soviets invaded Afghanistan; and US foreign policy became more and more intertwined with energy policy (Klare 2004). In the late 1970s, as oil prices climbed, federal subsidies expanded to include tax incentives for energy efficiency and alternative fuels. Once prices began to retreat in the1980s, however, public and media interest in energy issues waned, as did federal support for efficiency measures.

For more than forty years, presidents and members of Congress promised Americans low energy prices and a stable and secure supply. The Nixon administration (1969–1974) pledged to reduce energy imports and to secure "energy independence," and every subsequent president has dutifully made the same pledge. The Carter Administration (1977–1981) took the challenge more seriously than others, launching a war on energy to increase domestic production, reduce imports, and improve energy efficiency and conservation. Conservation was a major plank of the Carter approach, featuring a presidential address from a sweater-clad president who had turned down the White House thermostat to save energy. The Reagan administration (1981–1989) swept to office on a pledge to reverse the sense of limits and constraints reflected in Carter administration policies and gave priority to opening public lands for oil and gas exploration and increasing US military might to ensure an uninterrupted supply of oil imports. The difference between the Carter and Reagan approaches to energy policy mirrors the policy debate that continues today between those promoting conservation and efficiency on the one hand and those advocating greater production on the other. Over the decades, this debate has grown increasingly partisan, with Democrats (at least those from non-oil-producing states) generally preferring the former and Republicans the latter.

The Bush I administration (1989–1993) continued the Reagan policy of expanding domestic energy production. The Clinton administration (1993–2001) was blessed with an unusually long stretch of economic growth and relatively stable world oil production. Its efforts to raise energy taxes early in its term in order to promote conservation generated intense political opposition and the administration abandoned any notion of transforming energy policy. The Bush II years were dominated by the war with Iraq, global terrorism, and their implications for energy security, and the White House pursued an ambitious array of administrative actions designed to foster domestic oil and gas production. Despite President Bush's warning in 2006 that America was "addicted to oil," oil dependency remained a problem; imports accounted for 29 percent of total US energy consumption in 2007 (compared to 24 percent in 2009, after the 2008 recession) (US Department of Energy, Energy Information Administration 2010a). According to the US Department of Energy's Energy Information Administration (2011b), total US consumption of liquid fuels, mostly used for transportation, was 19.1 million barrels per day in 2010 and was projected to rise to nearly 22 million in 2035 (see figure 6.2).

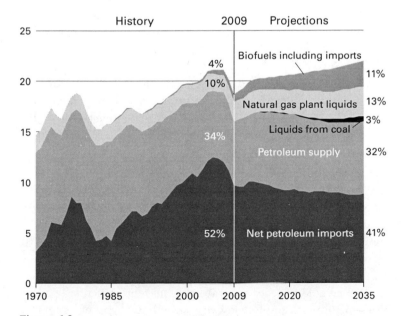

Figure 6.2
US Liquids Fuel Consumption, 1970–2035.
Source: US Department of Energy, Energy Information Administration 2011a, 2.

During the Bush II years, partisan conflicts stymied efforts to enact a new energy law aimed at increasing domestic oil production. The fight over opening Alaska's Arctic National Wildlife Refuge (ANWR) to energy development generated the most attention, with Republicans pushing for drilling and most Democrats opposing it (Little 2004). In April 2005, the new 109th Congress, flush with additional Republican seats in both chambers, which strengthened the party's power, moved quickly in response to high gas prices. The House bill would have opened ANWR for exploration and development; the Senate's bill included neither but incorporated an increase in fuel efficiency standards. The conference committee dropped the contentious issues but Congress did agree to update the tax incentives for clean-fueled vehicles. Before 2005, federal tax incentives for alternative fuels were limited to a $2,000 deduction for the purchase or retrofit of vehicles using natural gas, liquefied natural gas or petroleum, hydrogen, electricity (including hybrids like the Toyota Prius), or any fuel containing at least 85 percent methanol or ethanol. The 2005 law provided tax credits for purchasers of vehicles using hybrid gas-electric, advanced lean-burn, fuel cell, and alternative fuel technologies (Congressional Quarterly 2006). The 2005 law also broke new ground by establishing the RFS program, which required 7.5 billion gallons of renewable fuel to be blended into gasoline by 2012.

When the Democrats took control of the House and Senate in 2007, a new energy bill was high on their priority list. The most heavily debated provision in the 2007 energy bill was a proposed increase in the CAFE standards. Members agreed to require new cars to average 35 mpg by 2020, a significant increase over the existing 27.5 mpg standard and the first time Congress had raised the target since 1975. Enactment of the energy bill, the Energy Independence and Security Act of 2007 (P.L. 110–140), was one of the few times that the Democratic Congress and the Bush administration were able to fashion a bipartisan agreement (Broder 2007; Clayton 2007). The second key area of agreement was a significant expansion of the RFS program. Specifically, the law increased the volume of renewable fuel required to be blended into transportation fuel from nine billion gallons in 2008 to thirty-six billion gallons by 2022, at least twenty-one billion gallons of which must be from advanced biofuels such as cellulosic ethanol. In addition, the law established new categories of renewable fuel, set separate volume requirements for each, and required the EPA to apply life-cycle greenhouse gas performance threshold standards to ensure that each category of renewable fuel emits fewer greenhouse gases than the petroleum fuel it replaces. It also required manufactures to provide additional energy-related information on labeling of vehicles and tires (US EPA 2011d).

In its first two years, the Obama administration supported a number of measures to promote fuel efficiency and energy conservation. The financial rescue package provided a $7,500 tax credit for plug-in hybrids beginning in 2010 and the production tax credits for biodiesel and other biomass-derived diesels were extended through 2009. Tax credits were also provided for alternative refueling stations. In May 2009, the administration announced that the new CAFE standard of 35.5 mpg would be imposed in 2016, four years ahead of what Congress had mandated. New passenger cars would be required to meet a standard of 39 mpg (compared with 27.5 mpg in 2009), and light trucks would be required to get an average of at least 30 mpg (compared with 23 mpg). Auto companies agreed to the new standard after the State of California agreed to accept federal fuel efficiency standards and the companies were ensured of having to meet only one standard nationwide (Power and Conkey 2009).

Just two years later, the administration announced yet another round of CAFE standards requiring an average of 54.5 miles per gallon by 2025. Under the program, efficiency standards for automobiles would increase by 5 percent per year from 2017 to 2025; light trucks would be required to become 3.5 percent more efficient for the first four years and 5 percent annually thereafter (Vlasic 2011b). Figure 6.3 illustrates motor vehicle fuel efficiency trend since 1966. The administration estimated

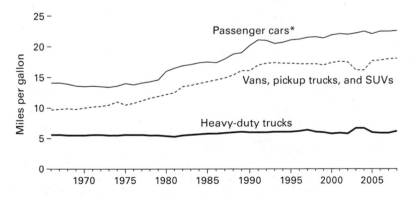

Figure 6.3
Motor Vehicle Fuel Economy, 1966–2008.
Note: *Motorcycles are included through 1989.
Source: US Department of Energy, Energy Information Administration 2010a, xxvii.

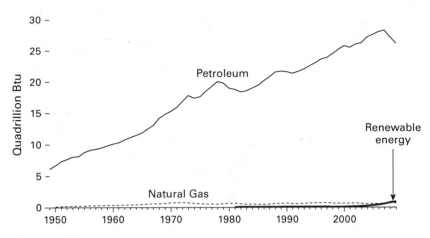

Figure 6.4
Transportation Consumption, by Major Source 1950–2009.
Source: US Department of Energy, Energy Information Administration 2010a, 39.

that the new rules would reduce oil consumption by 2.2 million barrels per day. In a sharp break from the past, automakers supported the move, at least in part because the administration had backed the $80 billion federal bailout of the industry in 2009. The industry had also returned to profitability and had learned how to build and sell smaller, fuel efficient cars; in fact, by 2011 six of the ten best-selling vehicles in the United States were small or midsize cars (Vlasic 2011a). In a sign that the politics of the issue had shifted, the new rules were also supported by the United Auto Workers and environmental groups.

As figure 6.4 shows, oil accounts for the vast majority of transportation fuel used in the United States. Biofuels, however, are an increasingly important source of transportation fuel, accounting for 4 percent of total, which is above the global average (International Energy Agency 2011a). The recent increase is a result of federal subsidies, incentives, and mandates to increase ethanol production, which is shown in figure 6.5 and discussed in greater detail in chapter 7.

Transportation Policy Options

Because of the steady growth in oil imports, the energy policy debate in the United States has emphasized increasing domestic oil and gas production to ensure steady supplies and low prices at the pump. Climate change and air pollution policies, however, have typically pursued an

	Gasoline pool* (million gallons/year)	Ethanol production (million gallons/year)	Annual growth (%)	Percent of gasoline pool
2000	128,662	1,630	11%	1.3%
2001	129,312	1,770	9%	1.4%
2002	132,782	2,130	20%	1.6%
2003	134,089	2,800	31%	2.1%
2004	137,022	3,400	21%	2.5%
2005	136,949	3,904	15%	2.9%
2006	138,378	4,855	24%	3.5%
2007	142,287	6,500	34%	4.6%
2008	137,797	9,000	39%	6.5%
2009	137,736	10,750	19%	7.8%

2,030 E85 stations (April 2010)

E85 average retail price (January 2010): **$3.36/gallon** (gasoline gallon equivalent basis), gasoline price: $2.65/gallon

Approximately eight million flex-fuel vehicles are on the road

Figure 6.5
US Ethanol Production and Growth in Gasoline Pool by Volume.
Note: *Includes ethanol.
Source: US Department of Energy, Energy Efficiency and Renewable Energy 2010, 101.

alternative agenda focusing on energy efficiency and renewable fuels. The challenge in integrating energy, air, and climate policies is to resist the allure of simply expanding domestic oil supplies, although the allure remains strong and expanding domestic production will likely be a key part of any climate and energy policy compromise.

Increasing Domestic Oil Production

There are a number of policy choices and trade-offs confronting the United States as it considers increasing its domestic oil supply. First, it must decide how to balance increased production with preservation of public lands, national parks, wildlife refuges, and other protected areas. The International Energy Agency's report (2008) on US energy concluded that the total recoverable resources within lands controlled by the federal government where access is prohibited or restricted are 113 billion barrels of oil and natural gas liquids and 21 trillion cubic meters of natural gas. Recoverable resources are defined as those that have been discovered as well as those that are likely to be. Onshore restrictions include the nineteen-million-acre Arctic National Wildlife

Refuge and protected areas in the Rocky Mountain states—national parks and monuments, wilderness and proposed areas, roadless forests, and other areas of environmental importance and sensitivity. National security-based energy policy suggests those lands should be opened for development but that would require considerable sacrifice of environmental protection.

Second, US policy makers must consider whether offshore drilling should be expanded, a question that became infinitely more complicated after the explosion of the Deepwater Horizon rig in the Gulf of Mexico in April 2010. Prior to the accident, offshore production had reached nearly 1.8 million barrels per day, or 33 percent of total US production (US Department of Energy, Energy Information Administration 2011b), even though drilling had long been prohibited along all coastal areas except the western Gulf of Mexico and parts of Alaska. Just weeks before the explosion, President Obama had proposed ending the moratorium and opening up much of the Atlantic coast, the eastern Gulf of Mexico, and the northern coast of Alaska to oil and gas drilling (Broder 2010a). The move was widely seen as an effort designed to foster agreement on a comprehensive energy overhaul. High oil prices at the time also contributed to demands to increase production, making it politically expedient. The accident prompted the Obama administration to impose a moratorium on deepwater oil and gas drilling; in October 2010 the administration lifted the ban and issued new rules imposing more stringent safety and environmental regulations on the industry. A few months later the White House reversed its decision to allow drilling off the Atlantic coast and in the eastern Gulf of Mexico and reinstated the ban on offshore drilling for at least the next seven years.

In 2009, offshore production accounted for about one-third of total US crude oil production and the US Department of Energy's Energy Information Administration (2010a) estimates there are 69.3 billion barrels of technically recoverable undiscovered crude oil in the outer continental shelf; this is in addition to the twenty-two billion barrels of proven crude oil reserves that lie offshore of Texas, Louisiana, Alaska, and California. Although offshore deepwater drilling costs are higher than for drilling in other areas, such as protected lands in the western United States, the size of these reserves is certain to keep the issue alive for the foreseeable future.

The same is true of offshore natural gas exploration. Natural gas is important because it is an valuable vehicle fuel, particularly for large trucks; some eight million cars in the world run on natural gas, although only a relatively few in the United States. Because it produces only about half the carbon of oil, and is now considerably cheaper, natural gas is increasingly seen as a transportation fuel that can be part of the transition to a low-carbon future. Although natural gas reserves are also difficult to measure, the US Department of Energy's Energy Information Administration (2010a) estimated that offshore production of natural gas in 2009 was 2.7 Tcf, or 13 percent of total US natural gas production. The EIA estimates that another 350 Tcf are technically recoverable. As is the case with oil, the scope of this potential resource will inevitably lead to pressure to develop it, and policy makers will thus have to resolve the difficult trade-off with environmental protection.

Although the United States has abundant supplies of natural gas, it also relies heavily on imports. The 2005 Energy Act encouraged the development of liquefied natural gas (LNG) facilities to accept shipments from abroad by streamlining the permitting process, but there are still issues of overlapping federal and state authority. Because most LNG import infrastructure is located in the Gulf of Mexico, there is considerable concern that it is vulnerable to disruption from hurricanes and tropical storms. It is generally easier to locate such facilities in the Gulf because there is already in place an extensive pipeline system and regulatory barriers are lower than elsewhere in the nation. And there is the challenge of refinery capacity. Declining domestic refining capacity has led to an increase in refined products being imported, now about one million barrels a day (International Energy Agency 2008). The permitting of these new sites is necessary and usually controversial, adding to the challenge of finding sites for major energy projects.

A related issue is whether the tax on oil company profits should be increased in order to capture their windfall profits or whether companies should be able to retain their profits so they can invest them in new supplies. In 2008, the top five US oil companies reported that their output had fallen by a total of 614,000 barrels a day. But they also reported record profits of $44 billion during the second quarter of 2008. Production had been steady at about ten million barrels a day until 2007, when it began to decline. Companies face a number of constraints, including mature fields and decisions by other countries to cut allocations of oil to US companies. Oil-producing nations have become much more assertive in controlling their oil. As late as the 1970s, for example, the large Western companies such as Exxon Mobil, BP, Shell, Chevron, and ConocoPhillips controlled more than half of the world's oil production. By 2008, they controlled 13 percent. One energy analyst argued that "there is still a lot of oil to develop out there which is why we don't call this geological peak oil. . . . What we have now is geopolitical peak oil" (Mouawad 2008a, A1). The world is not running out of oil but companies are running out of places to drill for it.

For this reason a windfall profit tax on oil profits that could be used to fund conservation and renewables makes sense because companies have only limited opportunities to use their profits to find new resources and they have recently spent less of their profits on exploration. In 1994, the top five companies spent 3 percent of their available cash to buy back their stock offerings and 15 percent on exploration. In 2007, by contrast, they spent 34 percent of their free cash on stock buy backs, thereby propping up the value of their stock, and only 6 percent on exploration. The trend may change as new areas are opened but current high prices provide a clear incentive for future drilling; the profits companies have earned are a result of dramatic increases in demand for petroleum and not a result of investments in new reserves (Mouawad 2008b).

There are significant reserves of unconventional oils in the form of oil shale, oil sand, coal-to-liquids and gas-to-liquids processing, and perhaps methane hydrate. The western United States, for example, is home to vast quantities of oil sands that have not as yet been economically recoverable but proponents are primed for a massive development. Canada also has significant oil sands resources but the lessons are sobering. As a case in point, Alberta's oil sands are believed to contain the equivalent of more than a trillion barrels of oil and by 2002 the province was providing one-third of Canada's oil production. The environmental impacts of oil sand development, however, are daunting. Oil sand operations are a major user of natural gas and extracting it requires large amounts of water. Moreover, the disruption to the land affected is enormous, as are the start-up costs (Deffeyes 2005).

Oil shale resources similarly represent enormously vast assets but their development also poses serious technological and environmental problems. Oil shale is an unconventional oil and gas resource found in solid, bituminous form in rocks. It has been developed in the past by crushing then heating the rocks to liquefy the oil and gas. The technology for converting oil shale to oil has been available for decades but the cost of producing has been much greater than that of conventional sources. Sweden and Estonia produced oil from oil shale but since the end of World War II it has not been economically viable because of the amount of energy required to heat the rock and the amount of waste generated. In the United States, oil shale is primarily found in the Green River formation that spans Colorado, Utah, and Wyoming. The resource represented in the formation could be eight hundred billion barrels, according to some estimates, and higher according to others. About 70 percent of the land containing oil shale is owned by the federal government, giving it great control over development (International Energy Agency 2008). In 2007, Shell Oil began exploring an alternative technology for extracting oil from shale, an in situ process that releases the oil and gas underground without the need for mining and crushing. Engineers inject hot fluids into holes drilled into the shale that release the oil and gas into producing wells that are also drilled in the formation. The amount of energy used is still high, but unlike the old approach, there is much less surface impact and gas can also be extracted. However, the process also requires large quantities of water, a challenge in the dry rocky areas of the Colorado Plateau (International Energy Agency 2008).   ·

Clearly, then, expanding domestic production of oil and gas is central to the energy policy debate; the challenge is to make sure it is part of the climate policy debate as well by linking any expansion of fossil fuel production to an increase in conservation, efficiency, and renewables. The end of the cheap oil era also reflects the fact that the environmental costs of developing new sources of oil and gas will be more expensive than in the past as well, and protecting against ecological damage will likely become increasingly difficult with high energy prices and inexorable political demands to drive them down. Just as contentious will be the difficult decisions about where to locate new refineries and other facilities and how to avoid siting them in communities that are already overburdened with unwanted and dangerous land uses such as incinerators, toxic waste dumps, power plants, and factories.

It is clear that opening new areas to drilling will not affect supplies and prices for several years but increasing long-term supplies will almost certainly have to be a central component of energy compromises and deals. The challenge will be to decide which areas are so ecologically fragile or economically important to tourism that they be insulated from development and to ensure that agreements to increase supply are matched with commitments to conservation and renewables.

Regulating the Efficiency and Emissions of Motor Vehicles
Although US energy policy will continue to emphasize expanding supply, even more important is a commitment to conserving oil. Petroleum-based products are critical components of the global economy; oil and natural gas are essential components of the fertilizers on which we depend to produce the world's food and are basic components of plastics,

chemicals, and other products central to modern life. As is true of other areas of energy policy, using petroleum energy more efficiently should be the policy priority because it saves a scarce resource, reduces costs, and produces numerous environmental and public health co-benefits. Much of the policy debate in this area to date has focused on improving fuel efficiency standards.

Fuel efficiency standards in the United States are lower than in other industrialized nations. In Japan, for example, fleetwide standards for new vehicles are 46 mpg, 43 mpg in the European Union, and 43 mpg in China. Until 2007, the standard in the United States had been 27.5 mpg for cars and 22.2 for light trucks. Meeting and raising fuel efficiency standards beyond those being implemented by the Obama administration is an obvious option but fuel efficiency standards do not reduce emissions from existing vehicles and new standards will likely encourage drivers to continue to use their old gas guzzlers. Other policies, such as federal or state gasoline taxes, will be needed to discourage driving (Crandall 2007). The current federal fuel tax is 18.4 cents for gas and 24.4 cents for diesel, and some have argued that increasing the tax could be an essential element of future transportation policy. Nevertheless, increasing the tax could be an essential element of future transportation policy, especially because it may be more cost effective than increasing CAFE standards. A study by the US Congress's Congressional Budget Office (2004) suggested that increasing the federal tax on gasoline would be the most direct way to reduce gasoline consumption because it raises the cost of driving and gives consumers incentives to purchase more fuel-efficient vehicles. According to the study, increasing the tax by 46 cents per gallon would achieve a 10 percent reduction in gas consumption in the long term, more than a 3.8 mpg increase in CAFE standards. Nevertheless, prospects for increasing the federal tax are slim in the near term. Republicans have refused to contemplate increases in any federal taxes and the Obama administration has indicated it will not pursue an increase (Power and Conkey 2009).

It may be that the future of clean car and fuel technologies depends on oil prices remaining high enough to force changes in consumer demand. After the oil embargo shocks of the 1970s, Detroit car makers rushed to produce cheap, fuel-efficient vehicles but the quality was poor and they shifted to producing SUVs and light trucks for which profit margins were much higher. Detroit was not alone in abandoning efficiency—Congress and presidents lost interest as well and oil companies stopped investing in alternative energy sources. Although it seems unlikely that oil prices will ever return to 1990s levels, because global demand is now so much greater, an expectation of price decline and a return of cheap oil will slow the development of these alternative technologies.

The political debate in recent years is emblematic of the allure of centering energy policy on maintaining low prices. Despite years of warnings of the seriousness of climate change, the national security costs of reliance on imported oil, and projections of increasing energy use from economic and population growth, policy makers have refused to engage in a serious debate on the topic and have instead tinkered around the edges and sought short-term political advantages. For nearly two decades, Republicans in Congress focused on opening the Arctic National Wildlife Refuge, which would have done little to address the fundamental problem, and Democrats proposed a modest increase in subsidies for renewables. In spring 2006, when gas prices spiked and policy makers from President Bush down focused attention on the need to reduce oil imports, congressional Republicans proposed giving US drivers $100 each to help with gas prices, and Democrats suggested a sixty-day suspension of the federal gasoline tax (Janofsky 2006). The lack of political courage has been breathtaking. Even in the midst of the debate over historic deficits and debt, Republicans have been unwilling to take on key constituents such as oil and gas companies. For their part, congressional Democrats were unwilling to challenge auto companies and auto workers. In 1990, for example, almost three-fourths of Senate Democrats voted for a bill that would require auto manufacturers to meet a 40 mpg average fuel economy standard by 2001; a 2005 proposal to require the same 40 mpg average by 2016 only garnered about half of the Democrats (Friedman 2006a, 2006b). What had changed, of course, was that energy prices were higher.

In order to ensure that recent progress in improving fuel efficiency and alternative fuels such as plug-in hybrids continues and accelerates, higher oil prices will be essential. We can either hope that somehow an era of plentiful and cheap oil will return or we can decide that a more prudent approach is to further diversify our sources and uses of oil. It is irrational to believe that low energy prices will return and that each American can continue to consume twenty-five barrels of oil per year, while Europeans use ten barrels and Chinese use two. A carbon tax or an increased gasoline tax is an efficient and effective means of ensuring that gas prices do not fall below a price that will discourage alternatives. Estimates for that range from $75 to $150 a barrel (Lowenstein 2008). Although the upper bound may be near politically impossible to pursue, ensuring that oil prices do not fall below $75 would send a clear signal that many alternative technologies should be developed. Rather than Congress choosing a particular technology to bless through tax breaks, a carbon tax helps increase the chance that more climate-friendly technologies will emerge through market competition. But all the political incentives point to tax breaks for specific technologies instead of a general tax increase.

The 1970s oil price shocks demonstrate the power of sharp price increases to shape fuel consumption. A similar reduction in driving occurred in 2008 when US gas prices rose well above $3 per gallon. As one writer put it, "High oil prices have accomplished what years of pleas from environmentalists and energy-security hawks could not: forcing the world's major automakers to refocus their engineers and their capital on devising mass-market alternatives to century-old petroleum-fueled engine technology" (White 2008b, R1). It will take a long time, however, to improve dramatically the fuel efficiency of US motor vehicles because new technologies require several years to develop and then put into production. Americans' attachment to their vehicles is difficult to weaken: for every American who rides a bike to work, 5 walk, 9 take public transportation, 21 carpool, and 154 commute alone in a car (Burning through Oil 2008).

Clean Car and Fuel Technologies

Vehicle designers have promised breakthroughs in new technologies for decades: ethanol-, hydrogen-, and electric-powered cars have been trumpeted as the new wave, only to be stymied by technological problems. Hydrogen has been touted as a replacement for gasoline in internal combustion engines or in powering fuel cells but the cost of storing and delivering hydrogen is still prohibitive. As mentioned previously, there is some interest in natural gas–fueled vehicles but there are only about 1,100 fueling stations across the country and only about half are open to the public. Most of the interest of the auto industry appears to focus on electric vehicles. The key factor is whether the cost of the battery technology will fall enough for these vehicles to be viable options. The costs include not only the battery technology but also the cost of designing and building a lighter car that requires less energy to propel and retooling factories and retraining workers. The good news is that refueling stations are as common as the electrical plug in any home or garage. If drivers can learn to recharge their cars during off-peak hours, the impact on the electric grid may be manageable. In addition, if smart technologies are employed to ensure recharging takes place during low-demand hours, the US grid could recharge tens of millions of electric cars (White 2008a).

Table 6.1
Gasoline and Its Alternatives in Motor Vehicles, 2008

Type of engine	Advantages and disadvantages
Hybrids: battery and electric motor for low speeds and gas engine for higher speeds	Significant fuel economy improvement in smaller vehicles, less so in larger ones, price premium of $2,500 to $8,000 or more
Mild hybrids: electric motor assists only gas engine	Less expensive than full hybrids but only modestly increase fuel economy
Plug-in hybrid: battery can be recharged by plugging it into an AC outlet	Much greater fuel efficiency, as high as 120 miles on the battery, but batteries are not yet available and are expected to be expensive
Flex fuel: ICE can run on gasoline or mix of gas and ethanol	Prices are not any higher, can be adapted to any size vehicle, reduces GHG emissions, ethanol is not widely available, and one gallon of it produces less energy than one gallon of gasoline
Fuel-cell vehicles: hydrogen gas and a chemical process combine to generate electricity for an electric motor	Only emission is water vapor but hydrogen as a fuel is not widely available and technology is too expensive for commercial use
Electric car: powered by a battery and electric motor	No emissions or noise, can be recharged from regular AC outlet but batteries are not yet available and technology is unproven
Clean diesel: advanced diesel engines burn low-sulfur fuel more cleanly	20 to 40 percent more mpg and more torque than gas engines, lower GHG emissions, cars and diesel fuel are more expensive

Source: Adapted from White 2008a.

Table 6.1 provides an overview of the current status of leading options to reduce carbon emissions from vehicles through improved efficiency and alternative fuels. These technologies all seem promising because they promise to reduce carbon emissions, but their future in US automaking depends on the health of the auto industry, in a kind of catch-22 dilemma. The future of the industry lies in technological innovations but companies may lack the cash to make the needed investments. The 2008 financial meltdown hit the big three Detroit automakers (GM, Ford, and

Chrysler) particularly hard, and GM and Chrysler filed for bankruptcy in 2009. The industry has since rebounded, recording strong profits and ample cash on their balance sheets and, for now at least, a professed commitment to their clean vehicle initiatives. The auto industry remains vulnerable, though, to the uncertain state of the economy.

CO_2 Emission Standards

Motor vehicle emission reductions under the CAA have been one of the most impressive environmental policy successes in history. Emissions of conventional pollutants (such as particulates, nitrogen oxides, sulfur dioxide, and carbon monoxide) have been reduced by more than 90 percent from preregulatory levels. In December 1999, for example, the EPA issued tier II tailpipe emission and gasoline standards that were phased in between 2004 and 2007 (through 2009 for vehicles over 6,000 lbs.) Those standards, for the first time, require the same emission standards for SUVs, pick-up trucks, and passenger cars and integrate efforts to reduce pollution through emission and fuel standards. The new standards promised to reduce NO_x emissions from cars by 77 percent and by 95 percent from SUVs and trucks, and the amount of sulfur in gasoline by 90 percent, by 2005. In January 2001, the agency issued new standards for heavy trucks and buses to reduce emissions by 90 percent beginning in model year 2007. The regulations also integrate efforts to produce cleaner engines and cleaner diesel fuel because the sulfur content of diesel fuel must be reduced in order for emission control equipment to work (US EPA 2007e).[1]

As explained previously, there are no control technologies currently available to capture or reduce CO_2 from motor vehicle emissions. In 2005, California petitioned the US EPA to allow the state to establish GHG standards for passenger vehicles beginning with the 2009 model year. The CAA allows California to establish standards more stringent than nationwide mandates set by the EPA. The state has a long history of using this provision to require new vehicles sold in the state to meet more stringent emission standards for conventional pollutants. California is the only state allowed to develop an alternative to national policies but any state wishing to adopt a California standard may do so.[2]

In California, motor vehicle emissions are responsible for about 40 percent of total GHG emissions. The proposed motor vehicle standard would reduce emissions by thirty million metric tons or 18 percent by 2020 and fifty million metric tons or 27 percent by 2030. Twelve other states had adopted the California standard by 2008 and state officials estimated that its implementation would reduce emissions by seventy-four million metric tons; six other states were considering adoption, which could bring reductions to one hundred million metric tons by 2020. The motor vehicle standards are a central element of California's goal, provided for in its Global Warming Solutions Act, to reduce its total GHG emissions to 1990 levels by 2020 (California Air Resources Board 2007).

In order to meet the standard, motor vehicles sold in California would have to achieve an average fuel efficiency of 40 mpg by 2016 (Simon 2008; Zabarenko 2008). Automakers aggressively lobbied EPA officials to reject the California waiver, arguing that it was too stringent and conflicted with the congressional mandate to increase the national fuel efficiency standard to 35 mpg by 2020. The Obama administration's agreement with California and the auto companies to accelerate the due date for that standard to 2016 in exchange for only one nationwide standard means California will have to find additional ways to reduce emissions.

Reducing Motor Vehicles Traveled

Although vehicles are much cleaner today, total transportation emissions continue to rise because people are driving more and keeping old, highly polluting cars longer (a problem similar to that of old coal-fired power plants operating longer than their design life because they are so cheap to operate). State efforts to enforce the emission standards have also been contentious and difficult. The 1990 law requires 181 areas to institute vehicle emissions inspection programs to ensure vehicles continue to comply with emission limits. Cities with serious ozone or carbon monoxide problems are required to have "enhanced" inspection and maintenance (I&M) programs that are more effective than the older, conventional I&M program in identifying emission problems. Because 20 percent of the vehicles on the road are believed to be responsible for 60 percent of emissions, the EPA expected the enhanced I&M programs to reduce VOCs, carbon monoxide, and nitrogen oxide emissions, and to do so at lower cost than other forms of air pollution control measures (US EPA, Office of Air and Radiation 1992).

Because of the cost of the new equipment and its impact on the auto inspection and repair industry, and the fear of inconvenience and delay in getting vehicles inspected, consumers and state governments have resisted the program. California was the first state to be permitted to develop an alternative system of testing at centralized locations and traditional service stations. Other states then began pressing the EPA for exemptions (Daniels 1995). After the 1994 congressional elections, the EPA gave states more time and discretion in regulating motor vehicle emissions, including I&M programs, employer carpooling requirements, and other programs, in order to head off congressional efforts to weaken the act. I&M programs have been less effective than expected in reducing emissions, particularly from high-emitting cars and trucks (National Research Council 2004).

A related area that has not worked as well is a provision in the CAA aimed at reducing vehicle miles traveled. The act requires that all federally funded transportation projects in areas that have not attained the national standards for conventional pollutants conform to SIPs: no federal agency may "approve, accept or fund any transportation plan, program or project unless such plan, program or project has been found to conform to any applicable implementation plan in effect" (42 U.S.C. 7506). The 1991 Intermodal Surface Transportation Efficiency Act provided funding for transportation projects that contribute to meeting SIP requirements, and air-quality standards in general, in ozone and CO nonattainment areas. These congestion mitigation and air-quality improvement, or CMAQ, funds, are distributed to states according to their share of the population living in nonattainment areas and levels of air pollution (US Department of Transportation, n.d.).[3] Similar to I&M programs, these transportation programs have been unpopular when they have tried to change driving patterns. As a result, vehicle miles traveled increased by 168 percent between 1970 and emissions of the six criteria pollutants (lead, carbon monoxide, particulate matter, volatile organic compounds, nitrogen oxide, and sulfur dioxide) fell by 63 percent (US EPA 20011a).

Vehicle Miles Traveled, Sprawl, and Land-use Patterns
The rise in vehicle miles traveled is also a function of urban sprawl and land-use planning. Land-use planning represents such a broad set of actions that the space here only allows for a very brief discussion that highlights the importance of the economic, social, and policy factors that have contributed to sprawl and its contributions to increased automobile travel.

Urbanization is a powerful demographic trend that has important consequences for climate change. Eighty percent of the US population resides in metropolitan areas and 60 percent of the world's people are expected to be urban dwellers by 2030. Urban development can have a positive impact on GHG trends: as urban areas become wealthier, residents invest more in environmental and other quality-of-life amenities. In addition, increased density can reduce per capita emissions. Low-density urban sprawl, however, has the opposite effect. Because of the growing urban environmental and carbon footprints, transportation policy must be integrated with climate and land-use policies (Kahn 2006).

The growth in urban areas in the United States is a result of a variety of economic and social factors as well as public policies. The US population has nearly doubled since the end of World War II, resulting in great pressure to surge beyond existing urban limits. Crime and other urban problems have contributed to the flight to suburbs, as have technological developments in communications and information processing that allowed for the dispersion of the work force, air conditioning that opened up development of the large cities of the South and Southwest, and the vast expansion of trucks and automobiles that made suburban life all the more attractive. As a result of sprawl, along with rising per capita income, public transportation greatly declined in the United States, from providing 35 percent of all urban transit at the end of World War II to less than 3 percent by the end of the century. Low energy prices have also made it possible for Americans to come to rely so heavily on personal motor vehicles for transportation as well as for heating, cooling, and lighting the large, detached homes and commercial and industrial facilities characteristic of sprawl. These and other factors that have driven sprawl are a result of powerful cultural and economic practices that will not be easily reversed and illustrate how difficult it will be to address these root drivers of high energy use in the United States (Nivola 1999).

Public policies have reinforced and been shaped by these economic and cultural factors, and that makes integrating climate, land use, and transportation policies more challenging. For example, although the decline in mass transit is a function of the powerful trends discussed previously, the way in which the United States has financed the construction and maintenance of highways has also been important. Highways have been funded through self-perpetuating mechanisms such as the federal trust fund, and states earmark income from toll roads and fuel taxes for highway use as well. In contrast to other countries where highways are funded from general tax revenues and must compete with other transportation options, US highways have flourished, and the extensive network of highways, built for national security and other reasons as well, contributes to sprawl. In the same vein, US taxes on motor vehicle fuels are much lower than those of other industrialized nations, except Canada. Lower electricity prices here than elsewhere are similarly a result of public policies, including energy subsidies, price controls during the 1970s and early 1980s, as well as abundant domestic sources of coal, natural gas, and hydroelectric power. Federal housing mortgage insurance and tax deductions for mortgage interest have also contributed to the suburban development. Local governments' dependence on property taxes to fund services encourages them to maximize the assessed value of real estate and minimize the associated cost of governmental services. Zoning regulation has traditionally separated residential and commercial land uses, contributing to sprawl and increased transportation demand (Nivola 1999). This discussion only scratches the surface in explaining the factors that have driven sprawl and the associated patterns of energy use. Effective integration will not be easy because it will require changing policies and practices that have long been very powerful determinants of energy use.

Policy Integration and Planning

If trends in sprawl continue, driven by growth in population and consumption, the demand on resources will be daunting. One estimate of the consequences of forty million new Americans living in the United States over the next two decades includes millions of miles of pipelines to carry an additional nine billion gallons of clean water and eight billion gallons of sewage, two million miles of new roads and other infrastructure for an additional 100 million more vehicles, and the development of the countryside into suburban sprawl at the rate of one football field every second of every day for three years, equal in size to Vermont, Massachusetts, Rhode Island, Connecticut, New York, New Jersey, Pennsylvania, Delaware, and Virginia combined (Flint 2006). Climate change policy will need to include efforts to reverse these unsustainable trends and will need to be integrated with strategies to reduce travel by putting homes, stores, and work places closer together and to make more efficient use of existing infrastructure. There is an extensive literature on smart growth, the new urbanism, sustainable development, and other concepts that seek to capture the idea of reversing sprawl and increasing planning in order to reduce the use of energy and other resources and impacts on ecosystems (Downs 1994; Flint 2006). Integrating climate and energy policy with these efforts to plan communities so that growth occurs in areas that are already built up or have already been developed (such as brownfield industrial sites) is critical. Overhauling zoning regulation so that it contributes to integrated communities, creating visioning scenarios that engage the public in considering alternative futures for their communities, and other strategies are promising because of the multiple benefits they promise that go beyond reducing energy use and GHG emissions to improve the quality of life in communities (Flint 2006).

Land-use planning provides a vehicle for exactly the kind of integrated policy making that climate policy requires. A climate-centered land-use plan could inventory the major GHG sources and sinks, identify the options for the largest and least expensive reductions, develop a mitigation plan and assign responsibilities for specific actions, and monitor, enforce, and assess the effort. Of course, many of the factors that determine GHG emissions are beyond the control of local officials, such as motor vehicle and power plant emissions. But local officials can create incentives through planning to encourage polluters to adopt the cleanest available technologies.

Planning should focus on pollution prevention and reduction through mass transit, reduced sprawl, higher-density housing, integrating commercial and residential development, and on protection of open spaces, farm lands, and ecologically important lands. As energy costs increase, preserving local farm lands will become increasingly attractive. The kinds of farming practices described in chapter 7 can reduce GHG emissions and increase carbon sequestration from agricultural production and related activities. Efforts to promote smart growth and sustainable communities and other policies are all ways to reduce GHG emissions and increase carbon sequestration (Szold and Carbonell 2002; Ruth 2006).

In short, land-use planning decisions can reinforce the policies described in other chapters of this book. They can reduce vehicle miles traveled and vehicle emissions and encourage more densely constructed housing that reduces heating and cooling costs. They can emphasize the rehabilitation of brownfields for commercial and industrial expansion and protect greenfields and open spaces for carbon sequestration (Pearson 2002). These are only a few of the possible policy options but all point to the importance of governments' capacity to plan. Planning is central to the idea of policy integration; governments need the ability to identify the interactions and consequences of different actions and behaviors and to devise solutions that minimize costs and maximize benefits.

The Future of Oil and Energy Policy

Dependence on imported oil has enormous consequences for US foreign policy, as documented in a voluminous literature (Roberts 2004; Goodstein 2004; Leggett 2005; Heinberg 2005; Simmons 2005; Tertzakian 2007). Michael Klare, for example, has chronicled the political and military consequences of imported oil for US military policy and entanglements in the Middle East and other areas of the world: "With domestic reserves facing long-term decline, we are becoming ever more dependent on foreign sources—and thus increasingly vulnerable to the violence and disorder that accompanies oil extraction in politically unstable and often hostile oil-producing countries" (Klare 2004, xv).

The unsustainability of oil imports is not just a function of political instability and conflict. US oil production steadily rose for more than a century before peaking at about ten million barrels a day in 1970; crude oil production was 5.3 million barrels per day in 2009. The quadrupling of prices in the early 2000s, reaching nearly $150 per barrel in 2008, has stimulated increased drilling in the United States, and extraction technologies are put to use to squeeze more oil from fields around the nation. But the large oil fields appear to be mostly tapped out; US production of crude oil has fallen every year before ticking slightly upward in 2009. In another sign of decline, average well productivity in 2009 was just over half of 1972 levels (US Department of Energy, Energy Information Administration 2010a).

Predicting oil supplies and prices is a daunting task (Huber and Mills 2005). Oil prices have been remarkably unstable in recent years, rising from $10 a barrel in 1999 to $145 a barrel in July 2008, and some oil industry analysts warned of $200 a barrel prices by the end of the year. Instead, as the financial credit crisis came to a head in fall 2008, economies around the world sputtered, demand fell in the United States and elsewhere, and oil prices dropped by nearly 50 percent (Mouawad 2008b). Two things seem clear, though: the era of cheap oil is over and climate change constraints will limit emissions from oil even if supplies remain plentiful. David Goodstein, for example, warns that "the world will soon start to run out of conventionally produced, cheap oil." If we are able to replace oil with coal and natural gas that are transformed into transportation fuels, "life may go on more or less as it has been—until we start to run out of all fossil fuels by the end of this century." But, he warns, "by the time we have burned up all that fuel, we may well have rendered the planet unfit for human life. Even if human life does go on, civilization as we know it will not survive, unless we can find a way to live without fossil fuels" (Goodstein 2004, 15).

Questions about oil supplies intersect with the threat of climate change in ways that greatly complicate energy policy making. A decline in petroleum use will result in reduced GHG emissions. But the development of alternatives such as oil shale, coal gasification, and oil sands will, if current trends continue, come at a very high environmental cost. This makes it all the more important to ensure that energy policy decisions be based on a careful analysis of the total costs of producing, transporting, and using energy. If we try to fill the gap between growing demand for petroleum and falling supplies with these unconventional fossil fuels, we will increase the threat of climate change. However, not filling the gap means unprecedented economic and social disruption.

7

Integrating Agriculture, Energy, and Climate Change Policies

Agricultural and related activities have significant implications for energy use, air and water quality, and climate change. Farming covers 40 percent of the globe (IASSTD 2009) and worldwide, agricultural and land-use decisions account for about one-third of human-driven global warming (Paustian et al. 2008). In addition, farming in the United States is very energy intensive. Producing food uses more fossil fuel than any other economic activity except for transportation. Moreover, agricultural production accounts for the majority of the food system's GHG emissions; an estimated 50 to 83 percent of emissions occur before food leaves the farm (Weber and Matthews 2008). In addition to being an important source of greenhouse gas emissions, though, agriculture is also a significant carbon sink, and this dual role shapes efforts to integrate agricultural, energy, and climate policies. For the most part, recent policy initiatives in the United States have exempted the agricultural sector from emission reductions and have instead emphasized carbon sequestration through tree planting, conservation programs, and other mechanisms. These policies are popular precisely because they promise to offset emissions from power generation and transportation, thus avoiding the need for painful emission-reduction efforts in those sectors. But the effectiveness, permanence, and other characteristics of terrestrial sequestration are problematic, and tree planting to offset emissions raises difficult issues about how to ensure that emission reductions actually occur. All this suggests how important policy integration is in this area as well as how difficult it may be to actually accomplish.

Discussing agriculture also focuses attention on questions about how to integrate climate mitigation and adaptation. Among the most serious risks of climate change is that it will affect snowmelt, rainfall, and temperature patterns, thus disrupting agriculture and food production. Some argue that a warmer climate will increase agricultural output and will expand areas where farming is feasible, and others contend that agricultural yields will decline. Despite disagreements on the overall consequences, it seems clear that the regional impacts on agriculture may be quite pronounced. The Southeast and Great Plains, for example, are typically viewed as likely to be harmed from global warming whereas northern states are expected to benefit from more favorable conditions for agriculture. Similarly, the impact of climate change on water will play a major role in determining how agriculture is affected by warming. The problem in many states that rely on irrigation, for example, is that most of the precipitation falls during the winter months, but most of the demand for water occurs during the hot, dry summer months. Excess precipitation must be stored in the form of mountain snowpack or in reservoirs, but warming may cause melting to occur earlier, requiring investments in new storage infrastructure (Siikamaki 2008).

This chapter focuses on the intersection of agriculture, energy, and climate changes and on the three primary strategies for mitigating climate change in agriculture: (1) reducing methane (CH_4), nitrous oxide (N_2O), and carbon dioxide (CO_2) emissions from agricultural operations, (2) increasing the carbon sequestration that occurs as a result of farming and associated land-use practices, and (3) producing biofuels to replace fossil fuels. There are significant co-benefits in pursuing these policy options in an integrated fashion. For example, chemical fertilizers require fossil fuels for their manufacture, distribution, and application; reducing their use and increasing natural fertilizers and organic farming can reduce water pollution, improve air quality, and lessen GHG emissions. Similarly, policies that encourage farmers to shift land from agriculture to conservation can reduce emissions while increasing the habitat available to foster biodiversity. Co-benefits are also possible with properly designed biofuel policies that could reduce GHG emissions while providing an important source of economic development in rural areas. Increasing the carbon content of soils through sequestration would improve their fertility and quality, stimulate water retention, and reduce soil erosion. Finally, efforts to improve the absorption of nitrogen could reduce loss of nutrients in runoff and improve ground and surface water quality; reduced methane emissions could enhance water and air quality.

We begin with a brief overview of agricultural policy and politics, explore how agricultural policy intersects with energy and climate policies generally, and then turn to a discussion of specific policies aimed at reducing GHG emissions from agricultural activity, encouraging carbon sequestration, and developing biofuels. Throughout, the emphasis will be on how these policies can be integrated with energy and climate policies.

Agricultural Policy and Politics

Agricultural policy has traditionally been aimed at supporting farmers in order to help ensure a stable food supply. During the Great Depression, the 1933 Agricultural Adjustment Act was enacted to ensure that crop prices remained high enough to provide a dependable income for farmers. Agricultural loans create a floor for crop prices, as do price supports or direct payments made when crop prices fall below a government-mandated level. Over time, other spending programs were added to promote conservation and soil protection, rural development, and nutrition. Farm subsidies have simultaneously been criticized as giveaways to farmers and defended as essential in preserving family farms. After years of reform proposals, in 1996, Congress enacted a farm bill that sought to reduce price supports and force farmers to depend more on market forces. A rapid decline in farm prices in the late 1990s, however, caused Congress to reverse course and provide more financial support for farmers, and the 2002 farm bill reinstated the price- and income-support programs. Farm subsidies peaked at $32 billion in 2000, then fell to about $16 billion in 2009 (Environmental Working Group 2011). If commodity prices continue to rise as they have in recent years, fed by global shortages and by increasing use of biofuels, spending for federal farm subsidies will continue to fall (Richert 2007).

The agricultural policy-making arena has become more crowded and complicated over time. Initially, farm policy was tightly controlled by the two congressional agriculture committees and lobbyists representing wheat, cotton, soybeans, rice, and the other major commodities produced by US farmers. These policy-making arrangements have been described by participants as the "old iron triangle," where "we'd all just sit down and work something out" (Richert 2007, 115). Not surprisingly, what they "worked out" was a policy characterized by the many subsidies noted previously (Browne 1988). Things began to change in the 1970s, when environmentalists and their congressional allies began to push for water, soils, and biodiversity conservation programs (Bosso 1987). More recently, specialty-food producers representing fruits, vegetables, nuts, wine, and other products have also entered the farm bill fray. Health and nutrition concerns are also complicating the politics of farm policy as the American Heart Association and American Cancer Society lobby for more funding for programs to increase the availability of fresh fruits and vegetables in school lunch programs and to low-income residents of urban areas. Biofuel industry representatives lobby for programs in their interests. Agricultural policy has been further complicated as globalization opened new markets and new competitors and international trade talks increasingly emphasize the importance of cutting US subsidies so that other countries can increase their exports to US markets. In fact, conflicts between the developed and developing countries over cuts in subsidies contributed to the collapse of global trade talks in 2008 (Richert 2007).

As a result, the politics of agricultural policy have naturally become much more complex, with many new groups seeking to join those who have been involved for decades. Advocates of carbon sequestration and biofuels, for example, seek to shape agricultural policy in the face of very powerful, well-organized, and long-established farm groups and a host of other groups that have joined the policy domain during the past few decades. As agricultural, energy, and climate change become more intertwined, the pressure grows for the agricultural committees to share responsibility with other congressional committees. Although the proliferation of actors greatly complicates policy making, it also creates opportunities for integrating these policy efforts with other climate-related polices because it introduces new perspectives to the agriculture arena. Indeed, with the debate over climate change so polarized, it is exceedingly unlikely that Congress will enact climate legislation any time soon. Therefore, if policy integration is to happen in the United States, it is more likely to occur through vehicles such as agriculture policy, where there already have been some tentative steps in that direction. Recent farm bills, for example, have included a host of provisions aimed at continuing and expanding the production of biofuels and sponsoring research on energy efficiency, rural energy self-sufficiency, the use of forests and woody biomass for energy production, and the development of the next generation of these fuels (US Department of Agriculture 2008). Agriculture policy's well-established pattern of subsidies has been adapted to a host of energy projects, including biorefineries and biofuel production, renewable energy projects in rural communities, and price supports for biomass crops and forest products. Table 7.1 outlines the major energy-related provisions of the 2008 Farm Bill.

Table 7.1
Energy Provisions of the 2008 Farm Bill

Bio-Refinery Assistance: Authorizes competitive grants to assist development and construction of demonstration-scale biorefineries that convert renewable biomass to advanced biofuels. Authorizes loan guarantees to fund development, construction, and retrofitting of commercial-scale biorefineries.

Repowering Assistance: Authorizes payments to encourage existing biorefineries to replace fossil fuels used to produce heat or power for operation of the biorefinery. Payments would be made for installation of new systems that use renewable biomass or for new production of energy from renewable biomass.

Bioenergy Program for Advanced Biofuels: Eligible producers are paid based on quantity and duration of advanced biofuel production and on net nonrenewable energy content of the advanced biofuel. Mandates a total of $300 million in funding for FY 2009 to FY 2012.

Rural Energy for America program: Provides grants and loan guarantees for energy audits, feasibility studies, and project development of renewable energy systems and energy efficiency improvements.

Biomass Research and Development Initiative: Funds competitive grants for research, development, and demonstration projects for biofuels and bio-based chemicals and products. Provides mandatory funding of $118 million for FY 2009 to FY 2012.

Rural Energy Self-Sufficiency Initiative: Provides grants to conduct energy assessments, formulate plans to reduce energy use from conventional sources, and install integrated renewable energy systems, which are defined as communitywide systems that reduce conventional energy use and incorporate renewable energy use.

Biomass Crop Assistance Program: Supports establishment and production of eligible crops for conversion to bioenergy and assists agricultural and forest landowners with collection, harvest, storage, and transportation of these crops to conversion facility. Assistance includes payments for up to 75 percent of cost of establishing an eligible crop, annual payments to support production, and matching payments of up to $45 per ton for two years for collection, harvest, storage, and transportation to a biomass conversion facility Contract terms are up to five years for annual and perennial crops and up to fifteen years for woody biomass. Eligible crops and other biomass do not include those eligible for commodity payments.

Forest Biomass for Energy: Encourages use of forest biomass for energy; priority project areas include developing technology and techniques to use low-value forest biomass for energy production, developing processes to integrate energy production from forest biomass into biorefineries, developing new transportation fuels from forest biomass, and improving growth and yield of trees intended for renewable energy.

Credit for Production of Cellulosic Biofuel: Provides temporary cellulosic biofuel production tax credit of up to $1.01 per gallon through December 31, 2012.

Modification of Alcohol Credit: Reduces tax credits from 51 cents in 2002 law to 45 cents per gallon in calendar year after annual production or importation of ethanol reaches 7.5 billion gallons.

Source: US Department of Agriculture, 2008. Titles IX, XV.

Agriculture and Climate Change Policy Options

Unlike other economic sectors, agriculture and forestry release and absorb greenhouse gases. About one-half of all CO_2 emitted from fossil fuels accumulates in the atmosphere; the rest is absorbed by plants, soils, and the oceans. On balance, agricultural soils absorb carbon, which helps offset agricultural-based emissions.

GHG emissions from US agriculture total 419 teragrams of carbon dioxide equivalents (Tg CO_2 Eq.) or about 6.3 percent of overall emissions, much less than electricity generation (33 percent) and transportation (27 percent). Although the amount fluctuates from year to year, table 7.2 shows that GHG emissions from agriculture have increased by 9 percent between 1990 and 2009 (US EPA 2011e), making the need for reductions from current levels even more important.

The primary greenhouse gases from agriculture are nitrous oxide and methane, with carbon dioxide a distant third. Figures 7.1 and 7.2 depict emissions from agriculture by type. The largest source of GHG emissions from agriculture is nitrous oxide emissions, about 222 million metric tons (MMT) (carbon equivalent) each year; they arise from nitrogen fertilizers and manure that is spread on agricultural fields, manure in

Table 7.2
GHG Emissions from Agriculture (Tg CO_2 Eq.) 1990–2009

Gas/Source	1990	2000	2005	2006	2007	2008	2009
CH₄	**171.2**	**186.7**	**190.1**	**191.7**	**198.2**	**197.5**	**196.8**
Enteric fermentation	132.1	136.5	136.5	138.8	141.0	140.6	139.8
Manure management	31.7	42.4	46.6	46.7	50.7	49.4	49.5
Rice cultivation	7.1	7.5	6.8	5.9	6.2	7.2	7.3
Field burning of agricultural residues	0.3	0.3	0.2	0.2	0.2	0.3	0.2
N₂O	**212.4**	**224.0**	**228.7**	**227.1**	**227.6**	**228.8**	**222.5**
Agricultural soil management	197.8	206.8	211.3	208.9	209.4	210.7	204.6
Manure management	14.5	17.1	17.3	18.0	18.1	17.9	17.9
Field burning of agricultural residues	0.1	0.1	0.1	0.1	0.1	0.1	0.1
Total	**383.6**	**410.6**	**418.8**	**418.8**	**425.8**	**426.3**	**419.3**

Note: Totals may not sum due to independent rounding.
Source: US EPA 2011e, 6-1.

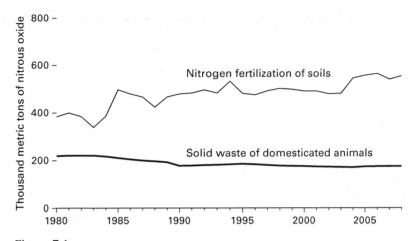

Figure 7.1
Agricultural Nitrous Oxide Emissions by Type, 1980–2008.
Note: Methane emitted as a product of digestion in animals such as cattle, sheep, goats, and swine.
Source: US Department of Energy, Energy Information Administration 2010a, 356.

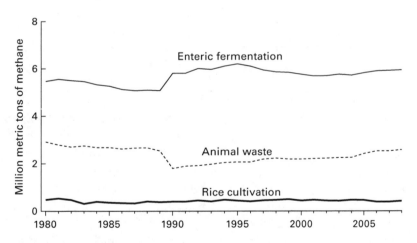

Figure 7.2
Agricultural Methane Emissions by Type, 1980–2008.
Note: Methane emitted as a product of digestion in animals such as cattle, sheep, goats, and swine.
Source: US Department of Energy, Energy Information Administration 2010a, 354.

storage, and crop residues. Methane from agricultural practices contributes another 197 MMT a year, primarily emanating from enteric fermentation in livestock. Manure management, rice cultivation, and burning of agricultural residues also contribute to methane and nitrous oxide emissions. Emissions from manure management increased more than 40 percent between 1990 and 2009, mostly as a result of an increase in the use of liquid systems, which produce greater emissions than composting or field spreading (US EPA 2011e). Carbon dioxide emissions in agriculture stem mostly from fossil fuel combustion in farm equipment but also include emissions related to the production of fertilizers, pesticides, and other products. Annual CO_2 emissions from farm energy use are approximately 47 MMT per year (US EPA 2011e).

Changes in agricultural practices can contribute in several ways to reducing GHG levels, such as increasing carbon storage in soils, reducing methane emissions from livestock and manure, reducing nitrous oxide emissions by improving fertilizer management, and increasing the production of bioenergy crops. Practices that would increase the level of carbon in soils include no till or conservation tilling, reducing fallow times, adding hay to annual crop rotations, and shifting to crops that produce higher residues. Even more effective is to shift lands from cultivation to conservation set-aside areas and planting grasses and trees. These practices can be instituted relatively quickly and at lower cost than many other climate mitigation actions. Agricultural-based GHG mitigation can thus serve as an immediate, low-cost strategy that buys time for the development of more long-term solutions (Siikamaki 2008).

Current trends in agricultural practices, independent of climate change policies, may also increase carbon sequestration and curtail GHG emissions over time if they are adopted more broadly. Conservation tillage is increasingly popular, and conservation set-aside programs for marginal lands could contribute to even more carbon sequestration. Crop yields have been increasing by about 1 to 2 percent a year; if that continues, more land could be shifted from food to biofuel production without leading to higher food prices or increased GHG emissions from farmers converting forests or grasslands to biofuel production. Fertilizer use and nitrous oxide emissions have leveled off since 1990, and using manure, nitrogen fertilizers, and irrigation more efficiently reduces nitrous oxide emissions, builds carbon stocks in the soil, and reduces the energy used to pump water (Paustian et al. 2006). Planting high-residue crops and grasses, such as corn and sorghum, leaves more plant matter in the field after harvesting. Similarly, reducing or eliminating fallow periods between

Table 7.3
Integrating Agriculture and Climate Change Policies

Increasing carbon stocks of soil:
• Reduce frequency and intensity of soil tillage
• Include more hay crops in annual rotations
• Produce high residue–yielding crops and reduce fallow periods
• Improve pasture and rangeland management
• Increase conservation set-asides and restoration of degraded lands

Improving the efficiency of nitrogen inputs and reducing nitrous oxide emissions:
• Use of soil testing to determine fertilizer requirements
• Better timing and placement of fertilizer
• Use of nitrification inhibitors and controlled release fertilizer

Reducing emissions of methane from livestock production and enteric fermentation:
• Improving animal health and genetics
• Using feed additives
• Increasing productivity of grazing systems

Replacing fossil fuels with biofuels:
• Using biomass to produce electricity
• Replacing gasoline and diesel in transportation fuels with biodiesel and cellulosic ethanol

Source: Adapted from Paustian et al. 2006, 59.

crops by planting winter cover crops that take up excess nitrogen in the soil will also increase plant residues. In any event, designing agricultural policies aimed at reducing GHG levels from agricultural operations, increasing carbon sequestration, and developing biofuels is a complex undertaking. Table 7.3 summarizes some of the ways agricultural and climate policies intersect and how policies could be better integrated.

Reducing Nitrous Oxide and Methane Emissions from Agricultural Operations

Nitrous oxide and methane emissions are responsible for about 80 percent of GHG emissions from agricultural activity. Nitrous oxide emissions, responsible for 60 percent of total agricultural emissions, come primarily from soil management activities such as fertilizer application and other cropping practices, and reducing those emissions is almost entirely a case of using fertilizers more efficiently (US EPA 2011e). Curtailing fertilizer use could dramatically reduce nitrous oxide and carbon emissions because fertilizer production is itself energy and GHG intensive

(Kleinschmit 2009). Some nitrous oxide emissions are inevitable, of course, because nitrogen is an essential element for highly productive soils, and the more nitrogen that is stored in these soils, the greater the releases into the atmosphere. Crop rotations that include legumes, which fix nitrogen in soil, would be desirable, as would greater use of perennial cropping systems, which reduce the need for tillage, builds soil through deeper root systems, provides better drought tolerance, and lowers fertilizer and pesticide requirements (Kleinschmit 2009).

Livestock are the primary source of methane emissions from agriculture. Cutting emissions through improving the efficiency of meat and milk production is key, as is improving the management of manure. For example, fertilizer is relatively inexpensive compared with other inputs and farmers often overfertilize. Because it is difficult to know how much to apply at the beginning of the planting season in anticipation of uncertain weather conditions, overfertilization seems to be rational. If best manure management practices were widely instituted, though, methane emissions could fall by 20 to 40 percent (Paustian et al. 2006). Because emissions from livestock digestive processes (called *enteric fermentation*) and wastes account for more than one-fourth of all agricultural GHG emissions, improving the efficiency of animal production so that fewer animals are used is essential. Dietary changes can also reduce methane emissions (Kleinschmit 2009). Improving the management of manure by efforts such as covering animal waste storage lagoons (and then capturing the methane as a fuel) are important innovations whose use could be expanded. This also produces co-benefits such as reducing odors and nitrates as a water pollutant. Programs designed to improve animal health and breeding can also increase the amount of milk or meat produced per unit of feed consumed, making them more attractive to ranchers (Paustian et al. 2006).

Carbon Sequestration

As explained previously, all agricultural emissions release about 150 MMT of GHG emissions each year. Improvements in agricultural practices could offset from 102 to 270 MMT of carbon equivalent over the next ten to thirty years, but there are numerous barriers to achieving these targets, and much more research is needed to improve the capacity of farm lands to sequester carbon and produce biofuels at minimum environmental cost (Paustian et al. 2006; Searchinger et al. 2008; Tilman et al. 2009).

The potential for carbon storage and GHG emission reduction from agricultural practices depends primarily on the cost of carbon or the magnitude of subsidies. If carbon is given a low price, carbon sequestration in soil and forest management are the most fruitful strategies. At middle prices, afforestation becomes more attractive, and it becomes the most promising approach at high prices, as do biofuels. Converting crop lands to forests is much more expensive than changing agricultural practices to increase carbon storage. Non-CO_2 mitigation efforts have significant benefits but they are not as great as for afforestation and biofuels. If carbon prices are as high as $50 per ton for CO_2, though, afforestation, biofuels, and other agricultural management efforts can produce significant GHG mitigation. A $50 per ton price for CO_2 is within the range of models that project what carbon price would be required to stabilize GHG levels. One model, for example, which examined what would be required to stabilize CO_2 levels at 550 parts per million (ppm), included carbon dioxide prices of from $20 to $90 per ton by 2050. In addition, the price of CO_2 in the EU Emissions Trading System (ETS) has ranged from $20 to $50 per ton, suggesting that the $50 price range for CO_2 might be feasible (Richards, Sampson, and Brown 2006).

There are significant geographic differences in the potential for carbon sequestration and its costs, and cost considerations will likely reduce sequestration below its potential. Farmers will naturally be hesitant to increase their susceptibility to risk through long-term carbon sequestration contracts and other agreements that could change as a result of economic, technological, and climate factors and uncertainties about the impacts of carbon sequestration on crop productivity. The availability of capital and access to credit is also a key concern, as are the costs of implementing sequestration projects. Policy approaches in which landowners bear the risks will be more controversial than those in which financial burdens are on taxpayers because costs or burdens are concentrated and benefits are widely dispersed. At the same time, though, the economic benefits could be considerable; producing biomass energy, for example, can create major opportunities for farmers to increase their income (Paustian et al. 2006; DeCicco 2009). The US Department of Agriculture estimates that the annual net return to farmers from offsets range from $1 billion per year from 2015 to 2020, to as much as $15 billion to $20 billion per year from 2040 to 2050 (Olmstead 2009).

If it is done carefully, agricultural carbon sequestration can yield a significant reduction in CO_2 levels. Croplands can be converted to grasslands or forests or to hay and pasture lands. Set-aside programs and restoration efforts for degraded lands include planting perennial grasses or trees that increase carbon stocks in soil as well as in above-ground biomass. Highly degraded sites such as reclaimed surface mines and saline soils are more difficult to restore but offer even greater carbon-storing benefits. The Conservation Reserve Program includes some thirteen million hectares of marginal croplands that have been set aside. This program has been effective in increasing carbon storage, particularly in more humid regions; one study estimated that the set-aside program produced an average of seven MMT of carbon equivalent sequestration a year. Creating and restoring wetlands is another way to increase sequestration but wetlands may also emit methane and a careful assessment of the prospects for net GHG benefits is essential (Paustian et al. 2006).

Carbon offsets have been included in some emissions-trading programs because they are an attractive way to increase the number of low-cost ways to reduce GHG levels. The Chicago Climate Exchange includes the National Farmer's Union Carbon Credit Program, which helps farmers market carbon credits from sequestration efforts. Similarly, the Regional Greenhouse Gas Initiative allows credits to be generated by reducing methane emissions from manure management (Siikamaki 2008).

As noted previously, agriculture's primary role in climate policy has been as an offset—the American Clean Energy and Security Act legislation adopted by the House in 2010 exempted agriculture and ranching from emission caps and listed specific agricultural practices that could be included in generating offsets for purchase by entities covered by GHG-reduction mandates, including conservation tilling, cover cropping, reduction of nitrogen fertilizer use, and biogas capture and combustion (Olmstead 2009). This approach blunted opposition from representatives from farm states because the offsets were designed to provide income to farmers and was politically popular because it allowed the energy and transportation sectors to avoid even deeper emissions reductions.

There are, however, significant challenges in mitigating GHG levels through sequestration. To begin, it is difficult to ensure long-lasting sequestration because it can be threatened by adverse weather, political instability, and climate change itself. Soils may become saturated and unable to store additional carbon within twenty to thirty years of shifts in farming practices, and, depending on the species of trees, from 70 to 150 years after afforestation. Carbon can also be quickly released into the atmosphere if farming practices revert to traditional methods and if grasslands and forests are converted to croplands for food or biofuel production (see the following section). Each type of soil may differ in terms of its ability to store carbon and the point at which it becomes carbon saturated and unable to sequester additional carbon. As is true for other mitigation efforts, agricultural practices must ensure they meet the standards for emissions reductions of being real, additional, and permanent, and that will be difficult because changes in agricultural practices can quickly result in carbon releases. Similar measurement and permanency problems exist with nitrous oxide emissions from soils because they are affected by soil and fertilizer management decisions as well as natural processes (Siikamaki 2008).[1] Finally, it is often exceedingly difficult to ensure that carbon offsets actually occur—a 2008 GAO study of EU offsets revealed systemic failures in certifying net GHG reductions (cited in Olmstead 2009).

Part of the policy debate focuses on the specific mechanisms for pursing carbon reductions. Governments, for example, can institute practices on public lands to serve as a model for increasing sequestration. They can create educational programs to encourage voluntary efforts. They can also issue command-and-control type regulations that mandate farmers to take certain actions such as dedicating a portion of their lands to carbon storage, but that kind of regulatory approach is rarely proposed because of its unpopularity with farmers. Most of the policy options receiving serious consideration fall between practice-based and results-based incentives; both seek to provide clear incentives for landowners. The practice-based approach to accomplishing these goals is to use existing programs aimed at other purposes that provide technical assistance and financial incentives for farmers to participate in conservation efforts. A major advantage of this approach is that the administrative structures are already in place and can be expanded relatively quickly and easily. These programs already have some carbon sequestration impacts, the incentives are popular among farmers, and monitoring requirements are less intrusive and expensive, requiring only a demonstration that the practices are occurring.

An alternative approach is to focus on results. Farmers could earn payments in the form of dollars per ton of carbon sequestered. The government would specify in advance a price per ton of carbon sequestered. Or carbon credits from sequestration could be designated offsets in a cap-and-trade program; this focuses attention on outcomes but requires clear methods for estimating GHG impacts of these changes in land use and management. One advantage of results-based programs is that they reward specific outcomes but these kinds of provisions are not typically used in agricultural policy and may therefore face some initial resistance (Richards, Sampson, and Brown 2006). Other factors besides opportunity costs must be taken into account in fashioning programs to attract farmers. Farmers already face many risks and uncertainties and may be hesitant to add new ones. For actions aimed at reducing emissions and increasing sequestration to have a long-term effect, long-term contracts are required, and that may be difficult to accept when technologies, weather, fertilizer and commodity prices, and other variables are so difficult to predict (Galik et al. 2009). These programs could be included in existing federal agricultural policies, and federal officials would be responsible for managing the programs, verifying claims of sequestration, and paying the incremental price increases. Or the program could be pursued through carbon contracts, in which farmers strike agreements directly with those interested in offsetting their own emissions through agricultural programs. The transaction costs of conducting negotiations, verifying the claims, monitoring compliance, and allocating risks are significant, although costs will fall with experience. Although workable in theory, it must be recognized that farmers may also resist the upfront costs that are needed for many of these investments (Paustian et al. 2006; Richards, Sampson, and Brown 2006).

The Promise of Biofuels

Biofuels offer perhaps the greatest hope for integrating climate, air, and energy policies but whether biofuels actually offer carbon savings depends largely on how they are produced (Fargione et al. 2008) and what goals biofuel policy makers seek to accomplish. To date, biofuel policies have been designed to serve multiple goals, including reducing GHG emissions, enhancing energy security, and promoting rural development (Galik et al. 2009). The results have been mixed, at least in part because policy makers have not always been clear about how to prioritize or balance those goals. The challenge becomes even greater, of course, if these policies are to be integrated with agriculture policy, which has typically sought to ensure food security as well.

Still, biofuels hold great promise. With the notable exception of corn ethanol, biomass as a fuel for heat, power, or transportation results is zero or near-zero CO_2 emissions. Life-cycle studies of biomass used to produce electricity have found that directly burning or gasifying biomass "displace[s] conventional fuels on essentially a one-to-one basis, reducing fossil fuel energy use by almost 100 percent, with corresponding reductions in fossil fuel emissions" (Paustian et al. 2006, 54). Fossil fuel energy savings for ethanol from residues and perennial grasses is about 102 percent because of the presence of lignin in the residues and grasses that serves as the energy source for the conversion process and results in excess energy. Replacing fossil fuels with fuels from these sources could result in significant cuts in GHG emissions and replace imported oil with domestic production. But the actual magnitude of reductions depends on a host of factors, such as the kind of energy source used to process the biomaterials into biofuels and how the agricultural lands used for carbon sequestration are managed.

Currently, the two largest uses of biofuels are burning biomass to produce steam and electricity and producing ethanol from corn grain for use in motor vehicles. But biofuels can be produced from a wide array of technologies, including burning biomass to produce heat and power, gasifying biomass to produce a synthetic gas that can fuel heat and power systems or serve as a transportation fuel, converting animal waste to methane used to produce heat and power, releasing and converting sugars in biomass to produce ethanol, and converting natural oils to fuels such as biodiesel. Biofuels can also be produced from a variety of products, including corn, soybeans, crop residues, trees, other woody crops, native grasses, and even algae.

Biomass currently supplies about 5 percent of the nation's annual energy production, and thus displaces only a small percentage of total fossil fuel use. But with improved yields, greater harvest efficiency, and expanded croplands, biomass could displace up to one-third of US gasoline consumption (Perlak et al. 2005; Galik et al. 2009; National Academy of Sciences, National Academy of Engineering, National Research Council 2009). Biomass production now occupies about 10 percent of US agricultural lands, but if just 15 percent of croplands were dedicated to bioenergy production, and yields were improved by two to four times, biofuels could provide another six to twelve exajuole (EJ) of primary energy.[2] The problem, however, is that technologies to turn agricultural residues and perennial grasses into ethanol are still in the development stage and are not yet commercially viable. If technologies can be developed so that energy crops do not compete directly with food production, biofuels could become even more important. For example, one study concluded that 30 to 40 percent of corn and wheat residue could be collected each year and, if it could be converted into ethanol, it could yield an additional 2.2 EJ of energy (Paustian et al. 2006).

Achieving such technological breakthroughs is no small feat, of course, and would likely require an enormous investment in biomass research

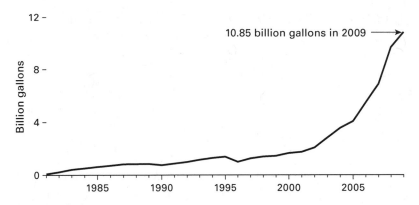

Figure 7.3
U.S. Ethanol Consumption, 1981–2009.
Source: US Department of Energy, Energy Information Administration 2010a, 290.

(Paustian et al. 2006). Even the biofuels we can produce now, such as ethanol, face other obstacles as well, including the "blending wall," the maximum amount of ethanol than can be blended at the current blending level of 10 percent. The United States consumes 140 billion gallons of gasoline annually, so the maximum amount of ethanol that could be blended is 14 billion gallons. Because the United States currently has thirteen billion gallons of ethanol capacity, the blending wall is an effective barrier to further growth of the domestic ethanol industry (see figure 7.3). Although E85 (fuel that is 85 percent ethanol and 15 percent gasoline) is an option, it provides only a very small share of the market, and expanding its production would require a massive investment in time and money. For starters, automobile makers would need to dramatically increase the production of flex-fuel vehicles and gasoline stations would need to install many more E85 pumps (Taheripor and Tyner 2008). In short, a significant increase in liquid biofuel production would require extensive new infrastructure, extending from the field, through refinement, distribution, and use (Galik et al. 2009).

The potential of energy production from crops depends on two key variables: whether yields will increase in the future and the amount of land available for energy crop production. Corn yield has increased some 400 percent since industrial fertilizers were first used and an additional 300 percent from advances in genetic breeding. But a major increase in biomass production would require breakthroughs in genetic manipulation of grasses as well as a significant expansion of the transportation infrastructure required to ship the products to processing facilities. A two-thousand-ton-per-day biomass facility, for example, would require trucks arriving every two-and-one-half minutes for twelve hours a day. Although this would undoubtedly have significant negative repercussions for those living near such plants, the high shipment costs of biofuel and dispersed areas of production make it a good candidate for small, widely distributed power plants, which could yield badly needed jobs in rural areas (Paustian et al. 2006).

Biofuel Policy Mechanisms
As with carbon sequestration, part of the biofuel policy debate focuses on the specific mechanisms for encouraging their production, distribution, and use. Despite its relatively brief history, there are many policies in place promoting the production and consumption of biofuels, so there is a great potential for overlap, redundancy, or conflict. Production tax credits, tariffs, mandates such as RFSs and low carbon fuel standards (LCFSs) are examples of policy approaches adopted by the federal government to encourage biofuel production and use, and it is likely that some of these options may be redundant or undercut one another. Furthermore, as Galik et al. (2009) note, state policies could either amplify or counteract federal policies, especially those involving subsidies. This is significant because, as of 2007, thirty-eight states had biofuel policies or incentives in place. Clearly, a great deal of coordination will be needed to ensure that biofuel policies are effective in achieving their goals.

As noted previously, the history of biofuel policy in the United States is marked by various subsidies and mandates. In part, subsidies are justified because biofuel markets are affected by uncertainty over many factors—the price of crude oil, technology, raw material supplies, and the implementation of renewable fuel standards, among others. Subsidies have clearly been essential to the US ethanol industry; indeed, according to one study, prior to 2005 the industry would not have existed without the subsidy (Taheripour and Tyner 2008). More broadly, using biomass to replace coal in generating electricity or gasoline in fueling vehicles requires subsidies or a carbon tax that raises the price of fossil fuels in order to make biomass energy competitive. Estimates of the cost of producing electricity from different fuels indicate that coal remains the cheapest option, and it is expected to remain so through 2025 (unless carbon emissions are taxed or limited). Biomass-based alternatives are currently two to four times more expensive than coal; that would obviously change should carbon be taxed. Using biofuels to replace gasoline is slightly more expensive than gasoline. If gasoline costs $11 per gigajoule (GJ) of energy produced, for example, ethanol from corn costs about $15 per GJ; for ethanol from biomass, the price varies greatly, from $13 to $30 per GJ. Bio-based ethanol may one day reach the price of gasoline but that would require a significant improvement in technology (Paustian et al. 2006) as well as other policies aimed at subsidizing its production. It may be that a variable subsidy would help alleviate much of the uncertainty over oil prices and would help in the creation of a cellulosic ethanol industry (Taheripour and Tyner 2008).

The ethanol subsidy is not the only example. The 2005 renewable fuels standard, for instance, requires domestic production of renewable fuels to displace 5 percent of total gasoline use in the country or 7.5 billion gallons a year in 2008, a goal that was easily met. The 2007 Energy Act increased the target to thirty-six billion gallons of biofuels by 2022. Biofuel production has been encouraged by a 51 cents per gallon tax credit, lowered to 45 cents in the 2008 Farm Bill, and a 54 cents per gallon tariff on imported fuel that also serves to favor domestic production (Taheripor and Tyner 2008). The 2008 Farm Bill also provided $1 billion in funding for bioenergy programs, including $320 million in loan guarantees for biorefineries and $250 million in grants and loan guarantees for farmers and small businesses to purchase renewable energy systems and invest in energy efficiency, $300 million to expand production of biofuels from crops and residue, and $120 million for biomass research and development (Siikamaki 2008).

Subsidies have also aided biodiesel production. A substitute for diesel fuel and an additive to improve the features of diesel, biodiesel is typically produced by combining soybean oil with methanol or sometimes waste grease and fats from restaurants and food processing. The development of biodiesel today is about where corn ethanol was twenty years ago. Production grew from a negligible amount in 2000 to four hundred million gallons in 2006, an increase that has been encouraged by commodity credit payments to farmers that produce crops for biodiesel and tax incentives for biodiesel production. It is apparent that if subsidies are large enough, they can produce clear changes in behavior; it is not clear, however, that the cumulative assortment of tariffs, production credits, loan guarantees, and mandates are either cost effective or environmentally beneficial.

There is, in fact, considerable debate over whether biofuels are the most cost-effective mechanism to reduce GHG emissions (Schlegel and

Kaphengst 2007; Galik et al. 2009). Indeed, some scholars argue that production tax credits, tariffs, and mandates are inefficient compared to putting a price a carbon. As a case in point, Galik et al. (2009, 9) suggest that "the implementation of a carbon price . . . represents a far more efficient mechanism to integrate biofuels into comprehensive climate policy. Assuming that the carbon price applies to all emissions tied to the production and use of biofuels, a carbon price provides a signal in direct proportion to a fuel's GHG footprint." By contrast, renewable fuel standards control only the rate of fuel production but not the quantity of GHG emissions (US EPA 2011d). As a result, mandates can encourage the production of biofuels, such as ethanol, that may actually increase net GHG emissions.

Others note that shifting cropland from food to biofuel production has contributed to higher food prices. Indeed, there is considerable evidence that corn and crude oil prices now move together. Higher gas prices mean greater demand for ethanol and thus induce more investment in ethanol production. That, in turn, means greater demand for corn, so corn prices rise in response, leading to higher food prices (Taheripour and Tyner 2008). Biofuels can be produced in significant quantities but they must come from feedstocks produced with much lower GHG emissions than traditional fossil fuels and with little or no competition with food production (Tilman, Hill, and Lehman 2006; Tilman et al., 2009). Feedstocks such as waste biomass or corn stover could be effective because they are rich in elements for maintaining soil fertility and carbon storage and help minimize erosion (Tilman, Hill, and Lehman 2006). Another option could be growing native perennials on abandoned or degraded agricultural lands, which because they are carbon poor would not result in large emissions when cultivated (Field, Campbell, and Lobell 2007; Fargione et al. 2008; Searchinger et al. 2008). An additional benefit is that such approaches would minimize habitat destruction and competition with food production while enhancing water quality (Fargione et al. 2008; National Academy of Sciences, National Academy of Engineering, National Research Council 2009).

It is possible that newer biofuels can be used to produce ethanol because they can be grown on marginal lands, use much less water, and thus do not compete with food production as corn-based enthanol does (Barta 2008a). Switchgrass and other native grasses can produce significantly higher energy yields than plant residues, ten tons per hectares compared with about two, and also contribute to improved soil health and reduced erosion. In addition, switchgrass and other biomass can substitute for coal in generating heat and power. Technologies are not yet in place, however, to convert switchgrass to transportation fuels and policies would need to ensure that switchgrass did not compete with land used for food production.

Others suggest that algae is the only fuel crop that does not result in environmental harm because it can be grown in wastewater or seawater and requires little more than sunlight and CO_2 to grow (Bourne 2007). Commercially viable technology for converting algae to fuel is not yet available, however. Corn, animal manure, Conservation Reserve Program (CRP) lands, agricultural residues, and energy crops are all part of a mix that could reduce significantly gasoline and diesel by as much as 80 percent if technological breakthroughs occur and prices of fossil fuels rise sufficiently, and if progress is made in accurately estimating GHG fluxes and carbon stock changes, tillage and other practices, fertilizer use, grazing practices, and other agricultural activities. Associated benefits include improving soil quality, reducing erosion, and improving air and water pollution.

Many scientists have concluded that biofuel production can actually contribute to higher GHG emissions because of the amount of carbon released when lands are cleared for planting crops (Naik 2008; Searchinger et al. 2008; Kleinschmit 2009). Whatever crops are grown as biofuels, it is imperative that we account for and prevent GHG emissions that result from the conversion of forests and grasslands to crop production (Searchinger et al. 2008; Galik et al. 2009; Searchinger et al. 2009; Wise et al. 2009). According to some calculations, such land-use change in the United States could increase GHG emissions by 50 percent (Searchinger et al. 2008). As a result, policies need to include the net GHG emission of sequestration from land-use change (Fargione et al. 2008). To some extent, policy makers have already recognized this issue. In 2007, for example, California included indirect land-use changes in the life-cycle accounting of biofuel-associated GHG emissions for its low carbon fuel standard. Similarly, the second version of the federal RFSs requires the EPA to use life-cycle accounting to determine which biofuels would qualify as reducing GHG and included land-use change in that calculation (Taheripor and Tyner 2008).

Climate, Energy, and Food

Part of the climate, energy, and agricultural policies challenge is resisting the demand for cheap energy and cheap food. Food and agricultural policies are built on the promise of inexpensive energy and highly processed food. Farm policies have encouraged the shift from solar and human energy to an input-intensive, fossil fuel–based system of "monocultures of corn and soy in the field and cheap calories of fat, sugar, and feedlot meat on the table" (Pollan 2008, 3). Public policies have encouraged the production of commodity crops that, because of subsidies, can be sold for less than it costs to produce them. Michael Pollan explains that "as this artificially cheap grain worked its way up the food chain, it drove down the price of all the calories derived from that grain; the high-fructose corn syrup in the Coke, the soy oil in which the potatoes were fried, the meat and cheese in the burger" (Pollan 2008, 3). In addition, farmers who receive commodity crop subsidies are prohibited from growing fruits and vegetables, a requirement demanded by California and Florida produce farmers in order to win their support for the commodity crop subsidy program.

There are several ways to reform agricultural policy that reduces fossil fuel use and improves the quality of food. As Pollan (2008) notes, we could preserve every acre of farmland then make it available to new farmers; we could decentralize and regionalize the food system so food is eaten close to where it is grown, making it fresher and less processed and using less energy to transport it. Livestock could be moved out of feedlots and back to farms; this would curtail the routine use of antibiotics in feed, reduce the problem of concentrated animal wastes that contaminate water supplies, and provide natural fertilizers for farms and thus replace chemical fertilizers. Pollan (2008) suggests that these policy shifts will result in myriad benefits, including improved human health and nutrition through eating a more varied diet with less meat and less chemically contaminated foods, improved animal well-being, improved water quality, reduced fossil fuel use, and healthier rural communities. All, he suggests, are part of a farm agenda that effectively integrates energy, climate, public health and nutrition, water quality, and agriculture.

Beyond Agricultural Policy

Until recently, agriculture policy was not considered in discussions of climate policy in the United States; this is ironic, given agriculture's vulnerability to the effects of climate change, as well its impacts on land, water, and energy use (Kleinschmit 2009). To date, though, much of the focus has been on agriculture's role in sequestering carbon, an admirable goal but one that falls far short of what is possible and necessary. In addition to mechanisms for banking carbon, we should pursue policies that enhance air, water, and soil quality, protect wildlife habitat, and provide food, fiber, and fuel (Olmstead 2009). Such an approach necessarily entails moving away from our current industrialized input and fossil fuel–intensive agricultural practices toward low input, resilient agricultural systems that serve multiple goals beyond carbon sequestration (Kleinschmit 2009). Bioenergy from low-input crops has a real potential to reduce GHG emissions from the agricultural and energy sectors, while providing economic development opportunities for rural communities (Tilman, Hill, and Lehman 2006).

Many of the technologies for reducing agricultural GHG emissions and for increasing carbon sequestration are quite feasible and can be instituted quickly. Although it is true there are many uncertainties about the precise rates of sequestration, rough estimates can work until more precise data are available. Offsets could be put in place for twenty to thirty years, halting the increase in emissions and buying precious time for more permanent reductions in GHG emissions from power plants and motor vehicles. There is always the danger, of course, that sequestration will be pursued instead of more difficult and unpopular mitigation policies, which reinforces the importance of taking a broad, integrated approach. Clear incentives for farmers and other land owners to change the way in which they use fertilizers and pesticides, irrigate lands, feed animals, and protect open spaces can be powerful change agents.

8

Climate Change, Policy Integration, and Ecological Sustainability

For readers who always begin books by reading the last chapter and for others who dozed off part way, here is what you missed. Although climate science still has many uncertainties, trends in the research since the 1990s clearly indicate that the threat of disruptive climate change is becoming more, not less, certain. Given the magnitude of the risks involved, the disruptions that are already occurring, and the way in which they are distributed in the world so that the poor are likely to be hurt first and worst by those changes, the case for taking action to reduce the magnitude of climate change is compelling.

Although there are many climate policy choices, thinking about them in an integrated fashion is essential. Many of the sources of greenhouse gases also produce conventional pollutants that threaten public health; coordinating regulatory efforts can produce more efficient and effective efforts. The co-benefits of reducing GHG emissions help strengthen the case for taking action that promises significant environmental and health benefits even if one is not yet convinced that climate change is a threat. The political saliency of energy, climate change, air pollution, agriculture, and other issues varies over time; indeed, in recent years energy security has dominated the discussion. But if trends in growing climate-driven disruptions continue, climate change policy will eventually come to dominate. It is a serious mistake, however, to frame the issues so narrowly because some policy options aimed at remedying one problem can make others worse. An integrated approach is thus essential.

Although the focus of this book has been on US policy options, the global scope of the climate challenge means that US policies must be part of a broader international effort. At the same time, our ability to help fashion a new global accord is limited by what policies can garner domestic political support. Global negotiations continue to rest on the deal struck in 1992, codified in the Framework Convention on Climate

Change, that the developed nations would reduce their emissions and at the same time assist developing countries to grow their economies by using cleaner technologies. Unfortunately, after a brief window of opportunity in 2009, Congress has abandoned that commitment, as have the leaders of some other industrialized nations, and policy action now seems unlikely. US climate policy makers face the daunting task of trying to get one side (either Congress or China) to move first to commit to GHG reductions so the other side will follow. This seems patently unfair to the Chinese, who only emit one-fourth the GHGs Americans do, and then have to count in their 25 percent the emissions from the production of much of the goods Americans buy and use. US budget and trade deficits, growing debt, and unfunded health and retirement obligations of $60 trillion (Yarrow 2008) make it all the less likely that it will be able to fund economic growth through clean energy in developing countries. China's enormous wealth will itself likely be the primary source of funding for its energy transformation, and its ability to scale up technologies may spread throughout the world (Friedman 2008). US policy making may be shaped more by global forces than itself be the driver of what happens around the world.

Domestic policy making focuses on determining the appropriate GHG emission–reduction targets, and, more important, how to achieve them. Just a few years ago, carbon-trading programs were thought to be the leading contender for the overall strategy to drive down emissions. Although a carbon tax is, in practical terms, a simpler and more effective approach to reducing emissions, carbon trading seemed more politically feasible. Either approach can help pursue the essential task of making sure that market prices include more of the true costs of producing and distributing goods and services. In an economy so rooted in markets, making markets work better by including environmental costs that are so easily externalized and not included in prices is a fundamental imperative. At this point, though, it seems unlikely that even carbon trading could muster sufficient support in Congress, with Republicans who had once embraced the idea now rejecting it out of hand as too costly and complicated.

Chapters 3 through 7 illustrate how policy integration might underlie energy, air pollution, transportation, and agricultural policies. The most effective and efficient way to pursue the co-benefits from reducing GHG levels is to make a massive investment in energy efficiency. This will require subsidies, incentives, grants, and other measures to provide the upfront capital required to finance these changes. Another priority is to reduce the use of coal in generating electricity because that is the primary source of GHG emissions. Coal is the dirtiest fossil fuel, producing carbon dioxide and other pollutants that threaten public and environmental health. But it also an efficient, plentiful, and domestic fuel, and simply ending our reliance on coal, as attractive as that sounds, is not now feasible because it is such a workhorse in generating electricity. Through a carbon tax or carbon-trading target, or new clean air regulations aimed at achieving national air-quality standards, coal emissions can be reduced by shifting to natural gas and by replacing old power plants with cleaner, more efficient ones. Eventually, we will no longer be able to burn coal; a key challenge here is that energy prices will have to remain high now in order to propel the transition, and US policy has long been dedicated to maintaining cheap energy. So the era of cheap, coal-fired electricity will need to end and it remains to be seen whether the public will embrace the notion that the climate, public health, and ecosystem benefits of GHG reductions will outweigh the costs of higher electricity prices.

Clearly, coal must also eventually be replaced with alternative fuels. Nuclear power is, in one sense, the clearest alternative because it can produce massive amounts of electricity but a direct comparison of the risks of climate change and nuclear power is difficult. Nuclear wastes last, in human terms, forever, and the threats posed by the proliferation of fuels that could be used to make nuclear weapons by rogue nations and terrorists are cataclysmic. Wind, solar, geothermal, wave, and other renewable sources could replace coal or nuclear power but electricity costs would be greater orders of magnitude. Those prices would almost certainly fall with economies of scale and technological advances but the problem is what to do during the next few decades. The choices are difficult. If we do not replace coal, we may commit to GHG levels that will be irreversible, but if we dramatically increase nuclear power, we greatly increase the associated risks, as illustrated by the events in Fukushima. If we make a massive investment in renewables and carbon sequestration of coal emissions, electricity bills will skyrocket. In the midst of a lengthy economic downturn marked by high unemployment and mounting deficits, there will be inexorable political pressure to avoid higher energy prices and to pass the climate problem off to others. Already we have seen that the zeal to slash spending has affected federal and state renewable energy and climate programs, which can only make things worse.

Transportation policy is in some ways more encouraging. We are already on the path to improving fuel efficiency standards. If gas prices stay high, it may be quite politically feasible; but if prices continue to fluctuate, as they did in 2008 and 2009, a carbon tax can help maintain the steady pressure that high prices produce to dampen interest in gas-guzzling vehicles. High fuel prices can also help address the challenge posed by ever-increasing vehicle miles traveled. Land-use planning, carpooling, mass transit, telecommuting, and other policies have only had a very limited impact on reducing driving because they impose unpopular constraints on individual choice, but they have so many co-benefits that ambitious climate change policies are all the more important.

Agriculture, climate, and energy policies need to be carefully integrated because of the impact of biofuels on food production and because carbon sequestration is one of the cheapest ways to reduce GHG levels. The technological and practical problems are considerable but sequestration is, like greater use of natural gas, one of the key bridging actions that can produce relatively immediate reductions in the atmospheric concentrations of GHGs and buy us some time as we develop renewable energy sources.

The policy options here are not mutually exclusive; all need to be pursued at levels of intensity and commitment that are orders of magnitude greater than current efforts. A commitment on the order of the Manhattan Project to develop the atom bomb in World War II, to fly to the moon before the Russians in the 1960s, represent the kind of massive commitment required. But these projects are not models for climate and alternative energy research because the energy effort needs to be broader and more ambitious, focusing not on one or a few options but a wide range of alternatives. Public policies will have to strike that elusive balance of partnering with private industry to subsidize basic research and stimulate technological innovation without subsidizing specific technologies.

There are two other ways of thinking about policy integration that deserve a brief discussion here. First, policies aimed at mitigating disruptive climate change must be integrated with those aimed at adapting to the changes that are already occurring and will likely accelerate. Second, climate policies, as broad and far-reaching as they are, intersect with a much broader set of issues surrounding sustainable development. This is particularly true in developing countries, where climate change policies must be carefully integrated with policies aimed at reducing poverty and increasing opportunity, well-being, and material consumption. The United States faces the dual challenge of deciding what role it will play in helping to fund the costs of adaptation around the world and how it will fund those costs at home.

Integrating Climate Mitigation and Adaptation

Given that climate change impacts are already occurring, adaptation is essential. Obama administration science adviser John Holdren argues we have three options: mitigation, adaptation, and suffering; the more we do of the first, the less of the second and third options will occur; the more we do of the first two, the less of the third we will have to endure. We are already doing some of each; the question is what the mix will be (Holdren 2007). The problem is that massive amounts of money will be needed for adaptation and mitigation. If a cap-and-trade program is enacted, for example, and allowances are auctioned, that money could be used to pay for clean energy investments. Similarly, if a carbon tax were instituted to discourage fossil fuel use and encourage energy efficiency and renewables, it could also generate a great deal of money. In order to reduce opposition to the cost of climate change policy, it may be necessary to make those policies revenue neutral and return the proceeds to taxpayers. Alternatively, it could be used to subsidize clean energy investments or to help pay for the costs of mitigation. In the end, we may compromise and do all three but the amount of money available will surely fall short of what is needed to spur innovation and pay for mitigation, and the more revenues are dedicated to those purposes, the less they can help reduce political opposition to higher energy costs.

Although some might argue that a focus on adaptation is an unfortunate surrender in the face of daunting mitigation challenges, efforts to adapt are inescapable. We will eventually pay in mitigation costs the climate changes we fail to prevent if we were to invest in energy efficiency, renewables, and carbon sequestration. The relationship between the two may not be linear; climate change is for now, at least, far too difficult to predict to allow for a precise relationship between mitigation and adaptation. One can argue that in the face of uncertainty it is better to invest in our capacity to adapt than to invest in mitigation because that approach gives us more flexibility to respond as we see what happens. It may work if climate change is gradual and its effects are manageable but it is a recipe for disaster if feedback mechanisms accelerate climate change and produce rapid and unmanageable climate disruptions. Decisions need to be made now about what benefits to enjoy and costs to impose on the current generation and which burdens to try to defer to succeeding generations.

The November 2007 Intergovernmental Panel on Climate Change (IPCC) synthesis report summarized their intersection this way: "Responding to climate change involves an iterative risk management process that includes both adaptation and mitigation, and takes into account climate change damages, co-benefits, sustainability, equity, and attitudes to risk" (IPCC 2007, 21). Adaptive capacity is intimately connected to social and economic development but is unevenly distributed across and within societies. Areas of the world already susceptible to the effects of adverse weather and environmental problems and lacking in resources to deal with these challenges will likely find such problems greatly magnified in the future. Adaptation strategies for coastal zones and other communities will likely be extraordinarily expensive, such as constructing or relocating seawalls and storm surge barriers and acquiring land to provide marshlands and wetlands as buffers against sea level rise and storm-driven flooding. Regulations and standards for building codes and land-use planning should be required to take into account climate change impacts. Furthermore, public health policies are needed to integrate traditional efforts with threats posed by climate change, such as the health impacts of heat episodes, polluted water, and the spread of infectious diseases. Plans for providing public services will need to incorporate increased demand for them in areas where significant climate change occurs. Transportation policies will also need to be integrated with climate change measures, including research for and the development of new infrastructure for areas with melting permafrost and increased drainage, and realignment and relocation of roads, rails, and other facilities. Although the primary focus of energy policy is on mitigating climate change, energy facilities and infrastructure such as power plants and transmission lines will also likely be damaged by disruptive climate change. Impacts range from death and destruction in areas unable to afford adaptive measures, such as coastal areas of Bangladesh and small Pacific island states, to economic disruptions in ski and coastal resort industries.

Nicholas Stern (2006) and others at the United Kingdom's Government Economic Service concluded that the costs of extreme weather could reach 0.5 to 1 percent of the world's gross domestic product a year by the middle of the century. If emission trends continued, the report warned that climate change could reduce per capita consumption from 5 to 20 percent. In addition, the impacts of climate change will disproportionately burden the poorest residents of the planet: "The challenge of adaptation will be particularly acute in developing countries, where greater vulnerability and poverty will limit the capacity to act. As in developed countries, the costs are hard to estimate, but are likely to run in the tens of billions of dollars" (Stern 2006, 21). After two years of debate engendered by the report, Stern and others reaffirmed in 2007 their conclusion that the "cost of action [to mitigate the threat] is much less than the cost of inaction" (Dietz et al. 2007, 231).

Roberts and Parks (2007), in a comprehensive study of the impacts of climate-related (not necessarily climate change–driven) disasters, found that the poorer nations of Asia, Africa, and Central America repeatedly suffered the greatest casualties from climate-related catastrophes such as flooding, droughts, hurricanes and other windstorms, and heat waves. The only climate-related disasters producing relatively high levels of casualties in developed countries are heat waves, such as those in Chicago in 1995 and Europe in 2003. Between 1980 and 2002, climate-related disasters claimed nearly 301,000 lives in Ethiopia, a fatality rate of 4.78 per thousand. During that same time, they rendered homeless some sixty-two million Bangladeshis, almost 46 percent of the total population. The top twenty countries that suffered fatalities from these kinds of disasters were all developing countries, except the United States, which ranked tenth in terms of the number of people killed (7,617) during this time. Although these climate-related storms were not necessarily driven by global warming, they demonstrate the magnitude of the impacts and their tremendous effects on poor countries.

Specific examples of communities threatened by climate change suggest how expensive adaptation would be. In Alaska, global warming has been blamed for warming the atmosphere and melting the sea ice in ways that threaten to cause houses and buildings to fall into the sea. Kivalina, a village north of the Arctic Circle, is located on a barrier reef in the Chukchi Sea and is home to the Inupiat. The cost of relocating the village is estimated to be about $400 million, or about $1 million for each of the village's four hundred residents (Barringer 2008; Gardner 2008). The actual costs of rebuilding or moving a community are relatively straightforward; much more daunting is determining how to address the loss of lives or the threat to indigenous communities whose culture, identity, and existence are intertwined with their traditional lands.

Adaptation poses daunting challenges to climate policy making in the United States and other developed nations. As difficult as it is to raise taxes to fund new clean energy programs or to create an incentive to use less energy, even more difficult will be the task of raising billions of dollars and more to help pay for the costs of adapting to a warming world.

Climate Adaptation Litigation in US Federal Courts

In the United States, the idea of how the costs of adaptation should be distributed is hardly an issue in any governmental forums, except federal courts. Climate change–related lawsuits are proliferating in the United States in the absence of federal regulatory action and US engagement in the Kyoto Protocol, and as a result of growing evidence that the consequences of climate change are not just future calamities but are already adversely affecting people and property.[1] What are termed *nuisance actions* are being brought by states and individuals against large corporations that emit large amounts of GHGs. Plaintiffs argue that property damage arising from weather events that are a result of climate change are ultimately caused by these large emitters of GHGs. Plaintiffs and others involved in these tort cases often liken them to the early tobacco cases, initially derided as improbable but eventually successful because of, among other factors, tobacco company officials' acknowledgment in internal documents of the health threat associated with smoking that conflicted with corporate policy statements. Critics of these cases persuasively argue that the courts are ill suited to decide these cases because climate change raises national and international issues that cannot be effectively addressed though the case-by-case patchwork approach of nuisance suits. By nature, court cases cannot directly result in the design of comprehensive GHG reduction policies.

A second problem is that the standards for nuisance and negligent suits appear quite difficult to satisfy. It will likely be challenging to get courts to rule that what companies have been doing for decades is now creating a nuisance. Public nuisance suits, for example, require plaintiffs to prove that defendants created an unreasonable interference with the exercise of a right such as access to public lands. Courts typically weigh the value of the defendants' activities with the harm suffered by the plaintiffs; plaintiffs must prove they have suffered from specific damages distinct from those incurred by the public as a whole. In negligence suits, plaintiffs must prove defendants owed them a duty, breached that duty, and caused harm. This requires showing that defendants had a duty to act reasonably and to take care to not cause the type of injury to those who are foreseeably at risk from those actions. For climate change, this might mean that plaintiffs must prove that they were in the "zone of foreseeable risk" from the conduct of utilities or automobile manufacturers. The problem is that such a duty might be understood as "a duty is owed to another person or class of persons, not the world at large," and climate change is "essentially a global environmental tort" (Hunter and Salzman 2007, 108).

The importance of these and others cases, however, lies not in the possibility that they will produce a rational, comprehensive solution to the problem of funding climate adaptation, or that they will even produce a partial policy solution, but in providing a forum for exploring the question of who is responsible for paying for climate adaptation costs. Courts are actually good public forums for exploring issues of responsibility to pay for harms. Are companies responsible for the damage produced by GHG emissions, even if they did not intend to do harm? Nuisance law does not require that polluters be branded as evildoers but rather focuses on compensating victims. The kind of fact finding that occurs in trials can help illuminate the trade-offs in thinking about justice, responsibility, and other issues that are at the heart of the debate over how to adapt to climate change.

For example, in the United States, negligence law suggests that because GHG emissions harm others, sources should take reasonable measures to reduce those emissions. Because adverse impacts have already occurred, sources should thus compensate those who have suffered harm. Before 1990, one could argue that it was not clear that GHG emissions were causing harm and it would not have been reasonable to expect sources to begin cutting back. However, since that time, there has been sufficient evidence that emissions were harmful that a reasonable response would be to take reasonable steps to reduce them. This, of course, then turns on what the "reasonableness" standard requires and that is exactly the kind of question courts deal with all the time. This is not likely to require an immediate halt to emissions but rather taking significant, prudent steps, as a legal obligation, to reduce the risk of harm. One cannot argue that if we reduce emissions and other nations (China, for example) do not, we are free from obligation; responsibility is attached to our behavior and its consequences even if others also contribute.

Justice and equity principles also empower courts to fashion equitable remedies to deal with unfairness. Climate change is harming some of the most vulnerable people on the planet, and they lack the resources to adapt. GHG sources have an obligation to compensate victims who have suffered as the result of an "unreasonable" willingness to reduce harmful behavior. Again, such an argument raises all kinds of questions about which damage can be attributed to climate change and how to calculate damages and apportion obligations but these are precisely the questions for which we should be seeking answers. If legislative bodies prefer to take over the task and develop comprehensive solutions, then let them proceed (Vanderheiden 2008).

If these cases were to proceed to settlement or decision, defendant companies would presumably pass on the costs of settlement to their customers. In this way, climate litigation can play an important role in helping to identify the costs of adaptation so they can be better incorporated into energy prices. In an economic system dominated by markets, fundamentally organized by markets, it makes a great deal of sense to focus on correcting those markets so they reflect the true costs of producing energy. Markets promise to produce decisions about production and consumption that reflect the interests of consumers and promote the most economically efficient use of the available resources. If markets reflect all the costs associated with goods and services, and consumers have perfect information about the costs and benefits of alternatives, then markets will be able to produce the benefits they promise. The task of law and policy is to ensure that, as much as possible, true cost prices dominate and accurate information is available because producers also have an incentive to maximize their profits by externalizing as many costs as possible.

All this is not to minimize the daunting tasks of actually deciding cases and awarding damages. Plaintiffs ask a few major companies that are responsible for only a tiny fraction of total global emissions to bear responsibility for all of the damages associated with global emissions. Plaintiffs may argue that the principle of strict, joint, and several liability has been established in other areas of environmental law and can be applied here. Under the Comprehensive Emergency Response, Compensation, and Liability Act or Superfund law, for example, there is no need for a showing of negligence or intent to harm but only that a hazardous substance was released by a potentially responsible party (PRP) and response costs occurred. A single party could be responsible for clean-up costs even though many other parties were also responsible for the harm. The Superfund liability rules have been widely criticized for being unfair to PRPs who are singled out for liability, and defenders argue that the parties benefited from the low cost of disposing of wastes in the past and should now bear the clean-up costs (Salzman and Thompson 2003). In the end, PRPs may seek to implicate as many other PRPs as possible in order to share the clean-up costs.

Although it seems difficult to envision litigation as an efficient and fair solution to the threat of climate change, the prospect of large damage awards or even the bad publicity that comes from a tort suit against major sources of GHG emissions may help build support for a national climate-change regulatory regime. The limited number of parties implicated in climate suits also raises the question of whether suits that seek to enjoin defendants from further GHG emissions or require reductions can produce an effective solution to the problem. The majority opinion in *Massachusetts v. EPA* (549 U.S. 497 (2007), 22–23) took up this issue in its analysis of standing, arguing that even though reducing emissions from motor vehicles through EPA regulations would not "reverse" global warming, plaintiffs could still seek EPA efforts to "slow or reduce" the problem; plaintiffs are not required to show that a "favorable decision will relieve [their] every injury" because a "reduction in domestic emissions would slow the pace of global emissions increases, no matter what happens elsewhere."

Because the problem of climate change is so broad and far-reaching, it seems at first blush to be exactly the kind of issue that courts are not well suited to address. But the experience so far suggests that it may be possible for the courts to play a positive role in helping to clarify statutory authority, focus attention on the compelling claim to compensate victims of disruptive climate change, and fashion a reasonable policy response to an enormously complex problem. It also suggests that international courts and courts in other nations might also have a role to play in investigating issues of who is responsible for paying the costs of adaptation to climate change and how those costs can become part of the prices we pay for the energy we use. In the United States, courts are best understood not as independent, justice-dispensing bodies, insulated from politics and the policy-making process, but from an interbranch perspective that emphasizes the interaction of the courts with the other branches of government. The interbranch theory of the courts suggests that the courts have a positive role to play in policy making because they provide a forum for issues that are not yet ripe for legislative action (Miller and Barnes 2004).

In short, climate change cases such as those in the United States are no substitute for major global programs aimed at funding the kinds of adaptive measures that are already needed on a large scale. But they are helping to clarify the responsibility of major GHG emitters and those who enjoy the goods and services produced by those emissions to include in the prices they pay the cost of the consequences of those emissions.

Integrating Climate Change and Sustainability

The concept of sustainability has been used for decades to assess the yield of natural resources such as forests because land managers have sought to ensure that resources are used no faster than they are replenished and could thus be used indefinitely. In the 1970s, ecologists and others broadened the notion to examine the extent to which economic activity, resource use, and pollution was consistent with the planet's carrying capacity. The World Conservation Strategy proposed the concept of sustainable development in 1980 (International Union for the Conservation of Nature 1980). But the idea of sustainable development gained real international prominence and attention with the publication in 1987 of the World Commission on Environment and Development's *Our Common Future,* which urged all nations to commit to the idea of sustainable development, defined as "development that meets the need of the present without compromising the ability of future generations to meet their own needs" (World Commission on Environment and Development 1987, 43).

The evolution of the concept of sustainable development from its early and rather precise formulation as sustainable yield to the more widely embraced but vaguely defined core principle guiding economic and environmental activity has made the term highly contested. For some, sustainability means that business as usual continues, that economic growth continues to be the priority but that it is good to try, whenever it is not too expensive or disruptive of economic goals, to minimize environmental damage and resource use. Alternatively, it might mean that industry needs to reinvent itself in ways that promote pollution prevention, energy efficiency, and technological innovation. Or it might mean that ecological and environmental goals are given roughly equivalent status, that they must be pursued in tandem and in innovative ways that promote a much wider range of values than are incorporated in market prices. Sustainable development might also be understood to mean that preserving the biosphere is the most important collective objective. As a prerequisite for every other human endeavor, it is to be given priority over any economic goal. The focus of this book has been on integrating climate with energy, air pollution, agriculture, transportation, land use, and other related policies, but this is all part of the integration of environmental and economic policy. That is the idea underlying sustainable development and the threat of climate change gives it new urgency.

The idea of a thick or rich notion of sustainable development calls for decisions harmonizing three "E"s—environmental protection, economic activity, and equity. This form of sustainability gives priority to ecological preservation rather than economic growth and recognizes that the economy is part of the global ecosystem and dependent on it. Underlying ecological and economic considerations is the importance of equity, fairness, and justice. Thick sustainability means that any effort to protect and conserve resources must recognize the great inequality in the distribution of resources and the importance of alleviating poverty. Those who have been marginalized in the past or are victims of injustices and discrimination should be given priority in the allocation of resources and the creation of opportunity. Those who live subsistence lifestyles are often most vulnerable to environmental degradation because their survival depends on healthy ecosystems. The pressure to survive may result in ecologically unsustainable practices or the high levels of consumption and waste generation of others may pose serious challenges to the health of the ecosystems on which gatherers, farmers, and hunters depend. Sustainability can provide the conceptual and ethical framework for responding to the claims of indigenous peoples for recognition of their land claims and for their self-determination. Although fairness to future generations is a traditional element of sustainability, fairness to current generations is at least as important.

It is, of course, possible to think about sustainability as primarily an ecological concept because of the centrality of a healthy biosphere for all life. But the central role ecological health plays in human flourishing requires that it include an equity and justice dimension because of the inequities and injustices that result from the way in which environmental threats are distributed in our society. Environmental law is fundamentally an issue of justice because it determines who will bear the burdens of pollution-producing activities. The harmful and adverse effects of polluting activities are rarely limited to those who profit from those activities. Even if the benefits of these activities vastly outweigh the costs and satisfy a cost-benefit test, if those costs are borne by the most vulnerable, politically weak, and economically marginalized citizens then the activities are morally suspect. As a leading expert on environmental justice has argued, "an abundance of documentation shows blacks, lower-income groups, and working-class persons are subject to a disproportionately large amount of pollution and other environmental stressors in their neighborhoods as well as their work-places" (Bullard 1994, 1). More broadly, one of the reasons why the threat of climate change is so morally charged is that those in the world who are the most vulnerable to risks such as melting glaciers and per-mafrost, sea level rise, the spread of disease, and shifts in plant and animal habitat are least responsible for the emissions that are driving climate change, and they largely lack the resources to adapt successfully to disruptive changes.

The breadth of the idea of sustainability gives it the potential to aggregate a wide range of interests under its umbrella but that breadth and generality poses challenges in translating the core concept into spe-cific decisions. Some argue that the idea of sustainability is most useful in narrow settings, where parties may be able to agree that certain prac-tices are not sustainable and should be changed but is too vague to illuminate broader issues (Jamieson 1994). Others argue that sustain-ability, similar to other transformative ideas, "promises to remake the world through reflection and choice, but its potential to engage people's hopes, imagination, and sense of responsibility may depend more on strategic uses of ambiguity than on conceptual precision and clarity." Sustainability is a powerful concept because it is "sufficiently ambiguous to be embraced by diverse interests, yet coherent enough to inspire move-ment in a particular direction" (Hempel 1999, 44). Sustainability has the potential to become one of the ideas, similar to justice, equality, and freedom, that create fundamental expectations for public and private behavior; it can also take shape in different contexts to provide specific guidance for action.

Sustainability is also consistent with an ecosystems approach. Knowl-edge of how ecosystems function, their productive capacity, required trade-offs, and long-term consequences, are essential moving forward.

Baseline data and inventories are required to assess changing conditions. An ecosystem approach must engage the public in a discussion of the benefits of ecosystem services, the costs and benefits of ecosystem use, and the trade-offs to be made (Costanza et al. 1997; Daily 1997). Local communities must be involved in decisions to ensure fairness in the distribution of benefits and costs and to engage local stakeholders in preserving ecosystem health. Accurate prices are critical; because prices of food, water, and other goods typically do not reflect the real costs to the environment of producing them, those costs are typically ignored or undervalued. Prices need to accurately reflect costs so we can make efficient trade-offs among competing values and set priorities for limited resources. The preservation of parks, wild lands, and other protected areas for recreation must be integrated with other efforts to preserve ecosystem services.

The methodology of sustainability builds on the idea of ecosystem services but goes beyond to include several other additional criteria for assessing policy choices, including pollution prevention, the precautionary principle and preservation of ecological values in the face of uncertainty, the development of economic indicators and measures that reflect depletion of natural resources, considerations of equity and distribution, and preservation of ecological conditions and options for future generations. Ecological sustainability places a major constraint on economics; only economic activity that is consistent with ecological sustainability is acceptable. Critical natural capital must be maintained so that the ecosystem services it provides are maintained; it cannot simply be harvested to generate economic wealth. Industrial activities, energy production, transportation, and consumption must be fundamentally transformed to avoid ecological disruptions and to protect regenerative processes.

Most significant, sustainability holds that ecological health simply outweighs economic growth as the primary public priority. Balancing environmental protection and economic growth is not enough; ecological values must come first and must define and limit what kinds and levels of economic activity are acceptable. Policy goals such as free trade and economic efficiency are subordinated to preservation of biodiversity, protection of wild lands, and reclamation of damaged areas. For precautionary reasons and because we do not know what the desires or utility functions of future generations will be, sustainability requires that we should ensure the preservation of as much of the natural world as possible as we balance meeting the needs of the current generation with the preservation of resources for future ones. Sustainability thus requires strong commitments to monitoring life-cycle assessments, feedback loops, and other means of ensuring that decision makers learn from experience and are able to make adjustments as learning occurs.

In sum, the three prongs of sustainability include the following commitments:

• Protecting ecological integrity, ecosystem services, and natural capital—ensuring that economic activity is within ecological limits, maintains ecological integrity, and protects key ecosystem services; meeting the needs of the present without compromising those of the future; ensuring sustainable yield of renewable resources while preserving and regenerating the natural capital base; and using adaptive management to respond to the dynamic nature of the environment

• Ensuring that economic activity is consistent with the environment in which it takes place—developing true-cost prices and ecologically sensitive economic indicators that reflect the depletion of natural resources, internalizing environmental costs in market exchanges, pollution prevention to reduce wastes and externalities most efficiently, regulating emissions to reduce externalities, reducing subsidies that have harmful environmental consequences, and creating incentives for reduced pollution through legal mechanisms

• Pursuing intra- and intergenerational equity—ensuring nondeclining per capita wealth; remedying current social, political, and economic inequality and the consequences of past inequities; fostering self-government and participation by all, especially by those who have been marginalized; and strengthening community, civil society, and social capital

Incrementalism, Prices, and Markets

One of the central questions in environmental policy making is whether the changes that will be required to preserve the biosphere and use natural resources sustainably can occur through traditional legal methods, policy-making models, and ways of thinking or whether these changes require new paradigms, approaches, and political structures. It is possible that current legal and political conceptual frameworks are sufficient and that incremental changes can produce the kinds of adjustments necessary. But incrementalism assumes that ecological change and the evolution of ecological risks are linear and that gradual policy adjustment and accommodation are sufficient. If we were to choose the incremental route, we would need to begin now, with tools such as life-cycle assessments, learn from our experience, and make midcourse adjustments designed to move in the direction of sustainability. The hope would be to build our capacity to make more effective policies so that as political demands create the will to pursue changes we are in position to embrace more ambitious policies that will ensure ecologically sustainable economic activity.

These approaches to framing some of the political challenges posed by climate change help focus attention on a key issue: can climate change be addressed effectively through some combination of markets and public policies or is a fundamental transformation to a new form of social, political, and economic organization required? It may well be that climate change requires such fundamental shifts in the way we produce and consume energy that nothing short of a radical transformation will be sufficient. Calling for a reframing of our conceptual frameworks and paradigms sounds compelling but it is also a risky way to talk about global environmental risks such as climate change because we may lose valuable time that could be used to begin the transition by trying to devise a radical restructuring of economic and social life. Our solutions may be inadequate, piecemeal, incremental, and ultimately insufficient but we will at least be making some changes in the right direction. Furthermore, a radical restructuring of society may take more time than environmental trends will allow. If we can begin to shift the direction of some of the most environmentally destructive practices immediately, then we will be in a better position to understand if sufficient policy innovation can occur within the existing discourse of industrialism to avoid catastrophic climate changes. The warning of climate scientists is clear: we have already begun to see climate changes; the question is whether we will be able to prevent the most serious possible disruptions from occurring.

This is also not a choice between markets and politics because most of the policy changes that are required to produce an ecologically sustainable energy system can be achieved by changing prices and market incentives. Economic and political pressure aimed at developing domestic fossil fuel sources may well be irresistible. They reflect a potent mix of goals aimed at protecting national security by developing domestic sources of energy and promoting economic growth through cheap electricity and gasoline. Making a major shift now toward energy efficiency and renewable energy sources, however, promises great benefits. Dramatically expanding efficiency efforts and the development of renewables would reduce greenhouse gas emissions and help reduce the threat of disruptive climate change. A major shift in this direction would also reduce air pollution, improve public health, and position US companies for economic opportunities in the future. A massive shift to renewable energy thus makes sense from the perspective of climate change, public health and air pollution, and also promises a long-term energy supply that enhances national security and strengthens the long-term economic sustainability of the US economy.

Although the challenges are real, transforming energy production is compatible, at least theoretically, with a variety of political motivations. For some, national security is the key driver. For others, ensuring the preconditions for economic growth and preserving environmental quality are paramount. Similarly, ethical arguments about our obligations to future generations or about improving the quality of life for those who currently live in poverty throughout the world can drive effective energy policy, just as can religiously rooted commitments to planetary stewardship. The way in which we produce and use energy permeates our lives and transforming its production and use will require a similarly broad set of actions. We are likely to fall short of the kind of transformation compelled by the idea of ecological sustainability and will also have to turn our attention to the great challenges of adapting to a less hospitable climate and a more constrained set of energy options. The sooner we take action, the more choices we will have to make that adaptation less painful and disruptive.

The Politics of Climate Policy

Some areas of policy are stable, characterized by incremental, marginal changes along a constant trajectory. Environmental policy has been much more uneven, though, with policy making occurring in fits and starts and with tipping points that produce abrupt shifts after long periods of inaction (Baumgartner and Jones 1993; Repetto 2007). The big changes in environmental policies in the United States throughout history have been the result of broad shifts in public opinion, often resulting from environmental crises and problems. Focusing events or crises that capture the public's attention are often thought to be required to overcome political inertia and the powerful interests that are threatened by policy changes. The Santa Barbara oil spills in the 1960s, for example, helped galvanize environmentalism. Similarly, the discovery of the "ozone hole" and television images of it in the 1980s pressured members of Congress and President Reagan to support the Montreal Protocol. There is no guarantee, however, that a crisis will prompt action. Even the shocking images of Americans struggling to survive Hurricane Katrina, which many assumed would compel support for climate change policies to reduce the threat of future catastrophic storms, did not provoke much policy response. It is exceedingly difficult to understand and assess policy developments when we are in the middle of watching them unfold. Future students and scholars will be able to explain climate and related policies during the first decade of the twenty-first century with clarity and insight. For the rest of us, we look for immediate indicators that suggest when we will be on the path to a more stable climate and a more ecologically sustainable world and for ideas on how to encourage that transformation.

Barring some technological breakthrough in energy that renders fossil fuels obsolete and replaces them with pollution-free sources, climate policy making will be a major policy priority for decades to come. As policy making evolves, a major element of that effort should be to craft policies that are carefully integrated horizontally, across related policy areas, and vertically, across levels of government. As we have argued, this is no easy task but it is essential to try to build on the many tentative steps we have already taken. Full or strong policy integration is still a distant hope, especially at the federal level, but integration is a matter of degree, not an all-or-nothing phenomenon. Companies and governments, for example, already employ life-cycle assessments, agriculture policy debates increasingly consider climate and energy concerns, and a number of states explicitly recognize the need to integrate climate, energy, and air pollution programs. Perhaps as knowledge of or experience with these efforts increases or diffuses to policy makers in other arenas, policy learning will occur.

One indicator of progress is whether policy debates tend to integrate a wide range of relevant factors rather than focus on the merits of individual options. If we continue to assess energy options without assessing their life-cycle impacts or if we ignore climate impacts when discussing energy independence, then we are likely to continue to enact policies that fail to develop effective solutions to the mix of problems confronting us. Integrative policy analysis helps us see more clearly the choices and trade-offs we must consider. It also makes the debate over options more complex and difficult, but, ultimately, more likely to lead us to design more effective policies.

A related indicator is whether we begin to see a shift in political discourse away from appeals to economic growth, low energy prices, and avoiding "economic harm." If climate and energy policy debates continue to begin and end with these reaffirmations, little will have changed. By contrast, if the discussion begins with the premise that we need to take whatever actions are required to secure a sustainable future and includes an honest assessment of how painful that might be, then the debate over what specific policies we should pursue will be meaningful. Similarly, if policy debates begin with the premise that we cannot afford to invest in conservation and more expensive alternative energy sources because other problems are more pressing, then climate change and energy security will be sacrificed, even though the failure to deal with these two challenges will make other problems all the more difficult to address.

Environmental protection imperatives clash with political imperatives in other ways. Environmental problems are typically long-term challenges, with causes that are rooted in well-established patterns and practices, with solutions that require similarly long-run thinking and action. These are major challenges for a political system famously dominated by short-term thinking and short-run incentives. Another challenge is that the benefits of environmentally protective policies often extend well into the future and the burdens of preventative costs and changes in behavior fall on current voters. Environmentalism is rooted in the idea of restraint, in ensuring that human activity remains within bounds set by ecological conditions and that the consumption of resources and production of wastes do not overwhelm ecosystems. By contrast, there may be no political value more universally embraced than the pursuit of economic growth and no presumption more pervasive than the idea that government's primary imperative, after national security, is an expanding economic pie.

Another indicator is how well the United States and other wealthy nations have been able to integrate the developing world in a global climate compact. Climate change will require emission reductions from all the major sources but before developing countries will place limits on their emissions, the United States and other industrialized nations will need to act first. If climate debates quickly turn to the argument that we cannot do anything in the United States because reductions here will be simply offset by increases in China and elsewhere, we will be deadlocked and the threat of climate change will grow unchecked. In the first decade of the twenty-first century, as the war in Iraq continued and the threat of Islamic terrorism hung over the United States, cutting oil imports was a powerful symbol of how to help insulate Americans from global forces they could not control. Calls for reducing energy imports and, to some extent, energy use itself are often intertwined with appeals to nationalism, independence, and autonomy. But serious action on climate change requires an alternative worldview, one that emphasizes our interdependence and that inextricably links Americans' future to that of the rest of the world. The more that energy policy is framed as an issue of us versus the rest of the world, the more daunting will be the task of convincing Americans to invest in renewable energy in developing countries or to help pay for the costs of adapting to disruptive climate events.

The vexatious characteristics of climate change, including the magnitude of the policy changes required, the complexity and interconnectedness of causes, the imposition of costs now to produce benefits in the future, and the inertia inherent in the policy-making process make progress toward policy integration particularly difficult. Evidence of growing climate crises, enlightened corporate and political leadership, and grassroots activism rooted in threats to local landscapes will all play a part in generating demand for an effective policy response. We cannot afford to fail, hoping instead that whatever partial and limited policy efforts we produce will reduce the magnitude of climate change and make adapting to an increasingly inhospitable climate seem possible.

Part of what has been missing in energy policy making to date is the political will to break through deadlocks by constructing significant policy compromises. Ronald Brownstein's (2006) political commentary nicely summarized the situation: "The key to greater energy independence isn't so much a scientific breakthrough as a political accommodation between the forces supporting more domestic production and those focused on greater conservation. And that won't come without the kind of hardball bargaining so far missing." Some decisions, such as a prohibition on building additional conventional coal-fired power plants and instead supporting only those employing the best clean-coal technologies available, are essential and, given the environmental costs of traditional coal combustion, no compromise is rational. But for most energy decisions, hardball bargaining is required. Every policy aimed at increasing domestic energy production, for example, should be matched by major commitments to improve efficiency and invest in renewables. We will need to employ all forms of current energy production and conservation technologies in order to meet national and global needs.

The obvious problem with this approach is that the partisan divide on energy and climate has widened, not narrowed, in recent years, primarily because Republicans have abandoned previously held positions on a range of issues. Just a few years ago, for example, leading Republicans voiced concerns about climate change and introduced numerous bills to address it. After a cap-and-trade bill passed the House of Representatives in 2009, however, Republicans attacked it for raising taxes and killing jobs, even though many of them had long supported the cap-and-trade approach. Indeed, climate change is now a litmus test in the Republican Party, with major figures backtracking from prior statements acknowledging that climate change is real or that it results from human actions.

Congressional Republicans have also decided that confrontation—not compromise—is a winning political strategy and now reflexively oppose anything supported by President Obama. For his part, Obama has made repeated efforts to strike the sort of grand compromise on energy outlined previously, only to be rebuffed. On issue after issue, he has offered concessions, only to see the opposition reject them as inadequate and instead demand even more concessions. After regaining control of the House of Representatives in the 2010 elections, Republicans see no need to negotiate with a president they believe is weak. For these reasons, the prospects for legislative progress appear dim.

The most admirable characteristic of environmentalism is its commitment to the future, to placing limits on our consumption of resources and generation of wastes so that the earth and its magnificent diversity will be enjoyed by those who come after us. It has embraced the idea of sustainability because of its promise to ensure that each generation takes care to ensure the ecological health and prosperity of succeeding generations. It is admirable not only because of its sense of responsibility for our actions and how they affect those who have no current political voice but because it is so infrequently found. The singular value that permeates so much of contemporary US policy making is our extraordinary willingness to burden future generations with debt that fuels our current consumption. Whether reflected in unfunded health care and retirement commitments, crumbling transportation infrastructure, wars financed not by tax increases but by tax cuts and borrowing, or in trillion-dollar bailouts to reckless financial institutions and individuals, a nearly fifteen-trillion-dollar-and-growing national debt is a stunning testament to our willingness to impose on our children and grandchildren the cost of living beyond our means. Climate policy clashes in dramatic fashion with the values that otherwise permeate our political economy. That mismatch may either spell the doom for securing a more ecologically sustainable world or it may inspire a change, rooted in climate policy, that can spread to other areas of our public policies. Let us hope it is the latter.

Notes

Chapter 1

1. Compared with corn ethanol, biodiesel requires much lower fossil fuel inputs because soybean crops require little or no nitrogen fertilizer. The market for biodiesel, however, is not expected to grow significantly because of high demand for soybean in food production and because biodiesel is currently from 50 to 90 percent more expensive than diesel fuel. Waste fat and oils could add as much as one billion gallons to biodiesel production (Paustian et al. 2006).

2. The US Department of Energy has spent almost $400 million on a variety of demonstration projects. Part of the research focuses on how to break down the cellulose: some processes use heat and others use enzymes and organisms. Another part centers on where the cellulose comes from. Switchgrass, a fast-growing grass found in the prairie states, is one option. Another option is a relative of sugar cane that grows without fertilizer and yields 50 percent more than corn and 100 percent more than switchgrass. Some researchers are working on converting corn stover—the matter left over after harvesting, as a source for ethanol. Algae is still another option; algal bioreactors are being developed that may be able to turn algae that are fed from carbon dioxide emissions of coal plants into rich algal crops that can be converted into biofuels or hydrogen (Tollefson 2008).

Chapter 3

1. The nation's energy intensity has been decreasing steadily because of technological innovation. The Bush administration's climate change policy was simply to continue that rate, setting the same target of a 17.5 percent reduction in emission intensity by 2012 (resulting in total emissions growing by an estimated 14 percent during that period).

Chapter 4

1. Hazardous air pollutants or air toxics include nearly 190 chemicals that threaten human health. Unlike the ambient pollutants, for which the EPA sets national standards for acceptable levels of these pollutants in the atmosphere, air toxics are controlled by placing emission limits on the different sources. These two different categories of air pollutants interact in complicated ways. Some air toxics such as toluene are also volatile organic compounds (VOCs) that contribute to ozone problems. Particulates may be coated with heavy metals and other toxic chemicals. Regulations that reduce emissions of the ambient pollutants may also reduce air toxics emissions and vice versa (US EPA 2007e).

2. Other studies have also heralded the benefits of the acid rain–emission trading program. A study by Resources for the Future concluded that the expected benefits of the program far outweigh the costs of compliance because of the flexibility it gives to utilities to find the cheapest ways to reduce emissions and to take advantage of trends in fuel prices and transportation costs. Industry groups estimated that the cost of reducing a ton of emissions under the traditional regulatory approach at about $1,500 per ton; the EPA's estimate was about $650 per ton. The actual prices of allowances available for purchase between 1993 and 1996 at the Chicago Board of Trade, where allowances are traded like other commodities, fell from $122 to $66 (Burtraw et al. 1997). According to a 1998 study of the president's National Science and Technology Council, the costs of administering the acid rain–emission trading program are lower than traditional regulatory schemes because it "eliminates the need to devise source-specific emission limits and to review control technologies and detailed compliance schedules." Lower costs are attributed to "cost reduction efforts and improved performance of scrubbers and changes in fuel markets"; it is difficult to estimate "future technological improvements, the more efficient use of existing technologies, and future economic conditions," but technological innovation, prompted by competition, seems to have fueled cost savings (National Science and Technology Council 1998, 93).

Chapter 5

1. H.R. 1424, the Emergency Economic Stabilization Act of 2008, Energy Improvement and Extension Act of 2008, and Tax Extenders and Alternative Minimum Tax Relief Act of 2008, which authorizes the secretary of the Treasury to establish a troubled assets relief program to purchase troubled assets from financial institutions, provides alternative minimum tax relief; extends expiring tax provisions and establishes energy tax incentives; and temporarily increases federal deposit insurance limits. The summary of tax incentives comes from www.energytaxincentives.org.

2. Information in this paragraph was previously published in Gary Bryner's "Challenges in Developing a Diverse Domestic Energy Portfolio: Integrating Energy and Climate Policy in the Western United States." *New York University Environmental Law Journal* 15 (2007): 104–105.

Chapter 6

1. Between 1991 and 1994, the EPA issued rules for gasoline Reid vapor pressure, tier I car and truck standards, cold temperature carbon monoxide emissions, oxygenated fuel credits, enhanced inspection and maintenance programs, the California pilot credit program, vehicle evaporative emissions, emission control diagnostics, clean fuels fleet, urban bus PM emissions, urban bus retrofits, enforcement of urban bus standards, revisions to motor vehicle certification procedures, testing protocols for fuels and additives, conformity of transportation projects with air-quality plans, reformulated gasoline, and onboard fueling vapor recovery controls. In 1994, the EPA issued a final rule for reformulated gas (US EPA, Office of Air and Radiation 1994).

2. See Section 209 of the act, which allows a state to "adopt standards . . . for the control of emissions from new motor vehicles . . . if the State determines that the State standards will be, in the aggregate, at least as protective of public health and welfare as applicable Federal standards" (42 U.S.C. 7543). Because there are no federal standards for GHG emissions from motor vehicles, the legal requirement was easily met. California also argued that the Supreme Court's ruling in *Massachusetts* v. *EPA* (549 U.S. 497 (2007)), which held that section 202(a) of the CAA authorizes the EPA to regulate GHG emissions, affirmed the EPA's authority to either issue standards or allow states to do so. Section 202(a) authorizes the EPA to issue standards for "any pollutant from any class or classes of new motor vehicles or new motor vehicle engines, which in his judgment cause, or contribute to, air pollution which may reasonably be anticipated to endanger public health or welfare" (42 U.S.C. 7521(a)).

3. The 1998 Transportation Equity Act amended the Intermodal Surface Transportation Efficiency Act (ISTEA) to extend the use of CMAQ funds in nonattainment areas. Metropolitan planning organizations, designated for each urban area having more than fifty thousand residents, must develop transportation plans that, among other things, minimize air pollution and coordinate their planning with transportation control measures included in relevant state implementation plans.

Chapter 7

1. What kind of land-use actions should be countable as an offset for GHG emissions has been an important international climate issue. Because of these challenges, the European Union Emissions Trading System does not allow offsets from agricultural practices. The Kyoto Protocol states that carbon sequestration resulting from replacing agricultural lands with forests can be used to offset emissions. Article 3.3 provides that "net changes in greenhouse gas emissions by sources and removals by sinks resulting from direct human-induced land-use change and forestry activities, limited to afforestation, reforestation, and deforestation since 1990" can be used to meet the commitments of each party to the agreement. Article 3.4 authorizes the parties to the treaty to develop additional guidelines and policies "as to how, and which, additional human-induced

activities related to changes in greenhouse gas emissions by sources and removals by sinks in the agricultural soils and the land-use change and forestry categories shall be added to, or subtracted from, the assigned amounts for Parties." In a subsequent meeting in Bonn, Germany, the signatories agreed that *cropland management, grazing land management,* and *revegetation* were defined as "eligible land-use, land-use change, and forestry activities" under Article 3.4.

2. A joule is a unit of energy, equivalent to the work required to produce one watt of power for one second. An exajuole is equivalent to 10^{18} joules. One exajoule is equal to approximately 948 trillion Btu.

Chapter 8

1. These cases should be distinguished from agency-forcing litigation brought by environmental groups that seek to enlist the courts' help in compelling government agencies to regulate GHG emissions or by industry groups that seek to block state regulatory efforts. The most well-known of these cases was the US Supreme Court's decision in 2007, in *Massachusetts* v. *EPA,* in which it ruled that under the CAA, the US EPA has the authority to regulate greenhouse gas emissions, that its decision to not regulate emissions was "arbitrary, capricious . . . or otherwise not in accordance with the law," and that it must do so unless it can demonstrate that "greenhouse gases do not contribute to climate change" or provide some other "reasoned justification."

References

American Association for the Advancement of Science. 2000. *AAAS Atlas of Population & Environment*. Berkeley: University of California Press.

Andrews, Richard N. L. 2006. *Managing the Environment, Managing Ourselves*. New Haven, CT: Yale University Press.

Associated Press. 2007. Bush Signs Broad Energy Bill. *New York Times*, December 19, A1.

Associated Press. 2011. Air Pollution off the Charts in Rural Wyoming. *Billings (MT) Gazette*, March 8. http://billingsgazette.com/news/state-and-regional/wyoming/article_8910eb78-49ae-11e0-bbc9-001cc4c03286.html.

Bachman, John. 2009. Appellate Court Tells EPA to Think Again about Ambient Standards for Particulate Matter. *EM*, May, 30–31.

Bachman, John, and Susan Wierman. 2008. Urgent CAIR Needed. *EM*, December, 6–10.

Barber, Benjamin. 1985. *Strong Democracy: Participatory Politics for a New Age*. Berkeley: University of California Press.

Barcott, Bruce. 2004. Changing All the Rules. *New York Times*, April 24. http://www.nytimes.com/2004/04/04/magazine/changing-all-the-rules.html?pagewanted=all&src=pm.

Barringer, Felicity. 2008. Flooded Village Files Suit, Citing Corporate Link to Climate Change. *New York Times*, February 27. http://www.nytimes.com/2008/02/27/us/27alaska.html.

Barta, Patrick. 2008a. As Biofuels Catch On, Next Task Is to Deal with Environmental, Economic Impact. *Wall Street Journal*, March 24, A2.

Barta, Patrick. 2008b. The Unsavory Cost of Capping Food Prices. *Wall Street Journal*, February 4, A2.

Baumgartner, Frank R., Jeffrey M. Berry, Marie Hojnacki, David C. Kimball, and Beth L. Leech. 2009. *Lobbying and Policy Change: Who Wins, Who Loses, and Why*. Chicago: University of Chicago Press.

Baumgartner, Frank R., and Bryan D. Jones. 1993. *Agendas and Instability in American Politics*. Chicago: University of Chicago Press.

Baumgartner, Frank R., and Beth L. Leech. 1999. *Basic Interests: The Importance of Groups in Politics and Political Science*. Princeton, NJ: Princeton University Press.

Begley, Laura. 2007. The Truth about Denial. *Newsweek*, August 13, 20–29.

Bennear, Lori Snyder, and Cary Coglianese. 2005. Measuring Progress: Program Evaluation of Environmental Policies. *Environment* 47 (2): 22–39.

Betsill, Michele, and Harriet Bulkely. 2003. *Cities and Climate Change: Urban Sustainability and Global Environmental Governance*. New York: Routledge.

Bezdek, Roger H., and Robert M. Wendling. 2006. The U.S. Energy Subsidy Scorecard. *Issues in Science and Technology,* Spring. http://www.issues.org/22.3/realnumbers.html.

Bohi, Douglas R., and Dallas Burtraw. 1997. SO2 Allowance Trading: How Experience and Expectations Measure Up (Discussion paper 97-24). *Resources for the Future,* February. http://classes.seattleu.edu/economics/econ468/green/Articles/SO2%20Allowance%20Trading.pdf.

Bosso, Christopher J. 1987. *Pesticides and Politics: The Life Cycle of a Public Issue*. Pittsburgh: University of Pittsburgh Press.

Bourne, Joel K., Jr. 2007. Green Dreams. *National Geographic*, October, 38–59.

Broder, John M. 2007. Bush Signs Broad Energy Bill. *New York Times*, December 19. http://www.nytimes.com/2007/12/19/washington/19cnd-energy.html.

Broder, John M. 2009. EPA Clears Way for Greenhouse Gas Rules. *New York Times*, April 17. http://www.nytimes.com/2009/04/18/science/earth/18endanger.html.

Broder, John M. 2010a. Obama to Open Offshore Areas to Oil Drilling for First Time. *New York Times*, March 31. http://www.nytimes.com/2010/03/31/science/earth/31energy.html.

Broder, John M. 2010b. EPA Limit on Gases to Pose Risk to Obama and Congress. *New York Times,* December 30. http://www.nytimes.com/2010/12/31/science/earth/31epa.html?_r=2&nl=todaysheadlines&emc=tha23.

Broder, John M. 2011. Obama Administration Abandons Stricter Air-Quality Rules. *New York Times,* September 2. http://www.nytimes.com/2011/09/03/science/earth/03air.html?_r=1&scp=1&sq=ozone%20rule&st=cse.

Brown, Anthony Cave. 1999. *Oil, God, and Gold: The Story of Aramco and the Saudi Kings*. New York: Houghton Mifflin.

Browne, William P. 1988. *Private Interests, Public Policy, and American Agriculture*. Lawrence: University Press of Kansas.

Brownstein, Ronald. 2006. Senator Could Play a Smarter Hand on Energy. *Los Angeles Times,* March 19. http://articles.latimes.com/2006/mar/19/nation/na-outlook19.

Brunner, Ronald D., Toddi A. Steelman, Lindy Coe-Juell, Christina M. Crowley, Christine M. Edwards, and Donna W. Tucker. 2005. *Adaptive Governance:*

Integrating Science, Policy, and Decision Making. New York: Columbia University Press.

Bryner, Gary C. 1987. *Bureaucratic Discretion: Law and Policy in Federal Regulatory Agencies*. New York: Pergamon Press.

Bryner, Gary C. 2000. Congress and the Politics of Climate Change. In *Climate Change and American Foreign Policy*, ed. Paul G. Harris, 111–130. New York: St. Martin's Press.

Bryner, Gary. 2007a. Challenges in Developing a Diverse Domestic Energy Portfolio: Integrating Energy and Climate Policy in the Western United States. *New York University Environmental Law Journal* 15: 73–112.

Bryner, Gary. 2007b. Congress and Clean Air Policy. In *Business and Environmental Policy: Corporate Interests in the American Political System*, ed. Michael E. Kraft and Sheldon Kamieniecki, 27–52. Cambridge, MA: MIT Press.

Bullard, Robert D. 1994. *Dumping in Dixie: Race, Class, and Environmental Quality*. Boulder, CO: Westview.

Burning through Oil. 2008. *New York Times*, April 20.

Burtraw, Dallas, Alan Krupnick, Eric Mansur, David Austin, and Deirdre Farrell. 1997. The Costs and Benefits of Reducing Acid Rain. *Resources for the Future*. http://ideas.repec.org/p/rff/dpaper/dp-97-31-rev.html.

California Air Resources Board. 2007. Frequently Asked Questions: Climate Change Emissions Standards for Vehicles. http://www.arb.ca.gov/cc/factsheets/ccfaq.pdf.

Cambridge Energy Research Associates. 2009. Press Release, June 23. http://www.cera.com/aspx/cda/public1/news/pressReleases/pressReleaseDetails.aspx?CID=10429.

Carbontrader. 2002. Investor Coalition Finds U.S. Corporations Face Multi-Billion Dollar Risk from Climate Change: Not Adequately Addressed by Boards, Investors, April 18. www.thecarbontrader.com/news124.007.htm.

Carey, John. 2004. Global Warming. *Business Week*, August 16, 69.

Center for Climate and Energy Solutions. 2012. Ethanol. http://www.c2es.org/technology/factsheet/Ethanol.

Chameides, William, and Michael Oppenheimer. 2008. Carbon Trading over Taxes. In *State of the Planet 2008–2009*, ed. Donald Kennedy, John Holdren, Janez Potocnik, and Daniel Cleary, 193–194. Washington, DC: Island Press.

Clayton, Mark. 2007. As Bush Signs Energy Bill, New Issues Come to the Fore. *Christian Science Monitor*, December 20, 2.

Clean Air Task Force. 2001. *Unfinished Business: Why the Acid Rain Problem Is Not Solved*. A Clear the Air Report. Boston: Clean Air Task Force.

Cleaning Up. 2007. *The Economist*, June 2, 13.

Columbia Daily Tribune. 2008. Congress Pulls the Plug on Incandescents. *Energy Central*, January 7. http://www.energycentral.com/center/news.

Congressional Quarterly. 2006. Energy Overhaul Includes Many Bush Priorities—but not ANWR. *2005 CQ Almanac*, 8-3. Washington, DC: CQ Press.

Conlan, Timothy. 1998. *From New Federalism to Devolution*. Washington, DC: Brookings Institution.

Costanza, Robert, et al. 1997. The Value of the World's Ecosystem Services and Natural Capital. *Nature* 387 (May 15): 253–260.

Crandall, Robert W. 2008. Are Higher Vehicle Fuel-Economy Standards Good Energy Policy? CQ Researcher, January 4. http://photo.pds.org: 5012/cqresearcher/document.php?id=cqresrre2008010406.

Daily, Gretchen C., ed. 1997. *Nature's Services: Societal Dependence on Natural Ecosystems*. Washington, DC: Island Press.

Daniels, Alex. 1995. Tempest in a Tailpipe. *Governing*, February, 37–38.

Danish, Kyle. 2009. Climate Change Policy Update, April 6. http://www.vnf.com/news-policyupdates-349.html.

Davies, J. Clarence, and Jan Mazurek. 1998. *Pollution Control in the United States: Evaluating the System*. Washington, DC: Resources for the Future.

Davis, Bob, and Douglas Belkin. 2008. Food Inflation, Riots Spark Worries for World Leaders. *Wall Street Journal*, April 14: A1.

Davis, Charles E. 2011. The Politics of Fracking: Regulating Natural Gas Drilling Practices in Colorado and Texas. Paper presented at the Annual Meeting of the Western Political Science Association, San Antonio, TX, April 19.

Davis, Sandra. 2011. Federalism, Renewable Energy, and the Qwest for Expanded Electricity. Paper presented at the 2011 Western Energy Policy Conference, Boise, Idaho, August.

DeCicco, John M. 2009. Addressing Biofuel GHG Emissions in the Context of a Fossil-Based Carbon Cap. Discussion paper prepared for the Environmental Defense Fund. University of Michigan, School of Natural Resources and Environment, Ann Arbor. http://hdl.handle.net/2027.42/76029.

Deffeyes, Kenneth. 2005. *Beyond Oil: The View from Hubbert's Peak*. New York: Hill and Wang.

Dietz, Simon, Dennis Anderson, Nicholas Stern, Chris Taylor, and Dimitri Zenghelis. 2007. Right for the Right Reasons: A Final Rejoinder on the Stern Review. *World Economy* 8: 229–258. http://personal.lse.ac.uk/dietzs/Right%20for%20the%20right%20reasons.pdf.

DiMento, Joseph, and Pamela Doughman, eds. 2007. *Climate Change: What It Means for Us, Our Children, and Our Grandchildren*. Cambridge, MA: MIT Press.

Downs, Anthony. 1994. *New Visions for Metropolitan America*. Washington, DC: Brookings Institution.

Duffy, Robert J. 2003. *The Green Agenda in American Politics: New Strategies for the Twenty-First Century*. Lawrence: University Press of Kansas.

Duffy, Robert J. 2011. Déjà vu All Over Again: Climate Change and the Prospects for a Nuclear Power Renaissance. *Environmental Politics* 20 (5): 668–686.

Easterbrook, Greg. 1995. *A Moment on the Earth: The Coming Age of Environmental Optimism.* New York: Viking.

Eckerberg, Katarina, et al. 2009. Institutional Analysis of Energy and Agriculture. In *Environmental Policy Integration in Practice: Shaping Institutions for Learning*, ed. Mans Nilsson and Katarina Eckerberg, 111–136. Sterling, VA: Earthscan.

Eilperin, Juliet. 2004. EPA's Wording Found to Mirror Industry's. *Washington Post*, September 22, A29.

Eilperin, Juliet. 2007. Warming Draws Environmentalists into Environmental Fold. *Washington Post*, August 8, A3.

Enviro News. 2009. Four New Coal Plants with CCS Technology for Britain, April 24. http://www.enviro-news.com/news/four_new_coal_plants_with_ccs_technology_for_britain.html.

Environmental Defense. 2008. The Cap and Trade Success Story. http://apps.edf.org/page.cfm?tagID=1085.

Environmental Working Group. 2011. Farm Subsidy Database: United State Summary Information. http://farm.ewg.org/region.php?fips=00000&progcode=total&yr=2009.

Fahrenthold, David A. 2009. Caps, Trades and Offsets: Can Climate Plan Work? *Washington Post*, May 26.

Fargione, Joseph, Jason Hill, David Tilman, Stephen Polasky, and Peter Hawthorne. 2008. Land Clearing and the Biofuel Carbon Debt. *Science* 319: 1235–1237.

Fialka, John J., and Greg Hitt. 2007. Roadblocks Remain to Energy Bill. *Wall Street Journal*, December 3, A4.

Field, Christopher B., J. Elliott Campbell, and David B. Lobell. 2007. Biomass Energy: The Scale of the Potential Resource. *Trends in Ecology & Evolution* 23 (2): 65–72.

Fiorino, Daniel J. 2006. *The New Environmental Regulation.* Cambridge, MA: MIT Press.

Fischer, Frank. 2003. *Reframing Public Policy: Discursive Politics and Deliberative Practices.* New York: Oxford University Press.

Flint, Anthony. 2006. *This Land: The Battle over Sprawl and the Future of America.* Baltimore: Johns Hopkins University Press.

Frank, Paolo, and Frieder Rubik. 2000. *Life Cycle Assessment in Industry and Business.* Berlin: Springer.

Friedman, Thomas L. 2006a. Let's (Third) Party. *New York Times*, May 3. http://www.nytimes.com/2006/05/03/opinion/03friedman.html?scp=1&sq=Friedman%20lets%20third%20party&st=cse.

Friedman, Thomas L. 2006b. A Million Manhattan Projects. *New York Times*, May 24. http://www.nytimes.com/2006/05/24/opinion/24friedman.html?scp=1&sq=friedman%20a%20million%20manhattan%20projects&st=cse.

Friedman, Thomas L. 2008. *Hot, Flat, and Crowded.* New York: Farrar, Strauss and Giroux.

The Frugal Cornucopian. 2008. *The Economist,* September 4.

Galik, Christopher, et al. 2009. *Integrating Biofuels into Comprehensive Climate Policy: An Overview of Biofuels Policy Options.* Duke University, Nicholas School of the Environment, Durham, NC.

Gardner, Gerald T., and Paul C. Stern. 2008. The Short List: The Most Effective Actions U.S. Households Can Take to Curb Climate Change. *Environment* (September–October): 12–24.

Gardner, Timothy. 2008. Alaska Town Sues 24 Energy Companies on Climate Change. *Reuters/Guardian,* February 27. http://www.sqwalk.com/blog2008/001242.html#gardner.

Geiser, Ken. 2004. Pollution Prevention. In *Environmental Governance Reconsidered: Challenges, Choices, and Opportunities,* ed. Robert F. Durant, Daniel J. Fiorino, and Rosemary O'Leary, 427–454. Cambridge, MA: MIT Press.

Gingrich, Newt. 2009. Our Tanks Are on Full. *Newsweek,* April 13, 43.

Golkany, Indur M. 1999. *Clearing the Air: The Real Story of the War Air Pollution.* Washington, DC: Cato Institute.

Goodstein, David. 2004. *Out of Gas: The End of the Age of Oil.* New York: W. W. Norton.

Griscom, Amanda. 2002. In Good Company: Cutting Emissions to Raise Profits. *Grist Magazine,* July 31. http://grist.org/business-technology/griscom-emissions1.

Hall, P. 1993. Policy Paradigms, Social Learning and the State: The Case of Economic Policy in Britain. *Comparative Politics* 25: 275–296.

Hansen, James E. 2005. Is There Still Time to Avoid "Dangerous Anthropogenic Interference" with Global Climate? Presentation at the American Geophysical Union, San Francisco, December 6.

Harris, Gardner. 2007. Surgeon General Sees 4 Year Term as Compromised. *New York Times,* July 11. http://www.nytimes.com/2007/07/11/washington/11surgeon.html?pagewanted=all.

Hawkins, David. 2000. *Memorandum to Environmental Groups.* Washington, DC: Natural Resources Defense Council.

Hawkins, David, and George Peridas. 2007, March. *No Time Like the Present: NRDC's Response to MIT's "Future of Coal" Report.* NRDC, Washington, DC.

Heinberg, Richard. 2005. *The Party's Over: Oil, War, and the Fate of Industrial Societies.* Gabriola Island, British Columbia, Canada: New Society Publishers.

Hempel, Lamont C. 1999. Conceptual and Analytic Challenges in Building Sustainable Communities. In *Towards Sustainable Communities: Transition and Transformations in Environmental Policies,* ed. Daniel A. Mazmanian and Michael E. Kraft, 43–74. Cambridge, MA: MIT Press.

Hirsh, Michael. 2009. The Lioness in Spring. *Newsweek,* April 13, 46–47.

Holdren, John P. 2001. The Energy-Climate Challenge: Issues for the New U.S. Administration. *Environment* 43 (1): 8–18.

Holdren, John P. 2007. Meeting the Intertwined Challenges of Energy and Environment. Speech before the American Association for the Advancement of Science, Washington, DC, October 17. http://www.aaas.org/news/releases/2007/media/1029barnard_holdren_ppt.pdf.

Howarth, Robert W., Renee Santoro, and Anthony Ingraffea. 2011. Methane and the Greenhouse Gas Footprint of Natural Gas from Shale Formations. *Climactic Change Letters.* DOI 10.1007/s10584-011-0061-5. http://www.springer.com/about+springer/media/springer+select?SGWID=0-11001-6-1128722-0.

Huber, Peter W., and Mark P. Mills. 2005. *The Bottomless Well: The Twilight of Fuel, the Virtue of Waste, and Why We Will Never Run Out of Energy.* New York: Basic Books.

Hughes, Siobhan. 2008. EPA to Loosen Controls on Power-Plant Pollution. *Wall Street Journal,* October 27, A3.

Hunter, David, and James Salzman. 2007. Negligence in the Air: The Duty of Care in Climate Change Litigation. *University of Pennsylvania Law Review* 155: 1741–1794.

IAASTD. 2009. *Agriculture at a Crossroads: The Global Report.* Washington, DC: Island Press.

International Energy Agency. 2008. *Energy Policies of IEA Countries: The United States 2007 Review.* Paris: IEA.

International Energy Agency. 2009. *Implementing Energy Efficiency Policies 2009: Are IEA Member Countries on Track?* Paris: IEA. http://www.iea.org/textbase/nppdf/free/2009/implementingee2009.pdf.

International Energy Agency. 2010. *World Energy Outlook 2010.* Paris: IEA.

International Energy Agency. 2011a. *Clean Energy Progress Report.* Paris: IEA. http://www.iea.org/papers/2011/CEM_Progress_Report.pdf.

International Energy Agency. 2011b. *Energy Efficiency Policy and Carbon Pricing,* August. Paris: IEA. http://www.iea.org/papers/2011/EE_Carbon_Pricing.pdf.

International Union for the Conservation of Nature. 1980. *World Conservation Strategy: Living Resource Conservation for Sustainable Development.* Gland, Switz.: IUCN, United Nations Development Programme, and World Wildlife Fund.

IPCC. 2007. Summary for Policymakers. In *Climate Change 2007: Synthesis Report.* Contribution of Working Group III to the Fourth Assessment Report of the Intergovernmental Panel on Climate Change, November. Cambridge, UK: Cambridge University Press. http://www.ipcc.ch/pdf/assessment-report/ar4/syr/ar4_syr_spm.pdf.

Jamieson, Dale. 1994. Sustainability and Beyond. *Discussion Paper PL 02.* Natural Resources Law Center, University of Colorado School of Law, Boulder.

Janofsky, Michael. 2006. Democrats Offer Alternative to Republican Energy Plan. *New York Times,* May 22. http://www.nytimes.com/2006/05/18/washington/18dems.html?scp=1&sq=Democrats%20Offer%20Alternative%20to%20Republican%20Energy%20Plan&st=cse.

Jasanoff, Sheila. 1998. Science and Judgment in Environmental Standard-setting. *Applied Measurement in Education* 11 (1): 107–120.

Johnston, Jason Scott. 2008. A Looming Policy Disaster. *Regulation* 31 (3): 38–44.

Jordan, Andrew. J. 2002. Efficient Hardware and Light Green Software: Environmental Policy Integration in the U.K. In *Environmental Policy Integration: Greening Sectoral Policies in Europe,* ed. Andrea Lenschow, 35–56. Sterling, VA: Earthscan.

Jordan, Andrew J., and Andrea Lenschow. 1999. Memorandum in *House of Commons, Environmental Audit Committee, First Report and Proceedings* (Series 1999–2000). EU Policy and the Environmental Agenda for the Helsinki Summit, House of Commons, London.

Jordan, Andrew J., and Andrea Lenschow. 2008. *Innovation in Environmental Policy? Integrating the Environment for Sustainability.* Northampton, MA: Edward Elgar.

Jordan, Andrew J., and Andrea Lenschow. 2010. Environmental Policy Integration: A State of the Art Review. *Environmental Policy and Governance* 20 (3): 147–158.

Kahn, Matthew E. 2006. *Green Cities: Urban Growth and the Environment.* Washington, DC: Brookings Institution.

Kettl, Donald F. 2002. *Environmental Governance.* Washington, DC: Brookings Institution.

Klare, Michael J. 2004. *Blood and Oil: The Dangers and Consequences of America's Growing Dependency on Imported Oil.* New York: Henry Holt.

Klein, Rick. 2006. Energy Gaps Seen in Bush's Budget. *Boston Globe,* February 8. www.boston.com/news/nation/washington/articles/2006/02/08/energy_gaps_seen_in bushs_budget.

Kleinschmit, Jim. 2009, December. *Agriculture and Climate.* Institute for Agriculture and Trade Policy, Minneapolis.

Klyza, Christopher McGrory, and David Sousa. 2008. *American Environmental Policy, 1990–2006: Beyond Gridlock.* Cambridge, MA: MIT Press.

Kolbert, Elizabeth. 2006. *Field Notes from a Catastrophe: Man, Nature, and Climate Change.* New York: Bloomsbury.

Kotas, Jerry. n.d. *Renewable Energy Project Ideas for Supplemental Environmental Project (SEP) Settlements.* National Renewable Energy Laboratory, Lakewood, CO.

Kraft, Michael E. 2004. *Environmental Politics and Policy.* 3rd ed. New York: Pearson Longman.

Kraft, Michael E. 2006. Environmental Policy in Congress. In *Environmental Policy: New Directions for the Twenty-First Century*. 6th ed., ed. Norman J. Vig and Michael E. Kraft. Washington, DC: CQ Press.

Kraus, Clifford. 2007. Exxon Accused of Trying to Mislead the Public. *New York Times*, January 4, A1.

Kraus, Clifford. 2008. Alternative Energy Suddenly Faces Headwinds. *New York Times*, October 21.

Lafferty, William M., and Eivind Hovden. 2003. Environmental Policy Integration: Towards an Analytic Framework. *Environmental Politics* 12 (3): 1–22.

Lafferty, William M., and Jorgen Knudsen. 2007. The Issue of "Balance" and Trade-offs in Environmental Policy Integration: How Will We Know EPI When We See It? A Co-ordinated Action under the European Union's 6th Research Framework Programme, CITIZENS-2004-4-4.2-Governmance for Sustainable Development DG Research. Ecologic-Institute for International and European Environmental Policy, Berlin. http://ecologic.eu/projekte/epigov/documents/EPIGOV_paper_11_lafferty_knudsen.pdf.

Langworthy, Lucinda Minton. 2009. This Decision Only Adds to the Chaos of the PM Regulatory Landscape. *EM*, May, 33.

Layzer, Judith. 2006. *The Environmental Case: Translating Values into Policy*. 2nd ed. Washington, DC: CQ Press.

Leggett, Jeremy. 2005. *The Empty Tank: Oil, Gas, Hot Air, and the Coming Financial Catastrophe*. New York: Random House.

Lehmann, Evan. 2011. House Republicans Open a Major Budget Battle, Proposing Deep Cuts into Energy, Environment, and Climate Spending. *New York Times*, February 14. http://www.nytimes.com/cwire/2011/02/14/14climatewire-house-republicans-open-a-major-budget-battle-61602.html?pagewanted=all.

Lenschow, Andrea. 2002. Greening the European Union: An Introduction. In *Environmental Policy Integration: Greening Sectoral Policies in Europe*, ed. Andrea Lenschow. Sterling, VA: Earthscan.

Lindblom, Charles E., and Edward J. Woodhouse. 1993. *The Policy-Making Process*. 3rd. ed. Englewood Cliffs, NJ: Prentice Hall.

Lipsky, Michael. 1983. *Street Level Bureaucracy*. New York: Russell Sage.

Little, Amanda Griscom. 2004. Energy Cronies Clamor for Reward. Grist.com, November 10. http://www.alternet.org/story/20467/energy_cronies_clamor_for_reward.

Loper, Joe. 2009. Energy Efficiency Programs: Are We Ready to Measure Success? Presentation to Energy Cost Recovery Conference, May 18. http://www.narucmeetings.org/Presentations/Loper%20EE%20EMV%20slides.pdf.

Lowenstein, Roger. 2008. What's Really Wrong with the Price of Oil. *New York Times*, October 19.

Lyons, Daniel. 2009. I, Robot: One Man's Quest to Become a Computer. *Newsweek*, May 25, 67–73.

MacKenzie, James J. 1989. *Breathing Easier: Taking Action on Climate Change Air Pollution, and Energy Insecurity.* Washington, DC: World Resources Institute.

Martelle, Scott. 2009. King Coal in Court. *Sierra* (May/June): 36–43.

Massachusetts Institute of Technology. 2007. *The Future of Coal: Options for a Carbon-Constrained World.* Cambridge, MA: MIT. http://web.mit.edu/coal/ The_Future_of_Coal.pdf.

Mazmanian, Daniel A., and Michael E. Kraft. 2009. *Toward Sustainable Communities.* 2nd ed. Cambridge, MA: MIT Press.

McFarland, James R., Howard J. Herzog, and Henry D. Jacoby. 2007. *The Future of Coal Consumption in a Carbon Constrained World.* Laboratory for Energy and the Environment, MIT, Cambridge, MA.

McKibben, Bill. 2007. Global Warning: Get Up! Stand Up! *Earth (Waukesha, Wis.)* (Spring): 22–25.

Miller, Mark, and Jeb Barnes, eds. 2004. *Making Policy, Making Law: An Interbranch Perspective.* Washington, DC: Georgetown University Press.

Mouawad, Jad. 2008a. As Oil Giants Lose Influence, Supply Drops. *New York Times,* August 19, A1.

Mouawad, Jad. 2008b. Oil Prices Slip Below $70 a Barrel. *New York Times,* October 17, A1.

Mufson, Steven. 2008. Power Switch. *Washington Post,* January 20, F1.

Naik, Gautam. 2008. Biofuels Hold Potential for Greater Levels of CO2. *Wall Street Journal,* February 8, A4.

National Academy of Sciences, National Academy of Engineering, National Research Council. 2009. *Liquid Transportation Fuels from Coal and Biomass: Technological Status, Costs, and Environmental Impacts.* Washington, DC: National Academy of Sciences.

National Association of Clean Air Agencies [State and Territorial Air Pollution Program Administrators and Association of Local Air Pollution Control Officials]. 1999. Reducing Greenhouse Gases and Air Pollution: A Menu of Harmonized Options, October. STAPPA/ALAPCO, Washington, DC.

National Research Council. 2004. *Air Quality Management in the United States.* Washington, DC: National Academies Press.

National Science and Technology Council. 1998. NAPA Biennial Report to Congress: An Integrated Assessment, May.

Nilsson, Mans, Katarina Eckerberg, and Goran Finnveden. 2009. Discussion: What Enabled EPI in Practice. In *Environmental Policy Integration in Practice: Shaping Institutions for Learning,* ed. Mans Nilsson and Katarina Eckerberg, 137–161. Sterling, VA: Earthscan.

Nilsson, Mans, Katarina Eckerberg, and Asa Persson. 2009. Introduction: EPI Agendas and Policy Responses. In *Environmental Policy Integration in Practice: Shaping Institutions for Learning,* ed. Mans Nilsson and Katarina Eckerberg, 1–2. Sterling, VA: Earthscan.

Nivola, Pietro S. 1999. *Laws of the Landscape: How Policies Shape Cities in Europe and America*. Washington, DC: Brookings Institution.

Nordhaus, William T. 2008. *A Question of Balance: Weighing the Options on Global Warming Policies*. New Haven, CT: Yale University Press.

Olmstead, Julia. 2009. *U.S. Climate Policy and Agriculture*. Minneapolis, MN: Institute for Agriculture and Trade Policy.

Owens, Susan 2009. Foreword. In *Environmental Policy Integration in Practice: Shaping Institutions for Learning*, ed. Mans Nilsson and Katarina Eckerberg, xvii–xviii. Sterling, VA: Earthscan.

Paustian, Keith, John M. Antle, John Sheehan, and Eldor A. Paul. 2006, September. *Agriculture's Role in Greenhouse Gas Mitigation*. Washington, DC: Pew Center on Global Climate Change.

Pearson, Holly L. 2002. Climate Change and Agriculture: Mitigation Options and Potential. In *Climate Change Policy: A Survey*, ed. S. H. Schneider, A. Rosencranz, and J. O. Niles, 307–335. Washington, DC: Island Press.

Pennell, William, Joel Scheraga, S. T. Rao, and Gary Foley. 2005. Air Quality and Climate Change. *EM*, October, 8–10.

Perlak, R.D. et al. 2005. *Biomass as Feedstock for a Bioenergy and Bioproducts Industry: The Technical Feasibility of a Billion-ton Annual Supply*. US Department of Energy, Oak Ridge National Laboratory, Oak Ridge, TN.

Persson, Asa. 2009. Different Perspectives in EPI. In *Environmental Policy Integration in Practice: Shaping Institutions for Learning*, ed. Mans Nilsson and Katarina Eckerberg, 25–47. Sterling, VA: Earthscan.

Pew Center on Global Climate Change. 2001. *An Overview of Greenhouse Gas Emission Verification Issues*, October. http://www.c2es.org/docUploads/emissions_verification.pdf.

Pinstrup-Anderson, Per, and Anna Herforth. 2008. Food Security: Achieving the Potential. *Environment* (September/October): 48–61.

Pless, Jacqueline. 2010. Regulating Hydraulic Fracturing: States Take Action. National Conference of State Legislatures, December. http://www.ncsl.org/documents/energy/FrackingPub1210.pdf.

Plumer, Brad. 2012. Why EPA's New Carbon Rules Won't Have Much Impact for Now. *Washington Post*, March 27. http://www.washingtonpost.com/blogs/ezra-klein/post/how-much-carbon-will-the-epas-new-power-plant-rules-actually-cut/2012/03/27/gIQAuaTDeS_blog.html.

Poffenberger, Clara. 2000. NSR Enforcement Initiative—A Historical Perspective. *EM*, April, 25–31.

Pollan, Michael. 2008. Farmer in Chief. *New York Times Magazine*, October 12. http://www.nytimes.com/2008/10/12/magazine/12policy-t.html?scp=4&sq=pollan&st=cse.

Pope, C., and I. I. I. Arden. 2004. Air Pollution and Health—Good News and Bad. *New England Journal of Medicine* 351: 1132–1134.

Pope, C. Arden, III, and Douglas W. Dockery. 2006. Health Effects of Fine Particulate Air Pollution: Lines That Connect. *Journal of the Air & Waste Management Association* 56: 709–742.

Pope, Charles. 1998. Opposition to Global Warming Treaty Is Cropping Up in Spending Bills. *Congressional Quarterly Weekly Report*, August 1, 2107–2108.

Power, Stephen, and Christopher Conkey. 2009. U.S. Orders Stricter Fuel Goals For Autos. *Wall Street Journal*, May 19, A1.

Power, Stephen. 2011. EPA Rule Targets Mercury Pollution. *Wall Street Journal*, March 17. http://online.wsj.com/article/SB10001424052748703899704576204583816132832.html.

Prasad, Monica. 2008. On Carbon, Tax and Don't Spend. *New York Times*, March 25, 27.

Quirk, Matthew. 2008. Blowback. *Atlantic*, October, 30–31.

Rabe, Barry G. 2004. *Statehouse and Greenhouse: The Emerging Politics of American Climate Change Policy*. Washington, DC: Brookings Institution.

Rabe, Barry. 2006. *The Expanding Role of U.S. State Renewable Portfolio Standards*. Arlington, VA: Pew Center for Climate Change.

Rabe, Barry. 2008a. The Complexities of Carbon Cap-and-Trade Policies: Early Lessons from the States. Governance Studies Paper. Brookings Institution, Washington, DC.

Rabe, Barry. 2008b. States on Steroids: The Intergovernmental Odyssey of American Climate Policy. *Review of Policy Research* 25 (2): 105–128.

Reitze, Arnold W., Jr. 2009. Federal Control of Carbon Dioxide Emissions: What Are the Options? *Boston College Environmental Affairs Law Review* 36 (2): 1–77.

Repetto, Robert. 2007. National Climate Policy: Choosing the Right Architecture. Publication 07-19, AEI-Brookings Center for Regulatory Studies, Washington, DC.

Reuters. 2002. U.S. Renewable Energy Use Falls to 12-Year Low, November 21. www.energycentral.com/sections/weekly,cfm?id=3473696.

Richards, Kenneth R., R. Neil Sampson, and Sandra Brown. 2006. Agricultural & Forestlands: U.S. Carbon Policy Strategies, September. Pew Center on Global Climate Change, Washington, DC.

Richert, Catharine. 2007. Shaping the Farm Agenda. *CQ Weekly*, January 8, 114–120.

Roberts, J. Timmons, and Bradley C. Parks. 2007. *A Climate of Injustice: Global Inequality, North-South Politics, and Climate Policy*. Cambridge, MA: MIT Press.

Roberts, Paul. 2004. *The End of Oil: On the Edge of a Perilous New World*. Boston: Houghton Mifflin.

Rosenbaum, Walter A. 2008. *Environmental Politics and Policy*. Washington, DC: CQ Press.

Rosenthal, Elizabeth. 2008. Europe Turns Back to Coal, Raising Climate Fears. *New York Times*, April 23. http://www.nytimes.com/2008/04/23/world/europe/23coal.html.

Royden-Bloom, Amy. 2009. Thinking Globally, Acting Locally: States Take the Lead on Global Warming. *EM*, April, 6–11.

Ruth, Matthias, ed. 2006. *Smart Growth and Climate Change: Regional Development, Infrastructure and Adaptation*. New York: Edward Elgar.

Sabatier, Paul. 1988. An Advocacy Coalition Framework of Policy Change and the Role of Policy-Oriented Learning Therein. *Policy Sciences* 21: 129–168.

Salzman, James, and Barton H. Thompson, Jr. 2003. *Environmental Law and Policy*. New York: Foundation Press.

Schattschneider, E. E. 1960. *The Semi-Sovereign People: A Realist's View of Democracy in America*. New York: Holt, Rinehart, and Winston.

Schlegel, S., and T. Kaphengst. 2007. European Union Policy on Bioenergy and the Role of Sustainability Criteria and Certification Systems. *Journal of Agricultural and Food Industrial Organization* 5: 1–19.

Schlesinger, William H. 2008. Carbon Trading. In *State of the Planet 2008–2009*, ed. Donald Kennedy et al., 191–192. Washington, DC: Island Press.

Science. 2006. Evangelicals, Scientists, Reach Common Ground on Climate Change. *Science* 311: 1082–1083.

Schoenbrod, David. 2005. *Saving Our Environment from Washington: How Congress Grabs Power, Shirks Responsibility, and Shortchanges the People*. New Haven, CT: Yale University Press.

Sclove, Richard. 1995. *Democracy and Technology*. New York: Guilford Press.

Searchinger, Timothy, Ralph Heimlich, R. A. Houghton, Fengxia Dong, Amani Elobeid, Jacinto Fabiosa, Simia Tokgoz, Dermot Hayes, and Tun-Hsiang Yu. 2008. Use of U.S. Croplands for Biofuels Increases Greenhouse Gases through Emissions from Land-Use Change. *Science* 319: 1238. http://www.sciencemag.org/content/319/5867/1238.full.html.

Searchinger, Timothy D. et al. 2009. Fixing a Critical Climate Accounting Error. *Science* 326 (October 23): 527–528.

Shogren, Elizabeth. 2004. EPA Is Lax on Coal Power Rule, Report Says. *Los Angeles Times*, October 1, 1.

Siikamaki, Juha. 2008. Climate Change and U.S. Agriculture: Examining the Connections. *Environment* (July–August): 36–50.

Simmons, Matthew R. 2005. *Twilight in the Desert: The Coming Saudi Oil Shock and the World Economy*. Hoboken, NJ: John Wiley.

Simon, Richard. 2008. EPA Chief Grilled over California Rejection. *Los Angeles Times*, January 25.

Sissine, Fred. 2012. Renewable Energy R&D Funding History: A Comparison with Funding for Nuclear Energy, Fossil Energy, and Energy Efficiency R&D. RS22858 Congressional Research Service, Washington, DC, March 12.

Smith, Joseph. 2005. Congress Opens the Courthouse Doors: Statutory Changes to Judicial Review Under the Clean Air Act. *Political Research Quarterly* 58 (March): 139–149.

Smith, Mark A. 2000. *American Business and Political Power: Public Opinion, Elections, and Democracy.* Chicago: University of Chicago Press.

Smith, Rebecca, and Stephen Power. 2008. After Washington Pulls Plug on FutureGen, Clean Coal Hopes Flicker. *Wall Street Journal,* February 2–3, A7.

Sorkin, Andrew Ross. 2007. A $45 Billion Buyout Deal with Many Shades of Green. *New York Times,* February 26. http://query.nytimes.com/gst/fullpage.html ?res=9907E2DE1E3EF935A15751C0A9619C8B63.

Stern, Nicholas. 2006. *The Economics of Climate Change: The Stern Review.* Cambridge, UK: Cambridge University Press.

Stone, Deborah. 2001. *Policy Paradox: The Art of Political Decision Making.* New York: W. W. Norton.

Szold, Terry S., and Armando Carbonell. 2002. *Smart Growth: Form and Consequences.* Cambridge, MA: Lincoln Institute of Land Policy.

Taheripor, Farzad, and Wallace E. Tyner. 2008. Ethanol Policy Analysis: What Have We Learned So Far? *Choices* 23 (3): 6–11.

Tertzakian, Peter. 2007. *A Thousand Barrels a Second: The Coming Oil Break Point and the Challenges Facing an Energy Dependent World.* New York: McGraw-Hill.

Tilman, David, Jason Hill, and Clarence Lehman. 2006. Carbon Negative Biofuels from Low-Input. High-Diversity Grassland Biomass. *Science* 314: 1598.

Tilman, David, et al. 2009. Beneficial Biofuels—The Food, Energy, and Environment Trilemma. *Science* 325 (July 17): 270–271.

Tollefson, Jeff. 2008. Not Your Father's Biofuels, Nature (February 21): 880–883.

Union of Concerned Scientists. 2004. The Colorado Renewable Energy Standard Ballot Initiative: Impacts on Jobs and the Economy. http://www.ucsusa.org/ clean_energy/solutions/renewable_energy_solutions/the-colorado-renewable -energy.html.

United Nations. 2002. United Nations Framework Convention on Climate Change, Articles 2 and 3. http://unfccc.int/resource/docs/convkp/conveng.pdf.

Urbina, Ian. 2011. Insiders Sound an Alarm on Natural Gas Rush. *New York Times,* June 25. http://www.nytimes.com/2011/06/26/us/26gas.html?_r=1 &scp=1&sq=urbina%20+%20insiders%20sound%20alarm&st=cse.

US Conference of Mayors, Climate Protection Center. 2011. Mayors Leading the Way on Climate Protection. http://www.usmayors.org/climate/protection/revised.

US Congress, Congressional Budget Office. 2004. Fuel Economy Standards versus a Gasoline Tax. Washington, DC: Congressional Budget Office, March 9. http://www.cbo.gov/ftpdocs/51xx/doc5159/03-09-CAFEbrief.pdf.

US Congress, Congressional Budget Office. 2008. *Nuclear Power's Role in Generating Electricity*. Congressional Budget Office, Washington, DC.

US Congress, Library of Congress, Congressional Research Service. 2002. Issue Brief for Congress, Energy Tax Policy, August 23.

US Department of Agriculture. 2008. *2008 Farm Bill Side-by-Side*. Washington, DC: USDA Economic Research Service. http://www.ers.usda.gov/FarmBill/2008/Titles/TitleIXEnergy.htm.

US Department of Energy. 2010. Secretary Chu Announces FutureGen 2.0, August 5. http://energy.gov/articles/secretary-chu-announces-futuregen-20.

US Department of Energy, Energy Efficiency and Renewable Energy. 2010. Renewable Energy Data Book, August. http://www1.eere.energy.gov/maps_data/pdfs/eere_databook.pdf.

US Department of Energy, Energy Efficiency and Renewable Energy. 2011. Commercial Building Initiative. http://www1.eere.energy.gov/buildings/commercial_initiative/goals.html.

US Department of Energy, Energy Information Administration. 2010a. Annual Energy Review 2009. DOE/EIA-0384, August. ftp://ftp.eia.doe.gov/multifuel/038409.pdf.

US Department of Energy, Energy Information Administration. 2010b. Levelized Cost of New Generation Resources in the Annual Energy Outlook 2011. http://www.eia.gov/oiaf/aeo/electricity_generation.html.

US Department of Energy, Energy Information Administration. 2011a. Annual Energy Outlook 2011: With Projections to 2035. DOE/EIA-0383, April. Washington, DC: US Department of Energy. http://www.eia.gov/forecasts/aeo/pdf/0383(2011).pdf.

US Department of Energy, Energy Information Administration. 2011b. Energy in Brief: How Dependent Are We on Foreign Oil? http://www.eia.gov/energy_in_brief/foreign_oil_dependence.cfm.

US Department of Energy, Energy Information Administration. 2011c. Energy in Brief: How Much of Our Electricity Is Generated from Renewable Sources? http://www.eia.gov/energy_in_brief/renewable_energy.cfm.

US Department of Energy, Energy Information Administration. 2011d. Renewable Energy Consumption and Electricity Preliminary Statistics 2010, June 28. http://www.eia.gov/renewable/annual/preliminary.

US Department of Energy, Energy Information Administration. 2011e. Renewable and Alternative Fuels: Trends in Renewable Energy Consumption and Electricity, 2009. http://www.eia.gov/renewable/annual/trends/pdf/trends.pdf.

US Department of Energy, Energy Information Administration. 2011f. Renewable Energy Explained: Incentives. http://www.eia.gov/energyexplained/index.cfm?page=renewable_home#tab3.

US Department of Energy, National Renewable Energy Laboratory. 2007. U.S. Life-cycle Inventory Database Project. http://www.nrel.gov/docs/fy05osti/37661.pdf.

US Department of Energy, National Renewable Energy Laboratory. 2009. U.S. Life Cycle Inventory Database Roadmap. DOE/GO-102009-2881. http://www.nrel.gov/docs/fy09osti/45153.pdf.

US Department of Transportation. n.d. Intermodal Surface Transportation Efficiency Act of 1991: A Summary. http://ntl.bts.gov/DOCS/istea.html.

US EPA, Office of Air and Radiation. 1992. Implementation Strategy for the Clean Air Act Amendments of 1990: The First Two Years, November.

US EPA, Office of Air and Radiation. 1994. Implementation Strategy for the Clean Air Act Amendments of 1990, May.

US EPA. 2005. Clean Energy–Environment State Partnership Program, Program Overview. http://www.epa.gov/statelocalclimate/state/partner/index.html.

US EPA. 2006. Inventory of U.S. Greenhouse Gas Emissions and Sinks, 1990–2004. Executive Summary, April. http://www.epa.gov/climatechange/emissions/usinventoryreport.html.

US EPA. 2007a. Cap and Trade: Acid Rain Program Basics, August 14. http://www.epa.gov/airmarkets/cap-trade/docs/benefits.pdf.

US EPA. 2007b. Key Elements of the Clean Air Act, June. http://www.epa.gov/air/caa/peg/elements.html.

US EPA. 2007c. Clean Air Interstate Rule. http://www.epa.gov/oar/interstateairquality.

US EPA. 2007d. Regulating Air Toxics. May. http://www.epa.gov/air/caaa/peg/toxcis.html.

US EPA. 2007e. Heavy-Duty Highway Diesel Program. August 16. http://www.epa.gov/otaq/highway-diesel/index.htm.

US EPA. 2008a. Acid Rain Program, October. http://www.epa.gov/airmarkt/progsregs/arp/basic.html.

US EPA. 2008b. Clean Air Mercury Rule, January 5. http://www.epa.gov/oar/mercuryrule.

US EPA. 2009. Proposed Endangerment and Cause or Contribute Findings for Greenhouse Gases under the Clean Air Act, April 17. http://epa.gov/climatechange/endangerment.html.

US EPA. 2010a. Fact Sheet: Proposal to Revise the National Ambient Air Quality Standard for Ozone, January 6. http://www.epa.gov/air/ozonepollution/pdfs/fs20100106std.pdf.

US EPA. 2010b. Briefing on Hydrofracking for Robert A. Sussman, January 27. http://www.nytimes.com/interactive/2011/02/27/us/natural-gas-documents-1.html#document/p1/a9895.

US EPA. 2011a. Air Quality Trends. http://www.epa.gov/airtrends/aqtrends.html.

US EPA. 2011b. Fact Sheet: Cross State Air Pollution Rule: Reducing the Interstate Transport of Fine Particulate Matter and Ozone. http://www.epa.gov/crossstaterule/pdfs/CSAPRFactsheet.pdf.

US EPA. 2011c. Fact Sheet: Proposed Mercury and Air Toxics Standard, March 16. http://epa.gov/airquality/powerplanttoxics/pdfs/proposalfactsheet.pdf.

US EPA. 2011d. Fuels and Fuel Additives: Renewable Fuel Standards. http://www.epa.gov/otaq/fuels/renewablefuels/index.htm.

US EPA. 2011e. Inventory of U.S. Greenhouse Gas Emissions and Sinks, 1990–2009. EPA 430-R-11-005, April 15. http://epa.gov/climatechange/emissions/downloads11/US-GHG-Inventory-2011-Complete_Report.pdf.

US Government Accountability Office. 2008. Advanced Energy Technologies: Budget Trends and Challenges for DOE's Energy R&D Program. GAO-08-556T, March 5.

Vanderheiden, Steve. 2008. *Atmospheric Justice: A Political Theory of Climate Change*. New York: Oxford University Press.

Victor, David. 2004. *Climate Change: Debating America's Policy Options*. New York: Council on Foreign Relations.

Vig, Norman J., and Michael E. Kraft, eds. 2006. *Environmental Policy: New Directions for the Twenty-First Century*. Washington, DC: CQ Press.

Vine, Edward L. 2003. Using Energy Efficiency to Achieve Air Quality Compliance. *EM*, May, 30–34.

Vlasic, Bill. 2011a. Car Makers Back Strict New Rules for Gas Mileage. *New York Times*, July 28. http://www.nytimes.com/2011/07/29/business/carmakers-back-strict-new-rules-for-gas-mileage.html?_r=1&emc=eta1.

Vlasic, Bill. 2011b. Obama Reveals Details of Gas Mileage Rules. *New York Times*, July 29. http://www.nytimes.com/2011/07/30/business/energy-environment/obama-reveals-details-of-gas-mileage-rules.html?emc=eta1.

Wald, Matthew. 2007. Calculating Energy Bill's Real Figures. *New York Times*, December 14, D1.

Wald, Matthew. 2012. Nuclear Power's Death Somewhat Exaggerated. *New York Times*, April 10. http://www.nytimes.com/2012/04/11/business/energy-environment/nuclear-powers-death-somewhat-exaggerated.html?_r=1.

Weber, Christopher, and H. Scott Matthews. 2008. Food Miles and the Relative Climate Impacts of Food Choices in the United States. *Environmental Science & Technology* 42: 3508–3513.

Weisman, Jonathan, and Siobhan Hughes. 2009. U.S. in Historic Shift on CO2. *Wall Street Journal*, April 18/19, A1.

Weiss, Dan and John Kinsman. 2008. The CAIR Vacatur Raises Uncertainty in the Power Generation Industry. *EM*, December, 11–13.

White, Joseph B. 2008a. Next Car Debate: Total Miles Driven. *Wall Street Journal*, February 5, D2.

White, Joseph B. 2008b. Why the Gasoline Engine Isn't Going Away Any Time Soon. *Wall Street Journal*, September 15, R1.

Wilson, Ken. 2008. Boulder Boosts Smart Grid. *EnergyBiz* (May/June), 106.

Wise, Marshall, Katherine Calvin, Allison Thompson, Leon Clarke, Benjamin Bond-Lamberty, Ronald Sands, Steven J. Smith, Anthony Janetos, and James Edmonds. 2009. Implications of Limiting CO_2 Concentrations for Land Use and Energy. *Science* 324 (29 May): 1183–1186.

Woodhouse, Edward J., and Dean A. Nieusma. 2001. Democratic Expertise: Integrating Knowledge, Power, and Participation. In *Knowledge, Power, and Participation in Environmental Policy Analysis*, ed. Matthijs Hisschemoller et al., 73–96. New Brunswick, NJ: Transaction Publishers.

World Commission on Environment and Development. 1987. *Our Common Future*. London: Oxford University Press.

World Resources Institute. 2004. *The Greenhouse Gas Protocol: A Corporate Accounting and Reporting Standard*. World Resources Institute and World Business Council for Sustainable Development, Washington, DC.

Yarrow, Andrew. 2008. *Forgive Us Our Debts: The Intergenerational Danger of Fiscal Irresponsibility*. New Haven, CT: Yale University Press.

Zabarenko, Deborah. 2008. EPA Expected to Lose Calif. Emissions Suit: Documents. *Reuters,* January 23. http://www.reuters.com/article/2008/01/23/environment-climate-california-epa-dc-idUSN2365074620080123.

Index

Acid rain
  air pollution and, 13, 26, 29, 60, 62,
    66, 71, 77, 88, 90–93, 100, 202n3
  carbon dioxide and, 92
  clean air politics and, 90–93
  climate policy and, 13, 26, 29, 60,
    62, 66
  coal and, 71
  fish and, 62
  forests and, 63
  George W. Bush and, 94
  health issues and, 90–93
  mercury and, 71, 90–91
  nitrous oxide and, 90–92
  power plants and, 29, 62, 90–94
  regulation and, 202n3
  sulfur and, 90–92
Adaptive governance (AG), 20–21
Adaptive management, 20, 192
  climate mitigation and, 181–184
  litigation over, 184–188
Afghanistan, 132
Agriculture
  algae and, 169, 174, 201n2
  American Clean Energy and Security
    Act and, 166
  biofuels and, 4, 156–159, 162–174
  biomass and, 158, 159t, 165–174
  cap-and-trade programs and, 167
  carbon dioxide and, 156, 160, 162,
    165, 168, 174
  carbon sequestration and, 151,
    155–158, 162–169, 171, 176,
    203n1

carbon tax and, 171
climate change and, 155–176
Conservation Reserve Program
  (CRP) and, 174
corn and, 4, 174 (see also Corn)
cotton and, 157
crop rotation and, 162, 164–165
droughts and, 164
energy policy and, 155–176
enteric fermentation and, 44,
  162–164
Environmental Protection Agency
  (EPA) and, 160, 162–163, 173–174
erosion and, 156, 173–174
ethanol and, 5, 159t, 163t, 168–173
farm bills and, 3, 5, 157–158, 159t,
  172
feedlots and, 175
fertilizers and, 6, 26, 141, 156,
  160–168, 170, 174–176, 201nn1,2
fossil fuels and, 155–156, 160, 162,
  168–176
Great Plains and, 156
greenhouse gases and, 155–156,
  160–169, 172–176, 176
health issues and, 157, 163t, 164,
  173, 175
Kyoto Protocol and, 203n1
land use and, 155
livestock and, 5, 42, 44, 162–164,
  175
lobbyists and, 157–158
manure and, 44, 46, 160, 162, 164,
  166, 174

Agriculture (cont.)
  marginal lands and, 4, 162, 166,
    173
  methane and, 26, 42, 47, 156,
    160–164, 166, 169
  monocultures and, 175
  National Farmer's Union and, 166
  nitrous oxide and, 156, 160–164,
    167
  nutrition and, 158
  oil and, 6, 169, 171–175
  pesticides and, 26, 162, 164, 176
  policy and, 26, 157–163, 175,
    178–180
  politics and, 156–159, 166
  ranching and, 166
  regulation and, 167
  renewable energy and, 158, 159t,
    171–173
  rice and, 46t, 157, 160t, 161f, 162
  soil conditions and, 4, 10, 26, 44,
    46, 91, 156–157, 160–167,
    173–174, 176, 203n1
  solid waste and, 119
  Southeast Plains and, 156
  soybeans and, 157, 169, 172, 175,
    201n1
  subsidies and, 5, 14, 65, 157–158,
    165, 171–172, 175
  sugar cane and, 3, 201n2
  switchgrass and, 173–174, 201n2
  taxes and, 159t, 165, 171–173
  UN Food and Agricultural
    Organization and, 5
  US Congress and, 157–158
  waste and, 164, 169, 173–175,
    189
  wheat and, 5, 157, 169
Air pollution
  acid rain and, 13, 26, 29, 60, 62, 66,
    71, 77, 88, 90–93, 100, 202n3
  Association of Local Air Pollution
    Control Officials and, 29
  Clean Air Act (CAA) and, 14 (see
    also Clean Air Act [CAA])
  Clean Air Interstate Rule (CAIR)
    and, 94–95
  clean air regulation and, 75–79,
    88–100
  climate policy and, 2, 6, 9, 12–14,
    17–18, 21, 25–30, 34–39, 48, 51
  congestion mitigation and air-quality
    (CMAQ) and, 148, 203n3
  emission standards and, 37, 57, 59,
    93, 99, 146–147
  energy efficiency and, 98–99, 101,
    108, 112, 113t, 117, 125
  energy policy and, 26, 29–30, 35,
    39, 77, 79–80, 86–88
  EPA and, 14, 202n2 (see also
    Environmental Protection Agency
    [EPA])
  fragmented policies and, 89
  fuel switching and, 98–99
  greenhouse gases and, 2, 4, 28–29,
    71–72, 78–79, 81, 86, 88, 90–95,
    98–100, 177–178
  health issues and, 2, 17, 96, 100
  leaded gasoline and, 78
  life-cycle analysis (LCA) and,
    30–33
  Massachusetts v. EPA and, 89, 187,
    203n2, 204n1
  methane and, 27, 156
  motor vehicle emissions and,
    129–130, 141–143, 146–147,
    203n1
  national ambient air-quality
    standards (NAAQS) and, 93–97,
    112
  National Association of Clean Air
    Agencies and, 29
  new source performance standards
    (NSPS) and, 96–97
  new source review (NSR) programs
    and, 97–98
  nitrogen oxides and, 93–94
  oil prices and, 77
  ozone and, 26, 42, 89, 93–96, 113t,
    129, 147–148, 195, 202n2
  particulate matter and, 13, 27, 71,
    80–81, 89–100, 112, 129, 146,
    148, 202n2
  penalties and, 29

politics and, 75–79
power plants and, 50
regulation and, 17, 30, 57, 75–77,
  83–84, 88–99, 187, 192, 202nn2,3,
  203n2, 204n1
Reid vapor pressure and, 203n1
renewable energy and, 30 (*see also*
  Renewable energy)
research into, 100
scrubbers and, 26, 92–93, 98,
  202n3
state action plans and, 112–114
State and Territorial Air Pollution
  Program Administrators and, 29
sustainability and, 189, 194–195
transportation and, 129, 136,
  147–148
volatile organic compounds (VOCs)
  and, 147–148, 202n2
wind farms and, 30
Algae, 169, 174, 201n2
Alliance to Save Energy, 111
Alternative energy. *See also specific*
  source
  American Recovery and
    Reinvestment Act (ARRA) and,
    104–105, 110
  carbon dioxide and, 127
  challenges of, 101, 117, 119–120,
    127
  cost of, 120–122
  electricity generation and, 114–122
  Energy Independence and Security
    Act and, 103, 110, 134
  energy policy and, 101–103, 105,
    108, 114, 117, 122–124, 130–136
  greenhouse gases and, 101–102,
    109, 111, 114, 120, 127
  green power and, 67, 126–127
  industry innovations and, 109
  managing demand and, 109, 111,
    113–114, 117, 122
  renewable energy and, 102–105,
    111–127, 134, 171, 174
  research in, 123–124
  subsidies and, 103–104, 115, 117,
    119, 126, 132

tax credits and, 102–104, 114, 117,
  119, 122
transmission lines and, 122–123
American Cancer Society, 158
American Clean Energy and Security
  Act (ACES), 50, 166
American Heart Association, 158
American Recovery and Reinvestment
  Act (ARRA), 82, 104–105, 110
Andrews, Richard N. L., 52
Arctic Circle, 183
Arctic National Wildlife Refuge
  (ANWR), 54, 134, 137, 143
Association of Local Air Pollution
  Control Officials, 29
Autonomy, 38, 197

Baker, James, 48
Bangladesh, 183
Barber, Benjamin, 21
Biodiesel, 103, 134, 163t, 169, 172,
  201n1
Biodiversity, 10–11, 119, 156–157,
  191
Biofuels
  agricultural policy and, 156–159,
    162–174
  carbon sequestration and, 164–165
  cellulose and, 4, 201n2
  cost-effectiveness of, 171–173
  croplands and, 4, 6, 169, 173
  Energy Act and, 3, 103
  energy efficiency and, 158
  ethanol, 3–6, 12, 65, 103, 115, 134,
    136, 144, 145t, 159t, 163t,
    168–173, 201nn1,2
  Farm Bill and, 3
  food and, 4, 6, 162, 166–167, 169,
    172–174, 180, 201n1
  fossil fuels and, 156
  greenhouse gases and, 4, 174
  increased use of, 115, 157
  jatorpha, 4
  lobbyists and, 158
  low carbon fuel standards (LCFSs)
    and, 171
  methanol, 134, 172

Biofuels (cont.)
miscanthus, 4
policy mechanisms for, 3, 171–174
promise of, 168–171
renewable fuels standard (RFS) and,
103, 134, 171, 174
subsidies and, 136
sustainability and, 180
tax credits and, 3, 159t, 171–173
transportation and, 134, 136
Biomass
agriculture and, 158, 159t,
165–174
alternative energy and, 103–104,
114, 125, 127
gasoline and, 169–174
land use and, 169
research for, 3, 169–170
transportation and, 134
Bipartisanship, 52–53, 105, 134
Brazil, 3
British Petroleum, 109, 139
Browner, Carol, 34
Brownfields, 151
Brownstein, Ronald, 197
Bush, George H. W., 48, 77, 133
Bush, George W.
climate policy and, 8–9, 49–50, 56,
201n1
new source review (NSR) programs
and, 98
oil and, 133–134, 143
power plant emissions and, 94
terrorism and, 133–134

Cameroon, 5
Canada, 62, 130, 140, 150
Cap-and-trade programs
agriculture and, 167
Clean Air Interstate Rule (CAIR)
and, 94
energy efficiency and, 119
greenhouse gases and, 13, 29,
36–37, 41, 50, 57–62, 64, 66–67,
91, 94–95, 119, 167, 181, 198
legal issues and, 54, 60
mercury hot spots and, 95

requirements for effective, 62–66
sustainability and, 181, 198
Carbon Credit Program, 166–167
Carbon dioxide
acid rain and, 92
agriculture and, 156, 160, 162, 165,
168, 174
air quality policy and, 83, 89–90
alternative energy and, 127
climate policy and, 14, 17, 26, 29,
41–49, 53–55, 57, 63
coal and, 71–72
difficulty of removing, 29
energy efficiency and, 98–99, 101,
110
fracking and, 86
fuel switching and, 98–99
greenhouse gases and, 17, 26,
41–49, 53–54, 57, 63, 72, 75, 79,
89, 156, 160, 162, 165, 179, 201n2
natural gas and, 75
power plants and, 81–83, 110
regulation of, 55, 89–90
state policies and, 55
storage of, 81–82
trading programs and, 63
transportation and, 14, 129,
146–147
US emissions rate of, 43–44
Carbon monoxide, 93, 129, 146–148,
203n1
Carbon sequestration
agriculture and, 151, 155–158,
162–169, 171, 176, 203n1
clean coal and, 81
climate policy and, 14, 44, 65, 81,
83, 84, 151, 155–158, 162–169,
171, 176, 179–181, 203n1
investment in, 65
power plants and, 81–82, 84
research and, 82, 164
sustainability and, 179–181
Carbon tax
agriculture and, 171
climate policy and, 13, 26, 41,
57–62, 67–69, 88, 90, 109, 119,
122, 143–144, 171, 178–181

Congressional Budget Office and, 87–88
energy efficiency and, 109, 119, 122, 181
as market-based incentive, 109
nuclear energy and, 88
regulation and, 13, 41, 57–62, 67–69, 88, 90, 109, 119, 122, 143–144, 171, 178–181
transportation and, 143–144, 180
Carbon trading, 63–66, 68, 122, 178–179
Carmona, Richard H., 9
Carter, Jimmy, 132
Cellulose, 4, 201n2
Center for Climate and Energy Solutions, 4
Chafee, John, 48
Chernobyl, 87
Chevron, 139
Chicago Climate Exchange, 166
China, 49, 80–81, 114, 129, 142, 178, 186, 197
Chrysler, 146
Chu, Steven, 82
Chuckchi Sea, 183
Clean Air Act (CAA)
acid rain and, 91
climate policy and, 14, 27, 49–50, 57, 60, 62
energy efficiency and, 112
EPA and, 203n2, 204n1
greenhouse gases and, 77–78, 88–91, 93, 95–97, 99, 203n2
regulations, 89–90
sulfur and, 78, 91, 93
transportation and, 146, 148
Clean Air Interstate Rule (CAIR), 94–95
Clean Air Mercury Rule, 95
Clean air politics
acid rain and, 90–93
air pollution and, 75–79, 88–100
carbon dioxide and, 89–90
climate change and, 99–100
congestion mitigation and air-quality (CMAQ) and, 148, 203n3

electricity generation and, 75–79
energy efficiency and, 112
EPA and, 76–79, 88–100
fuel switching and, 98–99
goals for, 75–78, 89–95
health issues and, 75–79, 89–90, 93–94, 96, 100
lowest achievable emission rate (LAER) and, 97
Massachusetts v. EPA and, 89, 187, 203n2, 204n1
national ambient air-quality standards (NAAQS) and, 93–97, 112
new source performance standards (NSPS) and, 96–97
new source review (NSR) programs and, 97–98
policy integration and, 75–79, 88–100
state action plans and, 112–114
Clean car technology, 144–146
Clean Coal Power Initiative, 81–82
Clean Water Act, 52, 76
Climate change, 12
acid rain and, 90–93
adaption litigation and, 184–188
agriculture and, 155–176
air pollution and, 26, 28 (*see also* Air pollution)
assessing, 6–10, 48, 177, 180
cap-and-trade programs and, 13 (*see also* Cap-and-trade programs)
carbon tax and, 13 (*see also* Carbon tax)
clean air regulation and, 88–93, 99–100
Clinton administration and, 48–49
coal and, 99–100
communities affected by, 183–184
complexity of, 17
deaths from, 183
disasters and, 183
droughts and, 89, 117, 122, 164, 183
emissions target strategies and, 57–58

Climate change (cont.)
  energy efficiency and, 108–109, 117,
    122, 125, 127
  energy intensity and, 49, 102, 108,
    201n1
  energy policy and, 35, 182
  energy supply and, 39
  EPA and, 9
  ethanol and, 3 (*see also* Ethanol)
  flooding and, 89, 182–183
  Framework Convention on Climate
    Change and, 48, 177–178
  framing debate of, 66–69
  George W. Bush and, 9, 49
  global policy response to, 41
  greenhouse gases and, 11, 58,
    61–66, 72, 75–80, 87–93, 99–100
  heat waves and, 89, 183
  institutional innovation and, 34–37
  integrating mitigation and adaption
    for, 181–184
  Intergovernmental Panel on Climate
    Change and, 51, 182
  methane and, 27
  NASA and, 7
  nuclear energy and, 87, 179
  oil and, 89
  one-atmosphere approach and, 28
  policy evolution of, 47–51
  policy integration and, 27–28,
    88–99, 181–184, 188–192
  politics and, 15, 51–56
  power plants and, 79
  regulation and, 27
  research on, 6–9
  scientific consensus on, 6–9
  state/local initiatives for, 52–54
  sustainability and, 188–199
  threat of, 1–2, 15, 17, 27, 38, 177
  transportation and, 136, 143, 148,
    150, 152–153
  windstorms and, 183
Climate Group, 109
Climate policy
  acid rain and, 13, 26, 29, 60, 62,
    66
  adaptation and, 181–188

  adaptive governance (AG) and,
    20–21
  adaptive management and, 20, 192
  air pollution and, 2, 6, 9, 12–14,
    17–18, 21, 25–30, 34–39, 48, 51
  cap-and-trade programs and, 13, 29,
    36–37, 41, 50, 57–62, 64, 66–67,
    91, 94–95, 119, 167, 181, 198
  carbon dioxide and, 14, 17, 26, 29,
    41–49, 53–55, 57, 63
  carbon sequestration and, 14, 44,
    65, 81, 83–84, 151, 155–158,
    162–169, 171, 176, 179–181,
    203n1
  carbon tax and, 13, 41, 57–62,
    67–69, 88, 90, 109, 119, 122,
    143–144, 171, 178–181
  Clean Air Act (CAA) and, 14, 27,
    49–50, 57, 60, 62
  Clean Air Interstate Rule (CAIR)
    and, 94–95
  Clean Air Mercury Rule and, 95
  Clinton and, 34, 48–49
  coal and, 13–14, 25–26, 41, 44, 49,
    52, 55, 63, 65–66
  emissions reduction targets and,
    57–58
  energy policy and, 11 (*see also*
    Energy policy)
  European Community
    Environmental Action Programme
    and, 21–22
  evolution of, 47–51
  food and, 174–175
  forests and, 2, 4–5, 14, 17, 44, 62
  fossil fuels and, 26–27, 38, 43–44,
    51–54, 67, 69, 79
  foundation for, 7
  fragmentation and, 18–36
  Framework Convention on Climate
    Change and, 48, 177–178
  framing debate for, 66–69
  gasoline and, 3–4, 25–26, 46, 50
  George W. Bush and, 8–9, 49–50,
    56, 201n1
  Global Warming Solutions Act and,
    147

health issues and, 2, 9–10, 13, 15,
  17, 26–28, 38, 49, 51–52, 60
incrementalism and, 192–194
Kyoto Protocol and, 49, 53,
  183–184, 203n1
legal issues and, 18–20, 33, 48, 50,
  52–53, 57, 60, 64, 184–190, 192,
  203n2, 204n1
life-cycle analysis (LCA) and, 30–33,
  122, 195
local initiatives and, 53–54
mercury and, 27, 49, 94, 95
mitigation and, 181–184
Montreal Protocol and, 195
National Environmental Policy Act
  (NEPA) and, 32–33
natural cycles and, 7
natural gas and, 26, 41–46, 57
new source performance standards
  (NSPS) and, 96–97
Obama and, 27, 34, 49–50, 59
options for, 55–66
ozone and, 26, 42, 89, 93–96, 113t,
  129, 147–148, 195, 202n2
policy evolution of, 47–51
policy integration and, 178–192
politics and, 6–9, 27, 34, 48–56, 59,
  194–199, 201n1
Reagan and, 48, 52
renewable energy and, 29–33,
  37–38, 41, 50–51, 59, 68
safety and, 49, 52
scrubbers and, 26, 92–93, 98,
  202n3
state initiatives and, 53–54
subsidies and, 35, 38
sulfur and, 26–27, 42, 49, 62, 66,
  94
sustainability and, 14–15, 20, 33,
  188–199
US Congress and, 3, 8–9, 14, 18, 20,
  27, 29, 34–38, 49–53, 59, 63, 178,
  195, 198
US emissions rates and, 41–47
wind energy and, 30, 44, 57, 65,
  179
Climate Registry, 63

Clinton, Bill, 34, 48–49, 77, 98, 133
Coal
  acid rain and, 71, 90–92
  alternatives to, 72, 74–75, 84, 86,
    88, 96, 101, 105, 119–120, 126,
    152, 171, 174, 179
  carbon dioxide and, 71–72
  carbon sequestration and, 14 (*see
    also* Carbon sequestration)
  clean, 80–82, 92, 99–100
  Clean Air Mercury Rule and, 95
  climate change and, 99–100
  electricity and, 13, 44, 71, 73–74,
    79–84, 92, 96, 171, 179
  energy efficiency and, 71, 79, 81,
    98, 101, 103, 105, 119–122, 126
  EPA and, 96
  ethanol refineries and, 4
  FutureGen and, 81–82
  gasification of, 153
  greenhouse gases and, 71–100
  Indian, 103
  low-sulfur, 66
  methane and, 74
  nitrogen and, 80
  politics and, 52, 72
  Powder River Basin and, 66
  power plants and, 13, 25–26, 49,
    55, 63, 71–72, 77–84, 93–95,
    98–99, 120, 122, 147, 197, 201n2
  price of, 41, 65–66, 73, 83, 92, 171
  refined, 103
  subsidies and, 80, 103, 150
  sulfur and, 77, 81, 92
  supply of, 71, 79, 80
  synfuels tax credit and, 80
  transportation and, 73
Coal-to-liquids processing, 140
Cold War, 131
Colorado Plateau, 141
Combined heat and power (CHP)
  processes, 98, 109
Command-and-control regulations,
  20, 30, 92, 167
Common Sense Initiative, 19
Compact fluorescent bulb (CFB),
  110

Comprehensive Emergency Response, Compensation, and Liability Act (CERCLA), 186–187
Congestion mitigation and air-quality (CMAQ), 148, 203n3
Congressional Budget Office (CBO), 87–88, 142
ConocoPhillips, 139
Conservation and Renewable Energy Reserve, 29
Conservation Reserve Program (CRP), 4, 174
Construction operating license (COL), 86–87
Corn, 201n2
  energy efficiency and, 174
  ethanol and, 3 (*see also* Ethanol)
  fertilizers and, 170
  greater demand for, 173
  high-fructose syrup and, 175
  as high-residue crop, 162, 169
  livestock feed and, 5, 173
  monoculture of, 175
  price of, 3, 5
  stover and, 173, 201n1
Corporate average fuel economy (CAFE), 26, 57, 134–135, 142–143, 145*t*
Cotton, 157
Croplands, 203n1. *See also* Agriculture
  biofuels and, 4, 6, 169, 173 (*see also* Biofuels)
  conversion to grasslands and, 165–166
  cotton and, 157
  cutting down trees for, 65
  environmentally sensitive, 4
  ethanol and, 6, 65
  expanded, 169
  marginal lands and, 4, 162, 166, 173
  pastures and, 166
  rice and, 46*t*, 157, 160*t*, 161*f*, 162
  soybeans and, 157, 169, 172, 175, 201n1

sugar cane and, 3, 201n2
wheat and, 5, 157, 169
Crop rotation, 162, 164–165
Crude Oil Windfall Profits Tax Act, 102

Davies, J. Clarence, 18–19
Deepwater Horizon rig, 138
Demand side management (DSM), 112
Demonstration projects, 81–82, 84, 127, 160*t*, 201n2
Dockery, Douglas W., 100
Droughts, 89, 117, 122, 164, 183
Dupont, 109

E85, 170
Eckerberg, Katarina, 24
Ecological issues. *See* Sustainability
Economic issues
  adaptation costs and, 184–188
  American Recovery and Reinvestment Act (ARRA) and, 82, 104–105, 110
  biofuel cost-effectiveness and, 171–173
  cap-and-trade programs and, 13, 29, 36–37, 41, 50, 57–62, 64, 66–67, 91, 94–95, 119, 167, 181, 198
  carbon tax and, 13, 41, 57–62, 67–69, 88, 90, 109, 119, 122, 143–144, 171, 178–181
  carbon trading and, 63–66, 68, 122, 178–179
  climate mitigation/adaption and, 181
  coal prices and, 41, 65–66, 73, 83, 92, 171
  community relocation and, 183–184
  Congressional Budget Office (CBO) and, 88, 142
  corn prices and, 3, 5
  costs of alternative energy and, 120–122
  Crude Oil Windfall Profits Tax Act and, 102
  economic harm and, 196

embargo shocks and, 131–132, 142
Emergency Economic Stabilization
  Act and, 202n1
energy efficiency and, 101, 124 (*see
  also* Energy efficiency)
energy policy and, 14 (*see also*
  Energy policy)
fertilizers and, 6, 168
fluorescent bulbs and, 110
food prices and, 5–6, 162, 173–175,
  191
gasoline prices and, 132
grants and, 80, 104, 159*t*, 172, 178
growth and, 1, 9–12, 36, 49, 56,
  76–77, 102, 108, 129–132, 178,
  188–196
incrementalism and, 192–194
legal issues and, 186–187 (*see also*
  Legal issues)
nuclear energy and, 72
oil prices and, 6, 25, 38, 77, 120,
  123, 132, 138, 141–144, 152,
  171–174
poverty and, 10–11, 180–181, 183,
  189, 194
power plant construction and,
  87–88
Social Security and, 24
subsidies and, 5, 14, 35 (*see also*
  Subsidies)
sustainability and, 189, 192–194
tariffs and, 3, 171–173
taxes and, 139–140 (*see also* Taxes)
Economies of scale, 179
Egypt, 5
Electricity
  alternative energy sources and,
    114–122
  clean air politics and, 75–79
  coal and, 13, 44, 71, 73, 79–84, 80,
    82–83, 92, 96, 171, 179
  energy efficiency and, 71–73, 78, 81,
    83, 92, 98–99, 101–104, 108–122,
    125–126
  grandfathered plants and, 97
  greenhouse gases and, 71–74, 82,
    88–90, 96, 99

long-term investments and, 27
mercury and, 27, 81, 83
natural gas and, 84–86
nitrous oxide and, 81
nuclear energy and, 73–74, 86–88,
  179
power plants and, 71–74, 77–78,
  88–96, 99–100
renewable energy and, 72–74, 86, 99
sulfur and, 27, 81
taxes and, 80, 83, 87–90
transmission lines and, 122–123
US emissions rates and, 72–75
utility companies and, 83, 92,
  96–97, 126
Embargoes, 131–132, 142
Emergency Economic Stabilization
  Act, 202n1
Emissions. *See also* Greenhouse gases
  congestion mitigation and air-quality
    (CMAQ) and, 148
  continuing trends in, 183
  EU Emissions Trading System and,
    203n1
  Framework Convention on Climate
    Change and, 48, 177–178 (*see also*
    Climate change)
  inspection and maintenance (I&M)
    programs and, 147–148
  Kyoto Protocol and, 49, 183,
    203n1
  lowest achievable emission rate
    (LAER) and, 97
  reduction targets and, 57–58
  standards for, 37, 57, 59, 93, 99,
    146–147
  tailpipe standards and, 146
  teragram measurements and, 41,
    160
  transportation and, 129–130,
    141–143, 146–147
  US rates of, 41–47, 72–75
End-of-pipe solutions, 19, 29
Energy Act, 3, 139, 172
Energy efficiency
  air pollution and, 98–99, 101, 108,
    112, 113*t*, 117, 125

Energy efficiency (cont.)
  Alliance to Save Energy and, 111
  alternative energy and, 102–103,
    105, 108, 114, 117, 122–124,
    130–136
  American Recovery and
    Reinvestment Act (ARRA) and,
    104–105, 110
  benefits of, 101
  biofuels and, 3, 103, 115, 158
  cap-and-trade programs and, 119
  carbon dioxide and, 98–99, 101,
    110
  carbon tax and, 109, 119, 122, 181
  challenges of, 105–108
  Clean Air Act (CAA) and, 112
  climate change and, 108–109, 117,
    122, 125, 127
  coal and, 71, 81, 98, 101, 103, 105,
    119–122, 126
  corporate average fuel economy
    (CAFE) and, 26, 57, 134–135, 142
  Crude Oil Windfall Profits Tax Act
    and, 102
  demand side management (DSM)
    and, 112
  economic issues and, 101
  Energy Act and, 3, 139, 172
  Energy Independence and Security
    Act and, 103, 110, 134
  Energy Tax Act and, 102
  Energy Tax Incentives Act and, 103
  Environmental Protection Agency
    (EPA) and, 108–109, 112–114, 127
  ethanol and, 3, 103, 115
  Farm Bill and, 159*t*
  food and, 26, 155
  fossil fuels and, 3, 101, 103, 115,
    117, 119–127
  Framework Convention on Climate
    Change and, 48
  fuel economy standards and, 26,
    48–49, 57, 143, 145*t*
  fuel switching and, 98–99
  generating electricity and, 71–73, 78,
    81, 83, 92, 98–99, 101–104,
    108–122, 125–126

  government bonds and, 111–112
  greenhouse gases and, 101–102,
    109, 111, 114, 120, 127
  green power purchasing programs
    and, 126–127
  home appliances and, 103, 110
  improving, 101–114
  industry innovations and, 109
  legal issues and, 102–105, 110, 117,
    124–125
  life-cycle analysis (LCA) and, 30–33
  lighting and, 110
  managing demand and, 109, 111,
    113–114, 117, 122
  natural gas and, 105, 119–122
  nitrous oxide and, 98–99, 113*t*
  no-regrets policy for, 48
  nuclear energy and, 105, 123–125
  ozone and, 113*t*
  policy integration and, 26–27, 179
  policy options for, 108–114
  power plants and, 13, 29, 81,
    98–99, 108–110, 114, 120, 122,
    124–126, 179
  public benefit fund (PBF) and, 112
  renewable energy and, 13, 102–105,
    111–127, 134–136, 141
  renewable portfolio standards
    (RPSs) and, 104–105, 114,
    124–127
  state action plans and, 112–114
  subsidies and, 132, 178
  sulfur and, 29, 98–99
  SUVs and, 26, 142, 146
  taxes and, 102–104, 109, 111, 114,
    117–122, 126, 132
  technology shifts and, 17
  transmission lines and, 122–123
  transportation and, 26, 57, 134–135,
    141–144, 142, 180
  US Congress and, 102–105, 109,
    114, 117, 126
  US history of, 101–105
  wind energy and, 101–104, 110,
    114–122, 125–127
Energy efficiency fund (EEF),
  111–112

Energy Improvement and Extension
Act, 202n1
Energy Independence and Security
Act, 103, 110, 134
Energy intensity, 49, 102, 108,
201n1
Energy policy, 13
agenda status of, 39
agriculture and, 155–176
air pollution and, 26, 29–30, 35, 39,
77, 79–80, 86–88
American Clean Energy and Security
Act (ACES) and, 50
American Recovery and
Reinvestment Act (ARRA) and, 82,
104–105, 110
Carter and, 132
climate change and, 26, 35, 182
Clinton and, 133
coal and, 79
economic impact of, 14
Energy Act and, 3, 139, 172
energy efficiency and, 101 (*see also*
Energy efficiency)
energy independence and, 3, 103,
110, 132, 134, 195, 197
Energy Independence and Security
Act and, 103
Energy Information Administration
and, 71, 73–74, 84–85, 103–105,
114–117, 125, 130, 133, 138–139,
152
Energy Tax Act and, 102
Energy Tax Incentives Act and, 103
fossil fuel infrastructure and, 17
framing of, 25, 27
fuel economy standards and, 26, 57,
143, 145*t*
future of, 152–153
George H. W. Bush and, 77, 133
greenhouse gases and, 52, 77,
79–80, 86–88
managing demand and, 109, 111,
113–114, 117, 122
oil and, 26, 117, 130–137, 152–153
policy integration and, 178–179
politics and, 9, 37–38, 51, 132

production costs and, 26
Reagan and, 133
renewable fuels standard (RFS) and,
103, 134, 171, 174
renewable portfolio standards
(RPSs) and, 104–105, 114,
124–127
sustainability and, 194, 196–197
transportation and, 130–137,
140–143, 150, 152–153
Energy Policy Act, 80, 86–88,
102–103
Energy Tax Act, 102
Energy taxes, 49, 102–104, 120, 132,
202n1
Energy Tax Incentives Act, 103
Enteric fermentation, 44, 162–164
Environmental Defense Fund (EDF),
55
Environmental impact statements
(EISs), 21, 23, 30–33, 101, 109,
119, 127, 140
Environmental issues
acid rain and, 13, 26, 29, 60, 62, 66,
71, 77, 88, 90–93, 100, 202n3
adaptive governance (AG) and, 20
agriculture and, 4, 157, 164,
172–174 (*see also* Agriculture)
American Clean Energy and Security
Act (ACES) and, 50
Arctic National Wildlife Refuge
(ANWR) and, 54, 134, 137, 143
biodiversity and, 10–11, 119,
156–157, 191
bipartisanship and, 52–53
cap-and-trade programs and, 13, 29,
36–37, 41, 50, 57–62, 64, 66–67,
91, 94–95, 119, 167, 181, 198
clean air politics and, 75–79,
88–100
Clean Water Act and, 52, 76
climate change and, 1 (*see also*
Climate change)
command-and-control regulations
and, 20, 30, 92, 167
Congress and, 20
economic growth and, 10

Environmental issues (cont.)
  end-of-pipe solutions and, 19, 29
  energy efficiency and, 13, 101,
    109–111, 119, 122, 127 (*see also*
    Energy efficiency)
  energy intensity and, 49, 102, 108,
    201n1
  European Community
  Environmental Action Programme
    and, 21–22
  expired statutes of, 20
  federalism and, 36–38
  fertilizers and, 6, 26, 141, 156,
    160–168, 170, 174–176, 201nn1,2
  fish and, 62, 91, 94, 122
  forests and, 2, 4–5, 14, 17, 44, 62,
    137, 158, 159t, 160, 162, 165–166,
    174, 188, 203n1
  Framework Convention on Climate
    Change and, 48
  global warming and, 7, 26, 42–44,
    48, 54, 75, 90, 147, 155–156, 183,
    187
  grasslands and, 4, 162, 166, 174
  greenhouse gases and, 4, 12, 72 (*see
    also* Greenhouse gases)
  increased knowledge on, 8
  institutional values and, 1
  integration challenges and, 18–25,
    29–39
  integration debates and, 15
  legal issues and, 18
  legislation and, 20
  less-developed nations and, 10–11
  life-cycle analysis (LCA) and, 30–33,
    122, 195
  Maastricht Treaty and, 21
  marginal players and, 23
  market-based regulations and,
    19–20, 109
  Montreal Protocol and, 195
  national ambient air-quality
    standards (NAAQS) and, 93–97,
    112
  National Environmental Policy Act
    (NEPA) and, 32–33
  oil and, 32, 89, 140, 144, 195

  population growth and, 129, 143,
    149–150
  Project XL and, 19
  protection mandates and, 1, 35, 52,
    60, 77, 100, 137, 139, 189, 191,
    196
  public health and, 13 (*see also*
    Health issues)
  public opinion and, 9
  recycling and, 31–32
  regulation and, 19, 20, 75–77,
    83–84 (*see also* Regulation)
  Reid vapor pressure and, 203n1
  restraint and, 1
  Santa Barbara spills and, 195
  set-aside programs and, 113t, 162,
    166
  sustainability and, 19, 177–179,
    182, 185–198, 204n1 (*see also*
    Sustainability)
  toxic substances and, 10, 34–35, 71,
    94, 96, 141, 202n2
  transportation and, 136–141, 144,
    146, 149, 153
  US climate policy and, 48–55,
    59–64, 67
  waste and, 67 (*see also* Waste)
Environmental Protection Agency
  (EPA), 35
  agriculture and, 160, 162–163,
    173–174
  air pollution and, 14, 202n2
  Browner and, 34
  cabinet-level, 34
  Clean Air Act (CAA) and, 203n2,
    204n1
  clean air politics and, 76–79,
    88–100
  climate change and, 9
  coal and, 96
  Common Sense Initiative and,
    19
  energy efficiency and, 113
  federalism and, 36
  fragmentation and, 18
  greenhouse gases and, 34, 71–79,
    85, 89–98, 100, 202nn1,2,3

health issues and, 93–94, 202n2, 203n2
Massachusetts v. EPA and, 89, 187, 203n2, 204n1
mercury and, 96
national ambient air-quality standards (NAAQS) and, 93–97
new source performance standards (NSPS) and, 96–97
new source review (NSR) programs and, 97–98
nitrous oxide and, 89
power plants and, 94–98, 108
Project XL and, 19
Reid vapor pressure and, 203n1
state action plans and, 112–114
statutory framework of, 18
sulfur and, 89, 91, 96–97
sustainability and, 187, 204n1
transportation and, 14, 129, 134, 146–148, 203nn1,2
US climate policy and, 41–52, 56
waste and, 35
Environment and Public Works Committee, 35
Equity, 55
legal issues and, 186
sustainability and, 182, 189–192
transportation and, 203n3
Erosion, 156, 173–174
Estonia, 140
Ethanol, 12
agriculture and, 5, 159t, 163t, 168–173
coal and, 4
corn stover and, 201n2
croplands and, 6, 65
energy efficiency and, 3, 103, 115
Farm Bill and, 159t
fossil fuel inputs and, 201n1
integration challenges and, 6
need for policy integration and, 3–6
policy integration and, 3–6
regulation and, 6
subsidies and, 65, 136, 171–172
transportation and, 134, 136, 137t, 144, 145t

Ethiopia, 5, 183
European Community Environmental Action Programme, 21–22
European Union Emissions Trading System, 203n1
Exxon Mobil, 52, 139

Farm bills, 3, 5, 157–158, 159t, 172
Federal Energy Regulatory Commission, 35, 50
Federalsim, 24, 36–38
Feedlots, 175
Fertilizers
agriculture and, 6, 26, 141, 156, 160–168, 170, 174–176, 201n1, 201n2
chemical, 26
cost of, 6, 168
crop rotation and, 165
emissions and, 162
food and, 141
greenhouse gases and, 27, 49, 80, 129, 146–148, 162–163, 166, 174
increased yields from using, 170
natural, 156, 160–161, 175
natural gas and, 26
nitrogen, 156, 160–164, 166, 201n1
oil and, 141
petroleum and, 26
Finnveden, Goran, 24
Fiorino, Daniel, 19–20
Fish, 62, 91, 94, 122
Flooding, 89, 182–183
Fluorescent bulbs, 110
Food. *See also* Agriculture
biofuels and, 4, 162, 166–169, 172–174, 180, 201n1
cheap, 174–175
climate and, 174–175
decentralized system for, 175
droughts and, 89, 117, 122, 164, 183
energy efficiency and, 26, 155
ethanol and, 4
fertilizers and, 141
fossil fuels and, 26, 155, 175
greenhouse gases and, 26

Food (cont.)
  higher prices for, 5–6, 162, 173
  maintaining stable supply of, 157,
    168
  mercury and, 91
  monocultures and, 175
  processed, 175
  real cost of, 191
  riots and, 5
  specialty, 157
  sustainability and, 157, 168,
    175–176, 180, 191
  transportation and, 5–6, 26, 54,
    141, 155, 175
  UN Food and Agricultural
    Organization and, 5
Ford Motor Company, 145
Forests
  acid rain and, 63
  biomass crops and, 158, 159t
  climate policy and, 2, 4–5, 14, 17,
    44, 62
  croplands and, 65
  energy production and, 158
  environmental issues and, 2, 4–5,
    14, 17, 44, 62, 137, 158–162,
    165–166, 174, 188, 203n1
  greenhouse gases and, 160, 162,
    165–166, 174
  Kyoto Protocol and, 203n1
  sequestration and, 5
  set-aside programs and, 166
  sustainability and, 188
  transportation and, 137
Fossil fuels
  agriculture and, 155–156, 160, 162,
    168–176
  biodiesel and, 201n1
  carbon tax and, 13, 41, 57–62,
    67–69, 69, 88, 90, 109, 119, 122,
    143–144, 171, 178–181, 181
  Clean Air Act and, 91
  climate policy and, 17, 26–27, 38,
    43–44, 51–54, 67, 69, 79
  energy efficiency and, 3, 101, 103,
    115, 117, 119–127
  ethanol and, 3

  food and, 26, 155, 175
  generating electricity and, 72, 74
  global infrastructure of, 17
  greenhouse gases and, 17 (see also
    Greenhouse gases)
  health hazards of, 91
  increased production of, 8
  industry interests and, 9
  new source performance standards
    (NSPS) and, 96
  nuclear energy and, 86
  security costs of, 51
  sustainability and, 193, 195
  transportation and, 129, 141,
    152–153
Fracking, 72, 85–86
Fragmentation, 1
  adaptive governance (AG) and,
    20–21
  adaptive management and, 20, 192
  clean air programs and, 89
  climate policy and, 18–36
  Common Sense Initiative and, 19
  decentralization and, 23
  EPA framework and, 18
  expired environmental statutes and,
    20
  institutional innovation and, 34, 36
  policy integration and, 18–21
  pollution-control technology and,
    18–19
  single media focus and, 18
  US federal system and, 23
Framework Convention on Climate
    Change, 48, 177–178
Fuel cells, 81, 103, 134, 144, 145t
Fukushima, 86–87, 179
FutureGen, 81–82

Galik, Christopher, 168–174
Gasoline
  air pollution and, 78
  biomass and, 169–174
  blended, 134, 170
  clean car technology and, 144, 145t
  climate policy and, 3–4, 25–26,
    46, 50

emission standards and, 146
EPA and, 193
lead and, 78
price of, 132, 171–172
Reid vapor pressure and, 203n1
sustainability and, 193
taxes and, 142, 142–143
transportation and, 3–4, 25–26, 46,
  50, 78, 132, 134, 142–146,
  169–172, 174, 193, 203n1
US consumption of, 170
General Electric, 110
General Motors, 145–146
Geology, 38, 82, 85, 139
Geothermal energy, 114–117, 122,
  125, 127, 179
Globalization, 10, 158
  poverty and, 10
  terrorists and, 35, 133, 179, 197
Global warming
  agriculture and, 155–156
  climate policy and, 7, 26, 42–44, 54,
    183, 187
  politics and, 90
  shale gas and, 75
  transportation and, 147
Global warming potential (GWP),
  42–43
Global Warming Solutions Act, 147
Golkany, Indur M., 78
Goodstein, David, 152
Gore, Al, 48
Government Economic Service,
  182–183
Grants, 80, 104, 159*t*, 172, 178
Grasslands, 4, 162, 165–166, 174
Great Plains, 156
Greenhouse gases
  agriculture and, 155–156, 160–169,
    172–176, 176
  air pollution and, 2, 4, 28–29,
    71–72, 78–79, 81, 86, 88, 90–95,
    98–100, 177–178
  alternative energy and, 101–102,
    109, 111, 114, 120, 127
  American Clean Energy and Security
    Act (ACES) and, 50, 166

biofuels and, 4, 174
cap-and-trade programs and, 13,
  29, 36–37, 41, 50, 57–62, 64,
  66–67, 91, 94–95, 119, 167, 181,
  198
carbon dioxide, 17, 26, 41–49,
  53–54, 57, 63, 72, 75, 79, 89, 156,
  160, 162, 165, 179, 201n2
carbon monoxide, 93, 129, 146–
  148, 203n1
carbon sequestration and, 65, 180
  (*see also* Carbon sequestration)
carbon tax and, 13, 41, 57–62,
  67–69, 88, 90, 109, 119, 122,
  143–144, 171, 178–181
carbon trading and, 63–66, 68, 122,
  178–179
Clean Air Act (CAA) and, 77–78,
  88–91, 93, 95–97, 99, 203n2
clean air politics and, 75–79,
  88–100
climate change and, 58, 61–66
coal and, 71–100
congestion mitigation and air-quality
  (CMAQ) and, 148
emission standards and, 37, 57, 59,
  93, 99, 129–130, 141–147
energy efficiency and, 101–102, 109,
  111, 114, 120, 127
energy policy and, 52, 77, 79–80,
  86–88
enteric fermentation and, 44,
  162–164
Environmental Protection Agency
  (EPA) and, 34, 71–79, 85, 89–98,
  100, 202nn1,2,3
federalism and, 36
fertilizers and, 162–163, 166, 174
food and, 26
forests and, 160, 162, 165, 188
Framework Convention on Climate
  Change and, 48, 177–178
gasoline and, 146
generating electricity and, 71–74, 82,
  88–90, 96, 99
Global Warming Solutions Act and,
  147

Greenhouse gases (cont.)
  health issues and, 40–51, 71–72, 75,
    77–79, 89–93, 129, 177–179, 184,
    186
  hydrochlorofluorcarbons (HFCs)
    and, 42
  industry innovations and, 109
  integration and, 12
  Kyoto Protocol and, 49, 183, 203n1
  legal issues and, 48, 76–82, 88–89,
    91, 93–94, 184–185, 187, 204n1
  local initiatives on, 53–54
  mercury and, 27, 49, 71, 81, 83,
    90–96, 110
  methane, 26–27, 42, 44–47, 74–75,
    86, 89, 156, 160–164, 166, 169
  motor vehicles and, 129–130,
    141–147
  natural gas, 71–75, 83–86, 88, 91,
    96, 98, 179–180
  nitrogen oxides, 27, 49, 80–81, 83,
    89–99, 113, 129, 146–148 (see also
    Nitrogen oxides)
  nuclear energy and, 72–74, 86–88,
    101
  oil and, 7, 26, 89, 169
  ozone, 26, 42, 89, 93–96, 113t, 129,
    147–148, 195, 202n2
  petroleum and, 44, 71, 109
  plethora of sources for, 11
  policy integration and, 2, 12, 27–29
  politics and, 6–7
  power plants and, 36, 46, 53–56,
    86–96, 99–100, 151, 176
  reduction goals and, 53–58, 64–65
  regulation and, 2, 34, 38, 57, 64–65,
    141–144, 177, 179, 187, 192,
    202nn2,3, 203n2, 204n1
  scrubbers and, 26, 92–93, 98, 202n3
  state initiatives on, 53–54
  sulfur and, 90–92 (see also Sulfur)
  sustainability and, 188
  SUVs and, 26
  teragram measurements and, 41,
    160
  transportation and, 14, 129–130,
    141–153, 203n2

  UN Conference on Environment and
    Development and, 48
  US Congress and, 75–79, 82, 87–91,
    100
  US emissions rates of, 41–47, 72–75
  volatile organic compounds (VOCs)
    and, 147–148, 202n2
  White House effect and, 48
  wind energy and, 72
  World Resources Institute and,
    63–64
Greenhouse Gas Protocol Initiative,
  63–64
Greenhouse gas registry, 53
Green power, 67, 126–127
Green River formation, 140
Gulf of Mexico, 7, 138–139

Hansen, James, 7
Health issues
  acid rain and, 90–93
  agriculture and, 157, 163t, 164, 173,
    175
  air pollution and, 2, 17, 96, 100
  clean air politics and, 75–79, 89–90,
    93–94, 96, 100
  climate policy and, 2, 9–10, 13, 15,
    17, 26–28, 38, 49, 51–52, 60
  EPA and, 93–94, 202n2, 203n2
  fossil fuels and, 91
  future policies for, 182
  George W. Bush and, 9
  greenhouse gases and, 2, 40–51 (see
    also Greenhouse gases)
  Medicare and, 24
  national ambient air-quality
    standards (NAAQS) and, 93–97
  nutrition and, 158
  Obama and, 89–90
  politics and, 9, 75–79, 89–90
  retirement and, 178, 198
  sustainability and, 189, 191, 194,
    198
  tobacco companies and, 184
  transportation and, 129, 141, 145
  volatile organic compounds (VOCs)
    and, 202n2

Heat waves, 89, 183
Holdren, John, 17, 181
Home appliances, 103, 110
House Energy and Commerce
  Committee, 35
Hovden, Eivind, 22
Hurricanes, 7, 9, 139, 183, 195
Hybrid vehicles, 103, 134
Hydraulic fracturing, 72, 85–86
Hydro, 150
  alternative energy and, 101, 103,
    114–122, 125, 127
  climate policy and, 44, 57
  generating electricity and, 72–74
Hydrochloroflurocarbons (HFCs), 42
Hydrogen, 81, 134, 144, 145*t*, 201n2

IBM, 109
Incrementalism, 192–194
India, 80–81
Inspection and maintenance (I&M)
  programs, 147–148
Integrated gasification combined cycle
  (IGCC) facilities, 83
Intergovernmental Panel on Climate
  Change (IPCC), 51, 182
Intermodal Surface Transportation
  Efficiency Act (ISTEA), 203
International Energy Agency, 80, 102,
  110, 125, 129, 136–141
Inupiat, 183
Iran, 130–132
Iraq, 130
Israel, 132
Ivory Coast, 5

Japan, 86, 105, 142
Jatorpha, 4
Johnson & Johnson, 109

Kivalina, 183
Koch Industries, 52
Kraft, Michael E., 20
Kyoto Protocol, 49, 53, 184, 203n1

Lafarge, 109
Lafferty, William, 22

Landfill gas, 29, 44, 103, 119
Land use
  agriculture and, 12, 17, 26, 155–
    156, 167, 174, 189
  alternative energy and, 119
  Arctic National Wildlife Refuge
    (ANWR) and, 54, 134, 137, 143
  biomass, 169
  Conservation Reserve Program
    (CRP) and, 174
  factories and, 141
  incinerators and, 141
  Kyoto Protocol and, 49, 183, 203n1
  oil and, 54, 133–134, 137–141, 143
  patterns in, 148–150
  planning for, 17, 151, 180
  policy integration and, 26
  power plants and, 141
  regulation of, 182
  soil conditions and, 4, 10, 26, 44,
    46, 91, 156–157, 160–167,
    173–174, 176, 203n1
  toxic waste and, 141
  transportation and, 34, 130,
    148–151, 180, 189
  urbanization and, 148–149
  zoning and, 34, 130, 150–151
Legal issues. *See also* US Congress
  adaption litigation and, 184–188
  awarding damages and, 186–187
  cap-and-trade and, 54, 60
  climate adaptation and, 184–188
  climate policy and, 18–20, 33, 48,
    50, 52–53, 57, 60, 64, 184–190,
    192, 203n2, 204n1
  Comprehensive Emergency
    Response, Compensation, and
    Liability Act (CERCLA) and,
    186–187
  energy efficiency and, 102–105, 110,
    117, 124–125
  equity and, 186
  expired environmental statutes and,
    20
  greenhouse gases and, 48, 76–82,
    88–89, 91, 93–94, 184–185, 187,
    204n1

Legal issues (cont.)
  Massachusetts v. EPA and, 89, 187,
    203n2, 204n1
  national ambient air-quality
    standards (NAAQS) and, 93–97
  National Environmental Policy Act
    (NEPA) and, 32–33
  nuisance actions and, 184–185
  potentially responsible party (PRP)
    and, 187
  suffering of plaintiffs and,
    184–185
  Supreme Court and, 89, 95, 203n2,
    204n1
  sustainability and, 189–190
  transportation and, 144–144, 147,
    150
Lenschow, Andrea, 22–23
Life-cycle analysis (LCA), 30–33, 122,
  195
Life-cycle inventory (LCI) database,
  30–31
Light emitting diodes (LEDs), 110
Lipsky, Michael, 21
Liquefied natural gas (LNG), 139
Livestock, 5, 42, 44, 162–164, 175
Lobbying, 37, 53, 75–76, 79, 95–96,
  157–158
Low carbon fuel standards (LCFSs),
  171
Lowest achievable emission rate
  (LAER), 97

Maastricht Treaty, 21
Manure, 44, 46, 160, 162, 164, 166,
  174
Marginal lands, 4, 162, 166, 173
Markey, Ed, 50
Massachusetts Institute of
  Technology (MIT), 82–83
Massachusetts v. EPA, 89, 187,
  203n2, 204n1
Mazmanian, Daniel A., 20
Mazurek, Jan, 18–19
McKibben, Bill, 54
Media, 132
Medicare, 24

Mercury
  acid rain and, 71, 90–91
  Clean Air Mercury Rule and, 95
  climate policy and, 27, 49, 94–95
  coal and, 94
  electricity production and, 27
  EPA and, 96
  fluorescent bulbs and, 110
  food and, 91
  generating electricity and, 81, 83
  George W. Bush and, 94
  new source performance standards
    (NSPS) and, 96
  regulation and, 96
Methane
  agriculture and, 26, 42, 47, 156,
    160–164, 166, 169
  air pollution and, 27, 156
  climate change and, 27
  coal and, 74
  emission issues and, 44–47, 75
  enteric fermentation and, 44, 162–
    164
  EPA and, 89
  global warming and, 44
  greenhouse gases and, 26–27, 42,
    44–47, 74–75, 86, 89, 156,
    160–164, 166, 169
  natural gas and, 42, 86
  shale gas and, 75
Methane hydrate, 140
Methanol, 134, 172
Mexico, 130
Mineral resources, 32
Miscanthus, 4
Monocultures, 175
Montreal Protocol, 195

NASA, 7
National Academy of Engineering,
  169
National Academy of Sciences, 51,
  169, 173
National ambient air-quality
  standards (NAAQS), 93–97, 112
National Association of Clean Air
  Agencies, 29, 99

National Environmental Policy Act (NEPA), 32–33
National Farmer's Union, 166
Nationalism, 131, 197
National Renewable Energy Laboratory, 30–32
National Research Council, 169
National Science and Technology Council, 202n3
Natural gas, 4
  carbon dioxide and, 75
  climate policy and, 26, 41–46, 57
  electricity generation and, 84–86
  energy efficiency and, 105, 119–122
  fertilizers and, 26, 141
  greenhouse gases and, 71–75, 83–86, 88, 91, 96, 98, 179–180
  hydraulic fracturing and, 72, 85–86
  liquefied (LNG), 139
  methane and, 42, 86
  natural, 156, 160–161
  transportation and, 134, 137–141, 144, 150, 152
Natural Resources Defense Council (NRDC), 55, 96
New source performance standards (NSPS), 96–97
New source review (NSR) programs, 97–98
Nigeria, 130
Nike, 109
Nilsson, Mans, 24
Nitrogen fertilizers and, 156, 160–164, 166, 201n1
Nitrogen oxides
  acid rain and, 90–92
  agriculture and, 156, 160–164, 167
  air quality policy and, 83, 93–96
  Clean Air Interstate Rule and, 94–95
  coal and, 80
  electricity and, 81
  energy efficiency and, 98–99, 113t
  EPA and, 89
  fuel switching and, 98–99
  George W. Bush and, 94

greenhouse gases and, 81, 83, 89–99, 113
politics and, 94
power plants and, 96–97
transportation and, 46, 129, 146–148
US emissions rate of, 46–47
Nixon, Richard M., 132
Northrop, Michael, 109
Nuclear energy, 38
  carbon tax and, 88
  Chernobyl and, 87
  climate change and, 87, 179
  climate policy and, 44
  constituency creation for, 24
  construction operating license (COL) and, 86–87
  economic issues and, 72
  electricity generation and, 73–74, 86–88, 179
  energy efficiency and, 105, 123–125
  fossil fuels and, 86
  Fukushima and, 86–87, 179
  greenhouse gases and, 72–74, 86–88, 101
  increased role of, 74
  power plants and, 86–88
  safety and, 72, 86–87
  Three Mile Island and, 87
  waste and, 72, 86–87
Nuclear Regulatory Commission, 35, 86
Nuisance actions, 184–185

Obama, Barack
  climate policy and, 27, 34, 49–50, 59, 181
  greenhouse gas reduction and, 82, 87, 89–90, 96, 98
  health issues and, 89–90
  oil and, 138
  Recovery Act and, 105
  sustainability and, 198
  transportation and, 135, 138, 142, 147
Ocean thermal energy, 103
Offshore drilling, 138–139

Oil
  acid rain and, 90
  addiction to, 129
  agriculture and, 6, 169, 171–173,
    175
  air pollution and, 77
  Arctic National Wildlife Refuge
    (ANWR) and, 54, 134, 137, 143
  Canada and, 140
  climate change and, 89
  Colorado Plateau and, 141
  consumption rates of, 129, 131
  corporate greed and, 25
  crisis of 1973 and, 123, 144
  Crude Oil Windfall Profits Tax Act
    and, 102
  Deepwater Horizon rig and, 138
  domestic, 133, 136–141
  embargo shocks and, 131–132, 142
  energy independence and, 132, 134
  energy levels from, 74
  energy policy and, 26, 130–137,
    152–153
  environmental issues and, 32, 89,
    140, 144, 195
  era of cheap, 25, 38, 141–143, 152
  fertilizers and, 141
  future of, 152–153
  gasoline and, 3–4, 25–26, 46, 50,
    78, 132, 134, 142–146, 169–172,
    174, 193, 203n1
  greenhouse gases and, 7, 26, 89,
    169
  Green River formation and, 140
  Gulf of Mexico and, 7, 138–139
  heating, 44
  horizontal drilling and, 85
  imported, 25, 38, 130–132, 136,
    143, 152–153, 169, 197
  land use and, 54, 133–134, 137–
    141, 143
  Obama and, 138
  offshore drilling and, 138–139
  OPEC and, 132
  Persian Gulf and, 130–131
  petroleum and, 26, 38, 44, 71, 109,
    117, 130–136, 140–141, 144, 153

  politics and, 52, 77, 129–134,
    138–139
  portability and, 101
  power plants and, 95
  price of, 6, 25, 38, 77, 120, 123,
    132, 138, 141–144, 152, 171,
    173–174
  production of, 131, 137–141,
    173–174
  public lands and, 132
  safety and, 138
  Santa Barbara spills and, 195
  shale and, 25, 140–141, 153
  soybean, 172, 175
  subsidies and, 80, 130, 132,
    171–172
  supply of, 25, 123, 131, 133,
    136–141, 152–153
  sustainability and, 195, 197
  tar sands and, 25
  transportation and, 129–144,
    152–153
  Western control of, 139
  windfall profits tax and, 139–140
Oil sands, 25, 140, 153
Organization of Petroleum Exporting
  Countries (OPEC), 132
Our Common Future (World
  Commission on Environment and
  Development), 188
Ozone
  energy efficiency and, 113t
  greenhouse gases and, 26, 42, 89,
    93–96, 113t, 129, 147–148, 195,
    202n2
  sustainability and, 195
  transportation and, 129, 147–148
  volatile organic compounds (VOCs)
    and, 147–148, 202n2
Ozone Transport Commission, 93

Parks, Bradley C., 183
Particulate matter
  air pollution and, 91–97
  national ambient air-quality
    standards (NAAQS) and, 93–97
Perfluorocarbons (PFCs), 42

Persian Gulf, 130–131
Pesticides, 26, 162, 164, 176
Petroleum
  energy policy and, 117, 130–136
  era of cheap oil and, 38
  fertilizers and, 26
  greenhouse gases and, 44, 71, 109
  transportation and, 44, 130–136,
    140–141, 144, 153
Photovoltaics, 115, 117
Policy
  adaptive governance and, 20–21
  adaptive management and, 20, 192
  agricultural, 157–163, 175–176
  American Clean Energy and Security
    Act (ACES) and, 50, 166
  biofuels and, 3
  Clean Air Act and, 91 (*see also*
    Clean Air Act [CAA])
  Clean Air Interstate Rule (CAIR)
    and, 94–95
  Clean Water Act and, 52, 76
  climate, 13 (*see also* Climate policy)
  command-and-control regulations
    and, 20, 30, 92, 167
  community-level, 21
  Comprehensive Emergency
    Response, Compensation, and
    Liability Act (CERCLA) and,
    186–187
  Crude Oil Windfall Profits Tax Act
    and, 102
  Emergency Economic Stabilization
    Act and, 202n1
  Energy Act and, 3
  Energy Improvement and Extension
    Act and, 202n1
  energy independence and, 3, 103,
    110, 132, 134, 195, 197 (*see also*
    Energy policy)
  Energy Independence and Security
    Act and, 103, 110, 134
  Energy Policy Act and, 86–88,
    102–103
  Energy Tax Act and, 102
  Energy Tax Incentives Act and,
    103

farm bills and, 3, 5, 157–158, 159*t*,
  172
Framework Convention on Climate
  Change and, 48
Global Warming Solutions Act and,
  147
health issues and, 182
Intermodal Surface Transportation
  Efficiency Act (ISTEA) and, 203
Kyoto Protocol and, 49, 183, 203n1
market-based regulations and,
  19–20, 109
Montreal Protocol and, 195
National Environmental Policy Act
  (NEPA) and, 32–33
new generation of, 19
no-regrets, 48
pollution prevention and, 18–19, 30,
  113*t*, 151, 188, 191–192
protection mandates and, 1, 35, 52,
  60, 77, 100, 137, 139, 189, 191,
  196
renewable energy and, 122–127
science gap and, 6–9
set-aside programs and, 113*t*, 162,
  166
state-level, 18, 37
Tax Extenders and Alternative
  Minimum Tax Relief Act and,
  202n1
transportation, 136–150, 203n3
Transportation Equity Act and,
  203n3
Policy change
  actors benefiting from, 24
  coalition of interests and, 38–39
  Colorado RPS and, 126
  integration and, 21–25
  learning and, 21–25
  politics and, 6–11, 39, 52, 56–57
  science and, 6–11
  sustainability and, 193–197
Policy integration
  acid rain and, 90–93
  adaptive governance (AG) and,
    20–21
  adaptive management and, 20, 192

Policy integration (cont.)
  agricultural policy and, 26, 155–
    163, 168, 173, 175–180
  benefits of, 38–39
  clean air regulation and, 75–79,
    88–100
  climate change and, 27–28, 88–99,
    181–192
  climate policy and, 11–41, 51, 57,
    63–64, 68, 72, 83, 86–93, 177–192
  command-and-control regulation
    and, 20, 30, 92, 167
  difficulty of, 23
  energy efficiency and, 26–27, 179
  energy policy and, 72, 83, 86–93,
    101, 112, 113*t*, 122–124, 178–179
  entrenched interests and, 23
  environmental issues and, 18–25,
    29–39
  European Community
  Environmental Action Programme
    and, 21–22
  external factors and, 23–24
  federalism and, 24, 36–38
  fragmentation and, 18–21
  greenhouse gases and, 2–3, 12,
    27–29, 180
  horizontal, 22–23, 36, 195
  increased knowledge and, 23–24
  institutional innovation and, 34–36
  land use and, 26
  life-cycle analysis (LCA) and, 30–33
  marginal players and, 23
  market-based regulations and, 19–
    20, 109
  motivation for, 25–29
  need for, 3–6
  paths to, 29–36
  reform and, 19–21, 24–25, 32
  renewable energy and, 122–127
  sectoral responsibility and, 22–23
  as slippery concept, 22
  sustainability and, 192–199
  transportation policy and, 26,
    129–130, 136, 146, 149–151, 180
  two approaches to, 180–181
  vertical, 22, 36–38, 130, 195

Policy learning, 11, 21, 23–24, 38,
  195
Politics. *See also* US Congress
  agriculture and, 156–159, 166
  air pollution and, 75–79
  Arctic National Wildlife Refuge
    (ANWR) and, 134
  autonomy and, 38, 197
  bipartisanship and, 52–53, 105, 134
  Carter and, 132
  clean air regulation and, 75–79,
    88–100
  climate change and, 51–56
  climate policy and, 6–9, 27, 34,
    48–56, 59, 194–199, 201n1
  Clinton and, 34, 48–49, 77, 98, 133
  coal and, 52, 72
  Cold War and, 131
  Democrats and, 11, 20, 49–52, 77,
    90, 132–134, 143
  energy policy and, 9, 37–38, 51, 132
  environmental issues and, 1–2
  federalism and, 24, 36–38
  George H. W. Bush and, 48, 77, 133
  George W. Bush and, 8–9, 49–50,
    56, 94, 98, 133–134, 143, 201n1
  health issues and, 9, 75, 77–79,
    89–90
  lobbying and, 37, 53, 75–76, 79,
    95–96, 157–158
  nationalism and, 131, 197
  nitrous oxide and, 94
  Nixon and, 132
  Obama and, 27, 34, 49–50, 59, 82,
    87, 89–90, 96, 98, 105, 135, 138,
    142, 147, 181, 198
  oil and, 52, 77, 129–134, 138–139
  polarization of, 52–53, 158
  politics and, 56–57
  pork barrel spending and, 68
  public opinion and, 9, 194
  Reagan and, 48, 52, 133, 195
  regulation and, 49
  renewable energy and, 119
  Republicans and, 8, 20, 49–55, 59,
    77, 90, 105, 119, 132–133,
    142–143, 178, 198

research and, 66
science and, 6–11
single media focus and, 18
terrorists and, 35, 133, 179, 197
White House and, 34, 37–38, 48,
    77–78, 90, 96, 100, 132–133, 138
Pollan, Michael, 26, 175
Pollution prevention, 18–19, 30,
    113t, 151, 188, 191–192
Pope, C. Arden, III, 100
Population growth, 129, 143,
    149–150
Pork barrel spending, 68
Poverty, 10–11, 180–181, 183, 189,
    194
Powder River Basin, 66
Power plants
  acid rain and, 29, 62, 90–93
  air pollution and, 50
  big dirties, 99
  carbon capture and, 82–84
  carbon dioxide and, 81–83, 110
  carbon sequestration and, 81–82,
      84
  Clean Air Mercury Rule and, 95
  climate change and, 79
  coal-fired, 13, 25–26, 49, 55, 63,
      71–72, 77–84, 93, 98–99, 120,
      122, 147, 197, 201n2
  construction costs and, 86–88
  construction operating license (COL)
      and, 86–87
  electricity generation and, 71–74,
      77–78, 88–96, 99–100
  end-of-pipe solutions and, 19, 29
  energy efficiency and, 13, 29, 81,
      98–99, 108–110, 114, 120, 122,
      124–126, 179
  gas-fired, 81, 98, 122
  greenhouse gases and, 36, 46, 53,
      55–56, 86, 88–96, 99–100, 151,
      176
  hydro, 125
  infrastructure for, 17, 182
  integrated gasification combined
      cycle (IGCC) facilities and, 83
  land use and, 141

nitrous oxide and, 96–97
nuclear, 86–88
regulation of, 36, 50, 94–98, 108
retrofitting older, 50
safety and, 86
service lifetime of, 82
subsidies and, 80
sulfur and, 96–97
transmission lines and, 17, 119,
    122–123, 182
waste and, 86–87, 141
working life of, 17
Prasad, Monica, 61
Project XL, 19
Public benefit fund (PBF), 112
Public lands, 132, 137, 167, 185

Ranching, 166
Reagan, Ronald, 48, 52, 133, 195
Recycling, 31–32
Reform
  agricultural, 157, 175
  policy integration and, 19–21,
      24–25, 32
  procedural, 24
Regional Greenhouse Gas Initiative
    (RGGI), 53
Regulation
  acid rain and, 90–93, 202n3
  agriculture and, 167
  air pollution and, 17, 30, 57, 75–77,
      83–84, 88–99, 187, 192, 202nn2,3,
      203n2, 204n1
  building codes and, 182
  cap-and-trade programs and, 13, 29,
      36–37, 41, 50, 57–62, 64, 66–67,
      91, 94–95, 119, 167, 181, 198
  carbon dioxide and, 55, 89–90
  carbon tax and, 13, 41, 57–62,
      67–69, 88, 90, 109, 119, 122,
      143–144, 171, 178–181
  carbon trading and, 63–66, 68, 122,
      178–179
  clean air, 75–79, 88–100, 203n2 (*see
      also* Clean Air Act [CAA])
  Clean Air Mercury Rule and, 95
  climate change and, 27, 88–93

Regulation (cont.)
  climate policy and, 51 (see also
    Climate policy)
  congestion mitigation and air-quality
    (CMAQ) and, 148, 203n3
  corporate average fuel economy
    (CAFE) and, 26, 57, 134–135, 142
  Crude Oil Windfall Profits Tax Act
    and, 102
  emission standards and, 37, 57, 59,
    93, 99, 141–147 (see also
    Emissions)
  environmental impact statements
    (EISs) and, 21, 23, 30–33, 101,
    109, 119, 127, 140
  environmental issues and, 19, 20,
    75–77, 83–84
  EPA and, 9 (see also Environmental
    Protection Agency [EPA])
  ethanol and, 6
  Federal Energy Regulatory
    Commission and, 35
  fracking and, 85
  greenhouse gases and, 2, 34, 38, 57,
    64–65, 177, 179, 187, 192,
    202nn2,3, 203n2, 204n1
  incremental reforms and, 21
  industry burden and, 49
  inspection and maintenance (I&M)
    programs and, 147–148
  Kyoto Protocol and, 184
  land use and, 182
  life-cycle analysis (LCA) and, 30–33
  mandates and, 25, 50, 52, 57, 60,
    68, 78–79, 113t, 126, 135–136,
    146–147, 157, 159t, 166–167,
    171–173
  Massachusetts v. EPA and, 89, 187,
    203n2, 204n1
  mercury and, 96
  methane and, 89
  motor vehicles and, 141–144
  national ambient air-quality
    standards (NAAQS) and, 93–97,
    112
  new source performance standards
    (NSPS) and, 96–97

  new source review (NSR) programs
    and, 97–98
  nitrous oxide and, 89
  Nuclear Regulatory Commission
    and, 35, 86
  power plants and, 36, 50, 94–98,
    108
  as protection, 55
  reflexive law and, 19
  regional differences in, 37, 63, 79
  renewable fuels standard (RFS) and,
    103, 134, 171, 174
  renewable portfolio standards
    (RPSs) and, 104–105, 114,
    124–127
  scrubbers and, 26, 92–93, 98,
    202n3
  sulfur and, 89, 91, 96–97
  transportation and, 66, 138–151
  waste and, 18, 35
Reid vapor pressure, 203n1
Renewable energy
  agriculture and, 158, 159t,
    171–173
  alternative energy and, 13, 101–105,
    111–127
  American Recovery and
    Reinvestment Act (ARRA) and,
    104–105, 110
  blended gasoline and, 134
  climate policy and, 29–33, 37–38,
    41, 50–51, 59, 68
  Conservation and Renewable Energy
    Reserve and, 29
  Crude Oil Windfall Profits Tax Act
    and, 102
  electricity production and, 72–74,
    86, 99
  energy efficiency and, 13, 101–105,
    111–127, 134–136, 141
  Energy Independence and Security
    Act and, 103, 110, 134
  Energy Policy Act and, 102–103
  Energy Tax Act and, 102
  Energy Tax Incentives Act and, 103
  geographical issues and, 119
  increased production in, 119–120

industry innovations and, 109
life-cycle analysis (LCA) and, 30–33
long history of, 101
managing demand and, 109, 111,
    113–114, 117, 122
National Renewable Energy
    Laboratory and, 30–32
policy integration and, 122–127
politics and, 119
portfolios and, 124–127
renewable energy and, 122–127
subsidies and, 104, 143
sustainability and, 179–181, 192,
    194, 197–198
transmission lines and, 122–123
transportation and, 134, 136–137,
    139, 141, 143
US history of, 101–105
waste and, 120
windfall profit taxes and, 102,
    139–140
Renewable fuels standard (RFS), 103,
    134, 171, 174
Renewable portfolio standards
    (RPSs), 104–105, 114, 124–127
Research
  acid deposition and, 62
  air pollution and, 100
  alternative energy and, 123–124
  biomass, 3–4, 69–70, 159*t*, 169–
    170, 172
  cellulose and, 4, 201n2
  climate change, 6–9, 177, 201n2
  energy, 8, 30, 35, 38, 102–104, 109,
    119, 122–124, 127, 158, 180
  greenhouse gases and, 49, 56
  National Renewable Energy
    Laboratory and, 30–32
  nuclear, 24
  politics and, 66
  sequestration, 82, 164
  stem cell, 9
  subsidies and, 64, 68, 80
  transportation and, 182
Resources for the Future, 202n3
Retirement, 178, 198
Rice, 46*t*, 157, 160*t*, 161*f*, 162

Roberts, J., 183
Rosenbaum, Walter, 34

Safety. *See also* Health issues
  air pollution and, 96 (*see also* Air
    pollution)
  climate policy and, 49, 52
  nuclear, 72, 86–87
  oil industry and, 138
  terrorists and, 35, 133, 179, 197
Salmon, 62
Santa Barbara oil spills, 195
Saudi Arabia, 130, 131
Sclove, Richard, 21
Scrubbers, 26, 92–93, 98, 202n3
Senegal, 5
September 11, 2001, 35
Set-aside programs, 113*t*, 162, 166
Shale, 25, 75, 85, 140–141, 153
Shell Oil, 109, 139, 141
Sierra Club, 55
Social Security, 24
Soil conditions
  agriculture and, 4, 10, 26, 44, 46,
    91, 156–157, 160–167, 173–174,
    176, 203n1
  erosion and, 156, 173–174
  fertilizers and, 6, 26, 141, 156,
    160–168, 170, 174–176, 201nn1,2
Solar energy
  agriculture and, 175
  climate policy and, 57
  dropping costs of, 120
  energy efficiency and, 101–103,
    114–122, 125, 127, 179
  greenhouse gases and, 72
Southeast Plains, 156
Soviet Union, 131–132
Soybeans, 157, 169, 172, 175,
    201n1
State and Territorial Air Pollution
    Program Administrators, 29
Stem cells, 9
Stern, Nicholas, 182–183
Stone, Deborah, 21
Street Level Bureaucracy (Lipsky), 21
Strong Democracy (Barber), 21

Subsidies
  agricultural, 5, 14, 65, 157–158,
    165, 171–172, 175
  alternative energy, 103–104, 115,
    117, 119, 126, 132
  basic research and, 180
  biodiesel, 172
  climate policy and, 35, 38, 57,
    64–65, 68
  coal, 80, 103, 150
  energy efficiency and, 132, 178
  Energy Policy Act and, 86–88
  ethanol, 136, 171–172
  mitigation costs and, 181
  oil, 80, 130, 132, 171–172
  pork barrel spending and, 68
  power plants and, 80
  reducing, 192
  renewable energy and, 104, 143
  research and, 68, 80
  transportation and, 130, 132, 136,
    143, 150
Sugar cane, 3, 201n2
Sulfur
  acid rain and, 90–92
  air quality policy and, 83
  Clean Air Act (CAA) and, 78, 91,
    93, 146, 148
  Clean Air Interstate Rule and,
    94–95
  climate policy and, 26–27, 42, 49,
    62, 66, 94
  coal and, 77, 80–81, 92
  electricity generation and, 27, 81
  energy efficiency and, 29, 98–99
  EPA and, 89, 91, 96–97
  flue gas desulfurization and, 98
  George W. Bush and, 94
  politics and, 94
  power plants and, 96–97
  regulation and, 89, 91
  scrubbers and, 26
Sustainability, 19
  air pollution and, 189, 194–195
  biodiversity and, 191
  biofuels and, 180
  breadth of, 190
  cap-and-trade programs and, 181,
    198
  carbon sequestration and, 179–181
  climate change and, 188–199
  climate policy and, 14–15, 20, 33,
    188–199
  concept of, 188–189
  economic issues and, 20, 189,
    192–194
  ecosystems approach and,
    190–192
  energy policy and, 194, 196–197
  Environmental Protection Agency
    (EPA) and, 187, 204n1
  equity and, 182, 189–192
  fats and, 201n1
  food and, 157, 168, 175–176, 180,
    191
  forests and, 188
  fossil fuels and, 193, 195
  gasoline and, 193
  greenhouse gases and, 188
  health issues and, 189, 191, 194,
    198
  incrementalism and, 192–194
  legal issues and, 189–190
  NEPA and, 33
  oil and, 152, 195, 197, 201n1
  policy change and, 193–197
  policy integration and, 188–192
  renewable energy and, 179–181,
    192, 194, 197–198
  taxes and, 184, 198
  thick, 189
  three commitments of, 192
  waste and, 192, 196, 198
  World Business Council for
    Sustainable Development and,
    63–64
  World Commission on Environment
    and Development and, 188
  World Conservation Strategy and,
    188
SUVs, 26, 142, 146
Sweden, 140
Switchgrass, 173–174, 201n2
Synfuels tax credit, 80

Tariffs, 3, 171–173
Tar sands, 25
Tax credits
  alternative energy and, 102–104,
    114, 117, 119, 122
  biofuels and, 3, 159*t*, 171–173
  coal and, 80
  Energy Policy Act and, 87
  Energy Tax Act and, 102
  hybrid vehicles and, 134
  synfuels and, 80
Taxes
  agriculture and, 159*t*, 165, 171–
    173
  alternative minimum, 202n1
  carbon, 13, 41, 57–62, 67–69, 88,
    90, 109, 119, 122, 143–144, 171,
    178–181
  Crude Oil Windfall Profits Tax Act
    and, 102
  electricity generation and, 80, 83,
    87–90
  energy, 49, 102–104, 120, 132,
    202n1
  Energy Tax Act and, 102
  Energy Tax Incentives Act and, 103
  gasoline, 142–143
  incentives and, 3, 57, 80, 103–104,
    117, 126, 132, 134, 172, 202n1
  oil and, 139–140
  petroleum development tax
    provisions and, 130–131
  renewable energy and, 102–103,
    139–140
  subsidies and, 35 (*see also*
    Subsidies)
  sustainability and, 184, 198
  Tax Extenders and Alternative
    Minimum Tax Relief Act and,
    202n1
  trading programs and, 61
  transportation and, 130, 132, 134,
    139, 142–144, 149–150
  windfall profit, 102, 139–140
  writing committee for, 35–36
Tax Extenders and Alternative
  Minimum Tax Relief Act, 202n1

Technology, 201n1
  agriculture and, 159*t*, 165, 168–
    176
  alternative energy and, 8, 119–124,
    127, 134
  biofuels and, 4
  breakthroughs in, 15
  clean energy, 10, 14, 27, 54, 56–57,
    68, 78, 81–83, 86–88, 92, 144–
    146, 151, 178
  control, 18, 46, 76, 80, 95, 129
  economies of scale and, 179
  emissions and, 27, 57, 97–98 (*see
    also* Emissions)
  energy efficiency and, 17, 104, 109,
    111
  environmental impacts and, 31, 52
  massive shifts in, 17
  National Science and Technology
    Council and, 202n3
  no-waste process, 24
  oil and, 140–141, 152
  politics and, 11, 21, 76
  recycling and, 32
  renewable energy and, 30, 41, 101,
    103, 119, 126
  subsidies and, 180
  sustainability and, 189, 195,
    197–198
  transportation and, 140–146, 149,
    151
  waste process, 24
Teragrams of carbon dioxide
  equivalent (Tg CO_2 Eq.), 41, 160
Terrorism, 35, 133, 179, 197
Thermal energy, 103, 114–118, 122,
  125, 127, 179
Three Mile Island, 87
Toxic waste, 10, 34–35, 71, 94, 96,
  141, 202n2
Transmission lines, 17, 119, 122–123,
  182
Transportation
  air pollution and, 129, 136,
    147–148
  biofuels and, 134, 136
  biomass and, 134

Transportation (cont.)
carbon dioxide and, 14, 129, 146–147
carbon tax and, 143–144, 180
Clean Air Act (CAA) and, 146, 148
clean car technologies and, 144–146
climate change and, 136, 143, 148, 150, 152–153
coal and, 73
congestion mitigation and air-quality (CMAQ) and, 148, 203n3
corporate average fuel economy (CAFE) and, 26, 57, 134–135, 142
deregulation and, 66
emission standards and, 37, 129–130, 141–147, 203n1
energy efficiency and, 26, 57, 134–135, 141–144, 142, 180
energy policy and, 130–137, 140–143, 150, 152–153
environmental issues and, 136–141, 144, 146, 149, 153
Environmental Protection Agency (EPA) and, 129, 134, 146–148, 203nn1,2
EPA and, 14
ethanol and, 134, 136, 137t, 144, 145t
food and, 5–6, 26, 54, 141, 155, 175
forests and, 137
fossil fuels and, 129, 141, 152–153
fuel economy standards and, 26, 48–49, 57, 143, 145t
gasoline and, 3–4, 25–26, 46, 50, 78, 132, 134, 142–146, 169–172, 174, 193, 203n1
Global Warming Solutions Act and, 147
greenhouse gases and, 14, 129–130, 141–153, 203n2
health issues and, 129, 141, 145
hybrid vehicles and, 103, 134
hydrogen and, 134, 144–145
inspection and maintenance (I&M) programs and, 147–148
Intermodal Surface Transportation Efficiency Act (ISTEA) and, 203

land use and, 34, 130, 148–151, 180, 189
legal issues and, 144–144, 147, 150
low carbon fuel standards (LCFSs) and, 171
motor vehicles traveled and, 147–150
natural gas and, 134, 137–141, 144, 150, 152
nitrogen emissions and, 46, 129, 146–148
oil and, 129–133, 135–144, 152–153
ozone and, 129, 147–148
petroleum and, 44, 130–136, 140–141, 144, 153
policy integration and, 26, 180
policy options for, 136–150
regulation and, 138–151
renewable energy and, 134, 136–137, 139, 141, 143
renewable fuels standard (RFS) and, 103, 134, 171, 174
research for, 182
subsidies and, 130, 132, 136, 143, 150
SUVs and, 26, 142, 146
tailpipe standards and, 146
taxes and, 130, 132, 134, 139, 142–144, 149–150
US Congress and, 130–135, 142–143, 147–148
vehicle miles traveled and, 148–150
Transportation Equity Act, 203n3
TXU Energy, 55

UN Conference on Environment and Development, 48
UN Food and Agricultural Organization, 5
United Kingdom, 25, 81, 82, 182
United States
adaptation costs and, 184–188
climate policy of, 41–69 (see also Climate policy)
Cold War and, 131
energy independence and, 3, 103, 110, 132, 134, 195, 197

EPA and, 41–52, 56 (*see also*
  Environmental Protection Agency
  [EPA])
federalism and, 24, 36–38
gasoline consumption of, 170
history of renewable energy in,
  101–105
hostage crisis and, 132
imported-oil dependence of, 25, 38,
  130–132, 136, 143, 152–153, 169,
  197
as oil production leader, 131
population growth in, 129, 143,
  149–150
Social Security and, 24
White House and, 34, 37–38, 48,
  77–78, 90, 96, 100, 132–133,
  138
US Agriculture Department, 4
US Congress
  agriculture and, 157–158
  climate policy and, 3, 8–9, 14, 18,
    20, 27, 29, 34–38, 49–53, 59, 63,
    178, 195, 198
  Conservation and Renewable Energy
    Reserve and, 29
  energy efficiency and, 102–105, 109,
    114, 117, 126
  greenhouse gases and, 75–79, 82,
    87–91, 100
  transportation and, 130–135,
    142–143, 147–148
US Department of Agriculture, 34,
  158, 165
US Department of Energy, 201n2
  climate policy and, 8, 30–32, 35
  demonstration projects and, 81–82,
    84, 201n2
  energy efficiency and, 103–105,
    113t, 114–118, 125
  Energy Information Administration
    and, 71, 73–74, 84–85, 103–105,
    114–117, 125, 130, 133, 138–139,
    152
  greenhouse gases and, 71, 73–74,
    79, 81–85
  transportation and, 130–138, 152

US Department of Homeland
  Security, 35
US Department of the Interior, 52
US Department of Transportation, 34,
  148
US Energy Information Agency, 111
US Government Accountability Office
  (GAO), 123, 167
US Supreme Court, 89, 95, 203n2,
  204n1
Utility companies, 83, 92, 96–97,
  126

Venezuela, 130
Volatile organic compounds (VOCs),
  147–148, 202n2

Waste
  agriculture and, 119, 164, 169,
    173–175, 189
  algae and, 174
  biomass, 173
  corn stover, 173
  decomposition in landfills and, 42
  end-of-pipe controls and, 19, 29
  EPA and, 35
  fats, 172
  fracking and, 85
  grease, 172
  landfills and, 42
  life-cycle analysis (LCA) and, 31–32
  manure, 44, 46, 160, 162, 164, 166,
    174
  municipal solid, 29
  natural processing of, 67
  nuclear, 72, 86–87, 125, 179
  oil shale and, 140
  potentially responsible parties
    (PRPs) and, 187
  power plants and, 86–87, 141
  process technologies and, 24
  production of, 1
  recycling and, 31–32
  regulation of, 18, 35
  as renewable energy, 120
  storage of, 72, 87
  sustainability and, 192, 196, 198

Waste (cont.)
  toxic, 10, 34–35, 71, 94, 96, 141,
    202n2
Wave energy, 103, 179
Waxman, Henry, 50
Wheat, 5, 157, 169
Wind energy
  climate policy and, 30, 44, 57, 65,
    179
  efficiency and, 101–104, 110,
    114–122, 125–127
  greenhouse gases and, 72
Windfall profits, 102, 139–140
Windstorms, 183
Wood
  biomass and, 158, 159t, 169
  paper and, 32
  particulate matter and, 91
  as renewable energy, 119–120
World Bank, 6
World Business Council for
  Sustainable Development, 63–64
World Commission on Environment
  and Development, 188
World Conservation Strategy, 188
World Resources Institute, 63–64

Zoellick, Robert, 6
Zoning, 34, 130, 150–151